Pitman
BUSINESS
ENGLISH 2

Susan Davies and Richard West

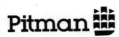

Pitman Publishing
128 Long Acre, London WC2E 9AN

A Division of Longman Group UK Limited

© Susan Davies and Richard West 1982

First published in Great Britain 1982
Reprinted in 1983, 1984, 1985, 1987, 1989, 1990

ISBN 0 273 01793 4

Printed and bound in Singapore.

Contents

Preface   v

Contents of Units 1–12   vi

How to use this book   viii

Unit 1   1

Unit 2   21

Unit 3   41

Unit 4   57

Unit 5   75

Unit 6   95

**Unit 7:   Applications and
            interviews**   113

Unit 8:   A clerical error   125

Unit 9:   Safety in the office   135

Unit 10: Waste in the office   145

Unit 11: The Film Society meeting   153

Unit 12: Flexitime   163

Pitman Spelling List   175

Index   177

Acknowledgements   181

Preface

This book is the second in a series designed for office workers, future office workers and for students who have to pass an English language examination as part of their commercial training. The first book in the series is for those using English at the clerical level; this book is for those using English at the secretarial level.

There are 12 units. Units 1–6 are divided into five sections:

Summary This section gives exercises on all the different kinds of summary you will be expected to write in the office – business letters, memos, telegrams and telexes. There are also exercises on statistics and diagrams used in the office. In addition, there are exercises to help you write the kind of summaries asked for in examinations.

Comprehension In this section you are given practice in understanding business texts, business documents, diagrams and written instructions. The exercises are designed to give you the skills necessary in understanding any document you may meet in the office.

Composition This section concentrates on giving you practice in writing business documents – letters, notes, memos, messages, telegrams, telexes, descriptions of statistics – and in completing business forms. There are also exercises on the types of composition required in examinations at this level.

Oral/Aural The work in this section gives practice in speaking and listening; it includes giving and receiving spoken messages, following and giving instructions, telephone techniques and problem solving.

Miscellany This is a special section at the end of all 12 units with exercises on grammar, punctuation, spelling, vocabulary and those areas of language which are important in office work. Special exercises called *Examination Preparation* are given in this section; each of these exercises gives practice in the skills you need to pass examinations.

PS exercises are given at the end of Summary, Comprehension, Composition and Oral/Aural. They are designed to help you do the work in each section and they cover problems in spelling, proof-reading, vocabulary, layout of business documents, British and American spelling, and the use of reference books.

Units 7–12
Each of these units is a series of related exercises based on an office situation. Problem solving and decision making play an important part in each unit. The assignments involve one or several of the language skills practised in units 1–6.

Throughout the book you will find sample questions from various examinations taken by students for office work at this level.

Susan Davies and **Richard West**

	Unit 1	Unit 2	Unit 3	Unit 4	Unit 5	Unit 6
Summary	Essential and inessential information 1	Summarising for telegrams and telexes 21	Relevant information in business documents 41	Summaries of business documents 57	Using charts and tables 75	Note summaries 95
PS	Proof-reading (1) 3	Compound words 23	Filing 44	Filing and indexing 60	Spelling – Telex code 78	Using numbering systems to display notes, outlines and reports 98
Comprehension	Bringing information to a text 5	Unfamiliar words 24	Diagrams in texts (1) 44	Diagrams in texts (2) 61	Written directions 80	Constructing complete texts 99
PS	Spelling – Sequences of letters 8	Writing formal definitions 26	Spelling – Problems with double letters 49	Spelling – Irregular spelling patterns 65	Instructions at the type-writer 82	British and American English 101
Composition	Making comparisons and recommend-ations 9	Organisation of a letter 27	Replies to letters 50	Business letters in examination questions 66	Using statistics 83	Expanding notes 103
PS	Ambiguity 12	Vocabulary of business letters 30	Word puzzles 52	Appropriate vocabulary for business letters 68	Vocabulary of statistics 85	Proof-reading (4) 105
Oral/Aural	Reporting messages 14	Telephone calls 31	Problem solving 53	Statistics 68	Sources of information 86	Oral instructions 106
PS	Proof-reading (2) 15	Spelling – Helping your memory 34	Two-word verbs 54	Words of comparison in interpreting a graph 71	Reference books 89	Examination instructions 108
Miscellany 1	Pronouns (1) 17	Paragraph division in business letters 35	Homophones 54	Spelling – Suffixes 72	Necessary conditions 91	Prepositions 110
2	Word families 18	Abbreviations 36	The apostrophe with letters and figures 55	Verbosity 73	Pronouns (2) 92	Spelling – Silent letters 111
3	Punctuation-semicolon (1) 18	Proof-reading (3) 36	Spelling – One word or two? 56	Tautology 73	Punctuation – commas 92	Dangling participles 112
Examination Preparation	*Due to/ Owing to* 20	*Only* 40	*Some, any* and *no* 56	Defining business terms 74	Form-filling 93	Punctuation of direct and indirect speech 112

Unit 7	Unit 8	Unit 9	Unit 10	Unit 11	Unit 12
APPLICA-TIONS AND INTERVIEWS 113	A CLERICAL ERROR 125	SAFETY IN THE OFFICE 135	WASTE IN THE OFFICE Background reading 145	THE FILM SOCIETY MEETING 153	FLEXITIME Background reading 163
1 Drawing up a job advertisement 114	1 Completing purchase requisition 125	1a Drawing up and completing an accident report form 135	1 Discussing ways of economising on the use of the telephone 146	1a Writing resolution minutes 153	1a Administering a questionnaire 164
2 Choosing candidates for interview 118	2 Locating errors in documents 127	1b Writing a notice of a meeting 135	2 Summarising in report form decisions reached at a meeting 148	1b Writing a letter of thanks 154	1b Collating the results of a questionnaire 164
3 Practising interview techniques 118	3 Agreeing on what went wrong 128	2a Listing hazards in the office 136	3a Writing a letter querying a telephone bill 148	2 Writing an agenda and a notice for a meeting 154	1c Summarising the results of a questionnaire 164
4a Drafting letter to a successful candidate 120	4a Solving a problem through discussion 128	2b Writing a notice giving rules for safety 136	3b Writing a letter of reply 148	3 Holding a meeting 155	2 Negotiating and reaching decisions within a meeting 165
4b Drafting letter to unsuccessful candidates 120	4b Reporting a problem and deciding on action 130	3 Writing a memo report 136		4a Designing and completing an order form 157	3a Writing an information leaflet 167
	5a Writing a tactful letter 130	4 Writing clear instructions 137		4b Writing a letter of enquiry 157	3b Writing a circular letter 167
	5b Writing a memo as follow-up to a decision 130	5 Making a requisition form 137			
	6 Summarising a series of documents 130				
British and American spelling 121	Using an index and table of contents 131	Consistent use of pronouns 139	Making suggestions 149	Word division 158	Pronouns (4) Substitution 168
eg and ie 122	Dictionary use – appropriate meanings 132	Proof-reading – word division (5) 140	Motions and resolutions 150	Appropriateness 158	Preparing telephone calls 170
Writing a Curriculum vitae 122	Punctuation – semicolon (2) 133	Report writing 141	Minutes 150	Prediction and proof-reading 160	Composing forms and question-naires 171
Indirect speech 124	Problems with pronouns (3) 134	Trap words 142	Vocabulary questions 152	Parts of speech 161	The examiner's point of view 173

How to use this book

Please don't write in the book.

<table>
<tr><td colspan="2"></td><td>Units 1–6</td><td>Unit 2</td><td>Unit 3</td></tr>
</table>

Unit 2	**Unit 3**	

Summary
Particular attention to summaries of business documents and abbreviated forms of office communication such as messages, memos, telegrams and telexes, as well as notes, statistics, diagrams and various visual presentations of information. *PS*

Comprehension
With special reference to business texts, commercial documents, instructions and visual presentations of data. *PS*

Composition
Concentrating on business letters, memos, messages, business forms and statistics, as well as types of composition required in examinations. *PS*

Oral/Aural
Including spoken messages, following and giving instructions, gathering information and telephone techniques. *PS*

Miscellany
Exercises on those areas of grammar, punctuation, spelling and vocabulary which often cause particular problems.

PS: Separate exercises on aspects of business English; can be used at the end of a lesson or for homework.

Examination preparation

Unit 2	Unit 3
Summarising for telegrams and telexes <div align="right">21</div>	Relevant information in business documents <div align="right">41</div>
Compound words <div align="right">23</div>	Filing <div align="right">44</div>
Unfamiliar words <div align="right">24</div>	Diagrams in texts (1) <div align="right">44</div>
Writing formal definitions <div align="right">26</div>	Spelling – Problems with double letters <div align="right">49</div>
Organisation of a letter <div align="right">27</div>	Replies to letters <div align="right">50</div>
Vocabulary of business letters <div align="right">30</div>	Word puzzles <div align="right">52</div>
Telephone calls <div align="right">31</div>	Problem solving <div align="right">53</div>
Spelling – Helping your memory <div align="right">34</div>	Two-word verbs <div align="right">54</div>
Paragraph division in business letters <div align="right">35</div>	Homophones <div align="right">54</div>
Abbreviations <div align="right">36</div>	The apostrophe with letters and figures <div align="right">55</div>
Proof-reading (3) <div align="right">36</div>	Spelling – One word or two? <div align="right">56</div>
Only <div align="right">40</div>	*Some, any* and *no* <div align="right">56</div>

Unit 10	Unit 11	Units 7–12
WASTE IN THE OFFICE	THE FILM SOCIETY MEETING 153	Each of these is an integrated unit consisting of a series of related assignments based on an office situation. The assignments combine several or all of the skills used in summary, comprehension, composition and oral/aural work. Each unit should be worked through from beginning to end as the outcome of one assignment may form input to subsequent ones.
Background reading 145	1a Writing resolution minutes 153	
1 Discussing ways of economising on the use of the telephone 146	1b Writing a letter of thanks 154	
2 Summarising in report form decisions reached at a meeting 148	2 Writing an agenda and a notice for a meeting 154	
3a Writing a letter querying a telephone bill 148	3 Holding a meeting 155	
3b Writing a letter of reply 148	4a Designing and completing an order form 157	
	4b Writing a letter of enquiry 157	
Making suggestions 149	Word division 158	*Miscellany*
Motions and resolutions 150	Appropriateness 158	
Minutes 150	Prediction and proof-reading 160	
Vocabulary questions 152	Parts of speech 161	*Examination preparation*

Unit 1

Summary: Essential and inessential information

Exercise 1 *To introduce the distinction between essential and inessential information*

Summarising is a widely-used skill both in the office and in examinations. Here are some of the documents which contain summaries:

PRECIS
A shortened version of a complete text, usually written in a required number of words. Most commonly found in examinations.

SUMMARY
A shortened version of a text, including information relevant only to a particular point or purpose.

SUMMARY OF CORRESPONDENCE
A shortened version of a series of letters or other documents. It should include all the main points.

MINUTES
A summary of the discussion and decisions taken in a meeting or debate.

CATALOGUES
Selective information containing essential points about products.

TELEGRAMS AND TELEXES
Abbreviated messages containing all the important information but leaving out any unnecessary words.

PRESS RELEASE
A brief statement from a company, organisation or government department prepared for the newspapers, radio and television.

All these documents require the separation of *essential* information from less important or *inessential* information. Work in pairs and decide which sentence in each of the following paragraphs is essential and which is inessential.

Example: One common method of correcting typing mistakes is known as 'opaquing correction fluid'. In other words, it is a fluid which covers the error with a paper-coloured film.
Essential: First sentence
Inessential: Second sentence

1 First of all, the trainees are told what skill is to be practised during the training session. This stage is called the 'briefing'.
2 The sun was shining brightly through the window as Mrs Lee entered the room. She announced that the examination results would be displayed in the college entrance hall the following afternoon.
3 At this point we should consider the qualifications required for suitable trainees. It is vital that all candidates should have good speeds and an adequate command of English.
4 The quotation we asked for came in this morning's post. It had been sent in a pale green envelope.
5 Generally speaking, light ink on dark paper is less effective than dark ink on light paper. For example, white ink on dark green paper is not recommended.
6 Miss Banda has been appointed as Typing Pool Supervisor. She has worked for the company for 12 years.
7 The lack of demand for the products of one industry will affect other industries which supply the raw materials to make these products. An instance of this was the fall in demand for ships, which led to a decline in the steel-making industry.
8 It was obvious that something was wrong in the stores section. It was soon discovered that petty theft was widespread.
9 I now come to my final point in my speech to you this afternoon. Because of increased demand and record sales, the company plans to build a new factory and employ 800 extra people.
10 This concentration of certain industries in certain areas is known as 'specialisation'. In other words, particular areas are said to specialise in the manufacture of certain types of product.

Exercise 2 *To show how writers introduce certain kinds of inessential information*

How can we tell which information is essential and which is inessential? Generally, we can say that the following types of information are inessential and can be left out of any summarising documents:

Examples
There has always been a tendency for some industries to concentrate in particular areas. For example, there is a concentration of vehicle manufacturers in the English Midlands.

Rephrasing and definitions

One common method of correcting typing mistakes is known as 'opaquing correction fluid'. <u>In other words</u>, it is a fluid which covers the error with a paper-coloured film.

Additions

The first thing to be said about the new airport – <u>especially</u> if you pay taxes to Manchester City Council – is that it will not be paid for by the city of Manchester.

In these sentences the writers used signposts to show that they were introducing examples, definitions or additions. The signposts have been underlined.

The paragraphs below all contain some inessential information – examples, definitions, rephrasings or additions. Work in pairs to find the inessential information. Decide why it is inessential. The writer's signposts will help.

Example: In industrialised countries, certain industries have developed extensively techniques for the mass production of goods. In other words, the manufacture of motor-cars, television sets, telephones, shoes and a whole range of other goods is carried out in large quantities.

(LC Bond, *Commerce and the World Outside*, Pitman, 1978.)

Inessential information: Second sentence.
Reason: Rephrasing, introduced by the signpost 'In other words'.

1 In business, goods are generally bought on credit, that is, they are paid for some time after delivery.
2 If goods are to be paid for later, then the seller will send an invoice to the buyer through the post. This is a document which informs the buyer of the quantity, description, price and value of the goods he has purchased.
3 Most businesses, especially those using machine accounting, do not show all these details but instead use a form of simplified accounting.
4 Many organisations, and particularly the larger ones, have turned more and more to the use of machinery for their office work.
5 It is important to know the quantity and value of goods in stock in order that the balance sheet can be completed. Stock may be defined as goods bought for sale, for manufacture and then for resale, or goods manufactured waiting to be sold.
6 Many other items appear on a stock sheet, which would run to several pages, and different types of stock would be grouped together. For instance, a furniture company might have Bedroom, Dining Room, Lounge, and Kitchen Furniture as main subdivisions, and under each of these further groupings would be made.

7 How does a business sell? How does it find its customers? It does so in the following ways:
a By advertising, that is, making itself known. Advertising takes all sorts of forms:
  i) Printed – eg leaflets, brochures, posters, etc.
  ii) Personal – ie using people, such as commercial travellers or sales representatives.
b By dealing with the enquiries received, for instance letters or telephone calls.
c By offering inducements to possible customers. Examples of such inducements range from free samples to longer credit terms than those offered by competitors.
d By offering goods in attractive packs. For example, the shape of the bottle, the design and colour of the label, and the choice of a name can do a great deal to sell bottled goods, eg perfumes, fruit juices, sauces and creams.

(Adapted from F C Thurling, *Office Practice Today*, 4th edn, Pitman, 1975.)

Exercise 3 *To practise recognising the purpose of sentences in a text*

Read the text below and then discuss the statements following in group- or class-discussion.

HOW ARE SALARIES AND WAGES DETERMINED?

[1]This is not so simple a matter as some people believe. [2]There are several major factors which decide the amount of pay received in a trade or profession. [3]The first factor is the general trade conditions in a country. [4]If, for instance, trade is good, there is a demand for employees, so the workers' pay tends to rise. [5]If, on the other hand, trade is bad or falling off, then the demand for workers drops, and pay tends to stabilise.

[6]Secondly, there are the conditions within a particular trade or profession. [7]For example, there are few craftsmen left in some of the old skilled trades (eg blacksmiths, carpenters) and therefore they can command good money. [8]If, however, a profession is over-crowded, that is, too many people are competing for the work available, then the monetary reward will be less than it would be if there were a shortage of labour within the trade or profession.

[9]Finally, there are the training requirements of the trade or profession. [10]Some work, eg medicine, law, accountancy and engineering, requires not only a high degree of ability but also a good education and a length of time in training. [11]It is expected, therefore, that those who satisfy the educational and training requirements in their chosen field of work will receive higher monetary rewards than those whose work does not require such qualifications.

(Adapted from F C Thurling, *Office Practice Today*, 4th edn, Pitman, 1975.)

Each of the statements below refers to one sentence in the text. Each statement says what the author is doing in a particular sentence. Work in groups or as a class to match each statement to a sentence (the sentences in the text have been numbered).

Example: The writer is giving an example of good conditions within a particular trade or profession.   = sentence 7

a The writer is illustrating what happens when there are good trade conditions in a country.

b He is giving examples of trades or professions with high training requirements.

c The writer is introducing the factors that determine salaries and wages.

d He is linking the title to the text.

e The writer is giving the third factor determining wages and salaries.

f He is illustrating what happens when there are poor trade conditions in a country.

g The writer is giving an illustration of poor conditions within a particular trade or profession.

h He is giving the first factor determining salaries and wages.

i He is showing how his example (given in the previous sentence) affects wages and salaries.

j The writer is introducing his second main point.

Exercise 4   *To use the essential information in a text to write a brief summary*

The essential information in the passage in Exercise 3 is found in the title and four sentences. Read the text through again to find these four sentences. Use them to make a summary of the text under the following headings:

Title
Introduction
First factor
Second factor
Third factor

PS: Proof-reading (1)   *To revise types of errors*

It is easier to find errors if you know the *types* to look for. With the following errors you need to know the typewriter keyboard. Use the diagram of the keyboard to describe each type of error. Rewrite each item correctly.

Type 1

a   `projessional`

b   `monable`

c   `lting`

Type 2

a   `$/"`

b   `LEFT?HAND`

c   `'No!8`

Type 3

a   `revognise`

b   `pernissible`

c   `superdede`

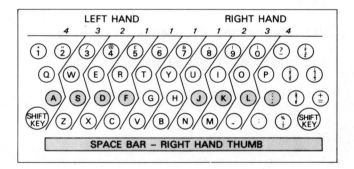

With the following types of error, you need to know typewriting conventions. Again, describe each type and write the correct versions.

Type 4

a   `If you don't understand something, ask.`

b   `Don't let your filing build up.`

c   `Make a note of every task to be done.`
      `Your memory can't be relied on for`
      `everything.`

Type 5

a Keep your desk tidy.Clear it after

every main job.

b It' s a good idea to keep out-of -date

diaries.

c Make sure allthe machines you use are

regularly serviced.

The remaining types of error are slips, ie errors made because concentration has lapsed. Describe these types of error.

Type 6

a Save all your photocopying to to do

at the same time.

b Clean your typewriter regularly and

and particularly after typing sten-

cils.

c With important documents, supervise

any photocopying yourself to make cer

certain the copies are good.

Type 7

a A filing sytem must be simple to use.

b There are many type of filing systems.

c The filing system used must suit the

kind of busness done.

Type 8

a Don't keep a miscellellaneous file.

b Evererything will be put into it and

it will become unmanageable.

c Keep a files list and display it to

help you and your boss rememember

where things are.

Type 9

a It's very difficult to chagne a

filing system once it is established.

b The right type of filing system

should be chosen in hte beginning.

c If you are working with a system you

don't like, wiat about a year before

trying to change it.

Type 10

a A typewriter is only as godd as the

person using it.

b A good secretary lokks after her

typewriter carefully.

c Endlles visits from the mechanic

can be avoided if the machine is

kept clean.

The following passage has examples of the types of errors given above. Find the errors and correct them.

WORD PROCESSORS

Word proccesors hace actually been around

since the 19608s in the form, firstly, of

of automatic typewriters, the princilpe

being that a key stroke could be recorded

in a memory and then re -used, with

editings en route if desired, in a

mechanised print-out sequence instead od

being (manuaaly) re-typed every time,

time, and later as sicple video machines

- memories that could display materual

on an elelementary type of screen before

it was printed out on papr.

Comprehension: Bringing information to a text

Exercise 1 *To identify the information that is missing from a message*

1–10 is a series of instructions; *a–j* is a list of pieces of information that the speakers leave out but expect the hearers to understand. Work in pairs. Match each message with the missing information.

1 'There's a package for Mr Lim in Hong Kong. Send it by registered post, please.'
2 'Type this on a memo form, please.'
3 'Send a telegram to the Bristol office telling them I can't make Friday's meeting, please.'
4 'Mr Brown, please.'
  'Sorry, this is extension 29.'
5 'Send this to the Kano factory, will you? Their telex number is in the book.'
6 'Here are the details for the agenda for tomorrow's meeting. Type them and put them on the notice-board in the canteen, please.'
7 'Send this to Mr Green, please. Mark the envelope "Confidential".'
8 'This letter came in this morning's post. Deal with it for me, will you please? RD Trading's address is Box 141, not 114.'
9 'Send this to Mr Brown, please. He's still overseas.'
10 'Type this for me, will you please. I need four carbons. And please try to get it right this time.'

a This is a private message.

b You made a mistake last time.

c This letter's been wrongly addressed.

d The contents are valuable.

e Send the message by telex.

f Send it by airmail.

g This is an internal message.

h You've got the wrong number.

i This is a public notice.

j The message is urgent.

Exercise 2 *To use a text to supply information missing from a table*

There is a table at the bottom of the following passage. The headings have been omitted from the four columns in the table. Read the passage carefully and supply the missing information.

SELECTING THE MEANS OF COMMUNICATION

In any office the majority of communications are of a routine nature and capable of being classified according to the purposes which they serve. The office manager should consider each class and lay down instructions as to the means to be used. In arriving at a decision as to the means of communication to be used in any circumstances, there are seven major factors to be considered:

a) *Speed* How urgent is the communication? How soon is a reply required? If the answer to both questions is 'Very', a telephone message should be sent.

b) *Accuracy* Will the information be received accurately? For example, figures spoken over the telephone are liable to be misheard, and the sender cannot check whether messages sent by telegram have been received accurately.

c) *Safety* What is the risk of losing the communication in transit? If an important legal document is to be sent through the post, it is prudent to send it by registered mail.

d) *Secrecy* Does it matter if unauthorised persons become aware of the information communicated? Appropriately marked letters are probably the easiest means of sending confidential information.

e) *Record* Is it necessary that the communication should be in writing for purpose of record?

f) *Impression* Is the communication in such a form as to produce the desired reaction from the person receiving it? In most instances a letter creates a better impression than a telegram or telephone call.

g) *Cost* All elements of cost must be taken into account. The greater proportion of cost usually lies in the stages of preparation rather than in transmission. For example, the cost of labour and material expended in preparing and posting a letter will far exceed that of postage.

Not one of these factors can be said to be of greater importance than the others and all must be given proper weight according to the circumstances. The table below indicates the relative facilities offered by some of the more commonly used methods.

	1..........	2..........	3..........	4..........
Speed	Fair	Fair	V. good	Good
Accuracy	V. good	V. good	Fair	Fair
Safety	V. good	Good	n/a	n/a
Secrecy	V. good	V. good	Fair	Fair
Record	V. good	V. good	Nil	Fair
Impression	V. good	V. good	Good	Good

It will be seen that cost has been omitted from the table. In any particular situation, cost must be considered in relation to the service required. If the cheapest means is selected first, the question to be answered is 'are the additional facilities offered by alternatives worth the additional expenditure?'

(Adapted from G Mills and O Standingford, *Office Organization and Method*, 6th edn, Pitman, 1978.)

Exercise 3 *To supply information missing from messages*

Read the following text and then answer the questions printed opposite.

IS A TELEX MACHINE NECESSARY – OR WORTH IT?

Telex is best described as 'typewriting by telephone'. An installation is fairly expensive – perhaps $1 000 a year.

The machines are available through the Post Office, but transmit using a separate line network from the telephone system and a separate scale of charges. There is no means of using voice on the system – conversations and other 'handshaking' must be typed.

Telex offers the following advantages:

Receiving messages
1 A 24-hour service – the machine can receive messages even when it is left unattended.
2 A printed copy of the message with up to six carbons.
3 Few nuisance and private calls.
4 Sales enquiries received by telex are usually serious.
5 Any inaccuracies in the message can be checked with the sender.

Transmitting
1 Messages can be transmitted at any time, irrespective of working hours or time zones.
2 Transmission times shorter and cheaper than the equivalent telephone call.
3 No need to find the correct person to receive the message, so long as the recipient is identified on the heading. If misdirected within a company, it can be rapidly redirected. The disadvantage, however, is the lack of secrecy that this involves.
4 Copies of all transmitted messages.
5 The automatic acknowledgement ('answerback') from the other end is a guarantee of receipt.

Will it save money?
Many offices find telex faster, easier and cheaper than either post or telephone. Considerable savings can be made by telexing overseas, rather than telephoning. If you are planning business transactions in the Middle East, a telex machine is *essential* – communication by telephone is frequently impossible, and there is the added problem that the Moslem Thursday/Friday week-end runs into the Saturday/Sunday week-end used elsewhere.

(Adapted from article in *Better Buys for Business*, Jan/Feb 1980.)

The statements below come from the passage. They all expect the reader to supply missing information for the message to be understood completely. What is the missing information? Choose the best answer from those offered.

Example: A telex installation is fairly expensive – perhaps $1 000 a year.
  a $1 000 is a lot of money.
  b There are other communication methods which are cheaper to install.
  c A telex machine is cheaper and more efficient if it isn't installed.

1 A 24-hour service – the machine can receive messages even when it is left unattended.
  a Some machines cannot receive messages when left unattended.
  b All machines can receive messages when left unattended.
  c Telex machines are usually left unattended.
2 A printed copy of the message with up to six carbons.
  a This is a useful facility which is offered by all methods.
  b This is a useful facility which other methods do not offer.
  c This is a useful facility but more than six carbons would be better.
3 Few nuisance and private calls.
  a Nuisance and private calls are a good thing.
  b Nuisance and private calls cannot be avoided.
  c Other methods involve more nuisance and private calls.
4 Sales enquiries received by telex are usually serious.
  a Sales enquiries made by telex are not always serious.
  b Sales enquiries made by other methods are never serious.
  c Many sales enquiries made by other methods are not serious.
5 Messages can be transmitted at any time.
  a This facility is not available with other communication methods.
  b It is not important when messages are transmitted.
  c Some machines cannot transmit messages when left unattended.
6 No need to find the correct person to receive the message.
  a Some methods of communication require the correct person to receive the message.
  b Telex messages are not normally addressed to one person in particular.
  c Many telex messages are not received by the correct person.

7 Copies of all transmitted messages.
  a This means that telex messages are not very secret.
  b This advantage is not offered by some other communication methods.
  c This facility is offered by all methods of office communication.
8 The automatic acknowledgement ('answerback') from the other end is a guarantee of receipt.
  a This is a useful service which is not available on all methods of communication.
  b This is a useful service which is not available on all telexes.
  c This is a useful service despite the fact that there is no means of using voice on the system.
9 If you are planning business transactions in the Middle East, a telex machine is *essential*.
  a A telex is of no use when planning business transactions in other parts of the world.
  b No one in the Middle East has a telephone.
  c Telex machines are useful rather than essential when planning business transactions in other parts of the world.
10 Is a telex machine necessary – or worth it?
  a The author concludes that a telex machine is not always necessary but is often worth it.
  b The author concludes that a telex machine is always necessary but not always worth it.
  c The author concludes that a telex machine is always necessary and is worth it.

Exercise 4 *To supply information missing from a table*

Use the text in Exercise 3 to complete the following table (compare the one in Exercise 2). Choose your answers from the following phrases: V good, Good, Fair, Poor.

	TELEXES
Speed	....
Accuracy	....
Safety	....
Secrecy	....
Record	....
Impression	....

PS: Spelling *Sequences of letters*

One way to improve your spelling is to take more care when you are looking at sequences of letters. Take care when you meet an unusual or unknown word in your reading; take care when you are looking a word up in a dictionary and, most important, take care when writing a difficult word.

One of the most commonly misspelt words appears six times in the following puzzle. What is the word? Can you find it six times?

S	E	P	A	R	A	T	E	S
E	E	R	T	Y	U	I	E	E
T	Y	P	A	S	D	T	O	P
A	S	D	A	H	A	M	N	A
R	T	Y	U	R	E	W	Q	R
A	P	O	A	W	A	S	D	A
P	A	P	O	I	U	T	R	T
E	E	W	M	N	B	V	E	E
S	E	T	A	R	A	P	E	S

In the following puzzle are 50 of the most commonly misspelt words. Each is hidden somewhere in the puzzle – it may be written vertically, horizontally, diagonally, forwards or backwards. Use the code around the puzzle to write down where each word is found.

Example: ACCOMMODATION (*i1–u13*)

ACCOMMODATION	MAINTENANCE
ACQUAINTANCE	MARRIAGE
ACQUIRE	NECESSARY
BEGINNING	NOTICEABLE
BELIEVE	OCCASION
CEILING	OCCURRED
CERTAINLY	ONUS
CHAOS	PIECE
CHOICE	PLANNING
COMING	PRECEDING
CORRESPONDENCE	PRIVILEGE
DEFINITE	QUIET
DISAPPOINT	REFERENCE
EQUIPPED	REFERRED
ESPECIALLY	SCARCE
EXERCISE	SECRETARY
EXPENSE	SEPARATE
EXTREMELY	SINCERELY
FRIEND	SUPPRESSION
HEIGHT	SURPRISING
IMMEDIATELY	TRANSFERRED
INDEPENDENT	UNDOUBTEDLY
LIAISON	USUALLY
LOSING	VALUABLE
LYING	VIEW

	a	b	c	d	e	f	g	h	i	j	k	l	m	n	o	p	q	r	s	t	u	v	w	x	y	
1	Z	A	C	C	O	M	O	D	A	T	I	O	N	U	S	T	E	G	E	L	I	V	I	R	P	1
2	V	C	I	E	L	I	N	G	K	C	L	E	F	D	E	R	R	E	F	S	N	A	R	T	R	2
3	A	Q	U	I	R	E	K	Y	N	E	C	G	U	N	D	O	U	B	T	E	D	L	Y	A	E	3
4	L	U	P	L	A	N	I	N	G	E	L	O	O	S	I	N	G	Y	L	L	A	U	S	U	C	4
5	L	A	I	I	L	H	Y	G	D	L	B	W	M	D	S	E	P	E	R	A	T	E	Z	I	E	5
6	U	I	H	N	D	P	E	E	C	U	N	M	O	M	S	T	N	I	O	P	P	A	S	I	D	6
7	B	N	T	G	E	X	P	L	I	T	R	U	E	J	O	C	A	S	I	O	N	B	E	S	I	7
8	L	T	E	F	F	P	C	O	R	R	E	S	P	O	N	D	E	N	C	E	M	L	P	U	N	8
9	E	A	I	L	I	A	I	S	O	N	F	M	A	I	N	T	A	I	N	A	N	E	A	R	G	9
10	V	N	U	U	N	F	D	I	N	D	E	P	E	N	D	E	N	T	I	C	W	O	R	P	T	10
11	A	C	Q	U	I	R	E	N	M	O	R	L	G	S	A	T	H	G	I	H	B	C	A	R	S	11
12	W	E	I	V	T	S	S	I	N	C	R	E	L	Y	Q	E	R	T	Y	O	P	A	T	I	O	12
13	Q	U	I	T	E	R	P	E	I	C	E	D	I	S	S	A	P	P	O	I	N	T	E	S	D	13
14	S	I	N	C	E	R	E	L	Y	U	D	E	F	I	N	A	T	E	R	C	V	G	H	I	O	14
15	A	S	E	R	T	N	C	V	B	R	D	E	R	U	C	C	O	M	E	I	N	G	N	E	E	15
16	R	E	X	E	R	C	I	S	E	E	L	Y	N	O	I	S	A	C	C	O	M	I	N	G	C	16
17	E	C	P	A	S	D	A	C	V	D	F	R	T	Y	S	U	P	P	R	E	S	S	I	O	N	17
18	F	R	E	I	N	D	L	A	E	R	T	A	S	D	F	G	L	I	A	S	I	O	N	S	A	18
19	E	E	N	M	E	R	L	R	T	S	U	S	S	U	A	L	Y	B	N	M	Q	L	N	O	N	19
20	R	T	S	D	F	C	Y	C	V	B	S	S	N	O	T	I	C	E	A	B	L	E	I	A	E	20
21	E	A	E	N	N	M	E	E	G	H	C	E	R	T	A	I	N	L	Y	H	E	I	G	H	T	21
22	N	R	T	E	R	T	R	A	N	S	F	C	R	E	E	D	B	I	G	I	N	N	E	C	N	22
23	C	Y	P	I	M	M	E	D	I	A	T	E	L	Y	R	E	F	E	R	E	D	F	B	N	I	23
24	E	X	T	R	E	M	E	L	Y	U	I	N	B	E	L	E	I	V	E	I	W	E	R	T	A	24
25	E	R	E	F	E	R	E	P	L	A	N	N	I	N	G	H	J	E	G	A	I	R	R	A	M	25
	a	b	c	d	e	f	g	h	i	j	k	l	m	n	o	p	q	r	s	t	u	v	w	x	y	

Composition: Making comparisons and recommendations

Exercise 1 *To use information from two sources (a catalogue and a textbook) to make a comparison*

Your boss, Mr Dobson, needs more filing cabinets. He has asked you to find the cheapest and the best. You work in a small office. You use a numerical filing system.

Use the information given to compile a table on the advantages and disadvantages of the two filing systems.

B *Information from a catalogue:*

	Price
— Two-drawer suspension cabinet 2 DFL 698 × 464 × 622 mm	67·88
— Three-drawer suspension cabinet 1321 × 464 × 622 mm, three drawers and one top drawer as cupboard	114·36
— Four-drawer suspension cabinet 1321 × 464 × 622 mm, steel with chrome handles, two-tone grey	90·92
— Standard unit, lateral cabinet, 170 × 79 × 30·5 cm, 5 shelves, open with roll-down cover	32·99 / 40·29
— Extension unit for lateral cabinet, 5 shelves, 170 × 30·5 cm, with cover / without cover	36·95 / 29·45

A *Information from a textbook:*

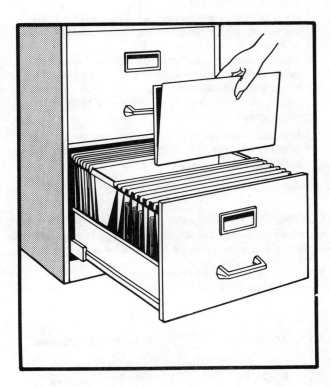

Lateral suspension

Lateral filing is the placing of one folder against another like books on a shelf. The folders are suspended laterally from rails. Space does not have to be allowed for opening drawers. A large number of files may be seen at the same time, but if they are not covered they may attract dust. A disadvantage of this method is the difficulty of reading file titles which are on their side, but this can be overcome by using a numerical system of filing.

Vertical suspension

A vertical suspension filing cabinet has drawers and the files are hung vertically. Papers can be inserted without removing the files. The files are suspended vertically from metal runners fitted inside the cabinet drawers which protect them from wear and tear. A disadvantage of using this method is the amount of space required not only for the cabinet itself, but for opening the drawers.

Now use the information you have collected to complete the following:

1 Vertical filing cabinets are ＿＿ expensive ＿＿ lateral filing cabinets.
2 Lateral filing cabinets take up ＿＿ space ＿＿ vertical filing cabinets.

3 The main difference between the two systems of filing is that ＿＿.
4 The files in the vertical system of filing have ＿＿ wear and tear ＿＿ those in the lateral system because ＿＿.
5 One advantage of the lateral system is that ＿＿ person can use it at the same time.

Exercise 2 *To complete a memo making a recommendation from a comparison*

Here is the memo written to Mr Dobson about the filing systems. Complete the message where the words have been left out.

MEMORANDUM

To: Mr Dobson   *From:* S Phiri
Date: 8 July 198–   *Subject:* Filing Cabinets

There are [1].......... systems of filing that would suit us: the lateral and the [2].......... systems.

The main difference is that in lateral filing the files are stored side by side like books on a shelf, and in [3].......... filing the files are arranged [4]...........

Lateral filing cabinets are much [5].......... (see a copy of the catalogue prices attached) and take up less [6]........... A disadvantage with lateral filing is that the files have to be [7].......... to consult papers inside, [8].......... with suspension filing there is no need to do this. With [9].......... filing the file titles are vertical and may be difficult to read; [10].......... as we have a [11].......... system of filing this is not a great [12]...........

I would recommend we purchase the lateral system as the [13].......... seem to outweigh the disadvantages.

How is the memorandum organised? Read through the message again. Is the message organised in the following way?
a Recommendation of one system.
b Reasons for the recommendation.
c A description of the two systems.

Discuss how the message is organised.

Exercise 3 *To compare features of photocopying machines and to match those features to requirements to make a recommendation in the form of a memo*

Your boss asks you to recommend a photocopier. The budget allows up to $2 000. Your firm does about 5 000 copies per month and this is likely to increase further. Your boss has specified that he does not want a treated paper machine. Use the table below to recommend one particular machine. Write your answer in the form of a memo.

Manufacturer	Model	Volume	Copies per minute	Price	Comments
BSD	9030S	••	6	471	Small desk top copier, treated paper
BSD	006S	•••	10	871	Roll feed, treated paper
BSD	965	•••	15	1 825	Plain paper copier
Quick Copy	111/10	••••	22	4 127	Plain paper, A3 size, optional meter
Quick Copy	116/3	••••	26	6 255	Similar to 111/10 but can also reduce copies
Quick Copy	74/11	••	8	825	Desk top copier, treated paper
Quick Copy	75/42	•••	10	2 680	Plain paper

(Adapted from *Better Buys for Business*, Issue No. 10, 1979.)

No of copies per month:
• 0 – 2 000
•• 2 000 – 5 000
••• 5 000 – 10 000
•••• Over 10 000

Exercise 4 *To list the information needed to make a recommendation*

Your boss has asked you to recommend a new desk for him. He has given no further information, such as how much money can be spent. The information below is from a catalogue. Use this to identify the questions you would need answered in order to make a recommendation. Write a memo to your boss requesting this information.

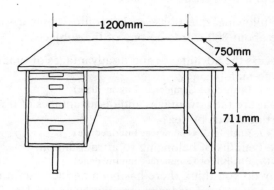

Clerical Desk MG7/T. A highly functional desk, suited to all clerical and secretarial purposes. Shown above, with panels and top **93462**, plus 3-drawer pedestal **93489** (left side), all in attractive Teak finish. Size: 1200mm × 749mm × 711mm (47¼″ × 29½″ × 28″), **£124.99.**

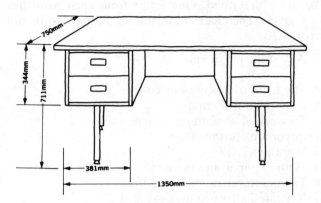

Clerical Desk MG5/T – this desk smartly combines with another to create extra desk-top working space. Top **93446**, shallow 2-drawer pedestals on both sides, **93497**. Dimensions: 1350mm × 750mm × 711mm (53″ × 29½″ × 28″), **£134.08.**

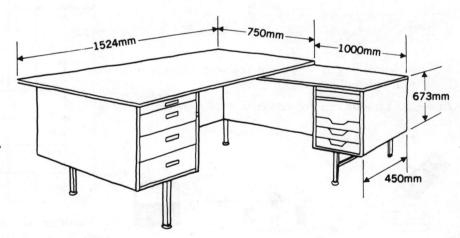

'L' Shaped unit MG6/M.
Mahogany finish and featuring practical 'L' shaped return unit. A perfect arrangement for standing additional items such as a typewriter, files or a desk-top calculator. Dimensions: 1000mm × 450mm × 673mm (39¼″ × 17¾″ × 26½″) MG6/M Desk in Sapele top **9325X**, and 3-drawer pedestal **93284**, **£201.92.** Size 1524mm × 749mm × 711mm (60″ × 29½″ × 28″). Return Unit Sapele Mahogany **93557**, **£82.54.** Return Unit Teak **93551**, **£87.85.**

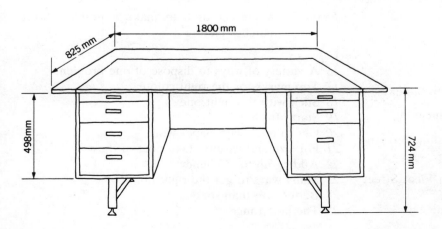

Executive Desk MG1/T – black inlay top and a choice of 2 and 3 drawer pedestals. Pedestals have pull-out flaps as standard. (The 3-drawer version has a pen tray, the 2-drawer a solid pull-out flap.) Illustrated here in Teak: **93403** (top), and 3-drawer pedestal on left **93489**, and 2-drawer pedestal on right **93470**. Dimensions: 1816mm × 825mm × 724mm (71½″ × 32½″ × 28½″), **£225.81.**

Exercise 5 *To answer an examination question which requires a comparison to be made*

The following questions each require comparisons. Write about 300 words on one of the subjects.

1 Discuss the advantages and disadvantages of running a one-man business.
(*LCCI*, English for Commerce, Intermediate)
2 What are the advantages and disadvantages of transporting goods by sea?
(*LCCI*, English for Commerce, Intermediate)
3 The benefits of belonging to a trade union.
(*LCCI*, English for Commerce, Intermediate)
4 Why do you think there has been an increase in the number of mail-order companies over the last few years?
(*LCCI*, English for Commerce, Intermediate)
5 The arguments for and against lotteries.
(*AEB*, English Language – Professional and Business Use)

PS: Ambiguity

How does something have more than one meaning?

a When you do not know where and when it is said.

Example: It's too hot to eat.

i)   *ii)*

b When something is shortened, eg in telegrams or newspaper headlines.

Example: London bus goes down well in America.

i)   *ii)*

Work in pairs to find two meanings for each of the following:
1 Judge hits out at violence.
2 86-year old man said to be critical
3 It's time to eat Grandma.
4 Flying planes can be dangerous.
5 The police were told to stop drinking on Sundays.

Other words which have more than one meaning:

a Words with a different spelling and the same pronunciation.

Example: *i)* **Their** offices used to be in Fleet Street but they
    ii) moved from **there** some time ago.

b Words with the same pronunciation and the same spelling with a different meaning or part of speech.

Example: *i)* The **file** was missing from the drawer and the papers inside were very important.
    ii) Her boss did not have much work to give her in her last job. She used to read novels, **file** her nails or write personal letters.

Complete the puzzle. The answers are pairs of words like those described. One letter from each word has been given. The clues are mixed up, and all words run across.

6 Any standard or rule
7 Not moving
8 The head of a school or college
9 Either/if it is so that
10 To work at something to improve a skill
11 Beyond or further than
12 Went by
13 Writing paper and materials
14 Temperature, rainfall, wind, etc
15 Repeated effort to improve a skill

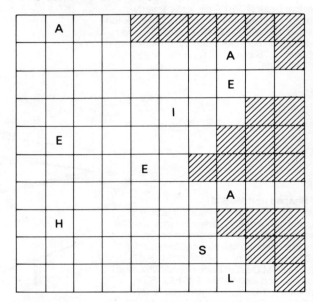

Advertising uses ambiguity. Match the following captions from advertisements with the pictures opposite. Use a dictionary if you have any difficulty.

Example: A perfect time to make a perfect choice matches picture *e*.

Captions
16 A variety of ways to dispose of one problem
17 Top marks for the right colour
18 Stick with the right one
19 Start afresh
20 Get to grips with paper work
21 For size and variety, take note of these
22 Adding up to efficiency
23 Many ways to get the right point
24 Better safe than sorry
25 The hole range

Oral/Aural: Reporting messages

Exercise 1 *Passing on information to fill in a business document*

Work in threes. Decide who is A, B and C. A: Copy the order form on page 17. B: Copy the Petty Cash Voucher on page 17. C: Copy the cheque on page 17.

1 B: A will give you some information. Pass this information on to C. Close your book while A gives you the message.

  C: Listen to the message that B gives you and use the cheque on p 17 to follow B's instructions.

  A: Read the following information to B so that C cannot hear:

> Make the cheque out to J Smith for $23·60. Put today's date and sign it.

2 C: B will give you some information. Pass this information on to A. Close your book while B gives you the message.

  A: Listen to the message C gives you and use the order form on p 17 to follow C's instructions.

  B: Read the following information to C so that A cannot hear:

> The order is for two four-drawer filing cabinets, model 161, at $39·02 each.

3 A: C will give you some information. Pass this information on to B. Close your book while C gives you the message.

  B: Listen to the message A gives you and use the petty cash voucher on p 17 to follow A's instructions.

  C: Read the following information to A so that B cannot hear:

> Make out a petty cash voucher for cleaning materials at $1·87. Put today's date and sign it yourself.

Now check that the information on the documents is correct.

Exercise 2 *To take notes to be able to remember a message*

Work in groups of three. A: Listen to a telephone conversation which B and C have. Take notes to remember the main points. Close your book while you are listening. When the conversation has finished, tell B and C what the message is. B and C: Read out the conversation below.

B: Good morning. Office Supplies Limited.
C: Ah, good morning. This is Mrs Yanchio of Star Travel Insurance. We rent a photocopier from you and we should like to order more paper.
B: Ah, yes. What model is the machine?
C: MP JFK 43.
B: And how much paper do you need?
C: 100 reams of A4.
B: White?
C: No. 25 reams each of white, blue, yellow and green.
B: May I have your account number please?
C: ST1 496, and could you deliver to our Enugu Road office?
B: Yes, fine. So you want 25 reams each of white, blue, yellow and green A4 paper for an MP JFK 43 machine, and your account number is ST1 495?
C: Yes, but the account number is ST1 496, not 495.
B: ST1 496. Your order will be delivered on Wednesday to your Enugu Road office.
C: Thanks very much.
B: Goodbye.

A: Report back the main points to B and C. B and C: Check that A has all the details correctly.

Exercise 3 *To use documents to have a telephone conversation which then has to be reported back accurately*

A: Use the *memo* for your telephone conversation with B.

B: Use the *reservation form* to guide your conversation with A.

C: Listen to A and B. Make notes. When the conversation is complete, report to A and B what you have heard.

A and B: Check that C has given all the information correctly.

A:

> **MEMORANDUM**
> *Technoproducts Ltd,* PO Box 1549,
> Singapore 0922
> Tel: 7758700
>
> *To:* A   *Date:* 30 October 198–
>
> *From:* Albert Ong   *Subject:* Hotel Booking
>
> Please phone and book one night at the International Motel for Wednesday 9 November in my name.

B:

```
International Motel
Reservation Form
Name: .....................................................
Address: ...............................................
       .....................................................
       .....................................................
Tel No: ...................................................
Dates: ....................................................
No of nights: .........................................
Single/double: .......................................
```

In the same groups, A: Use the information in the *memo* below to have a conversation with C. C: Use the information in the *insurance renewal form* below as a guide for your conversation with A.

A:

```
MEMORANDUM

To: A              From: Mr Scudder
Date: 30 October 198–   Subject: Car Insurance

Please phone the Reliance Insurance Company
to renew my policy on the car. The car is a Ford
GFS, the number is VK 9267, the policy number
is 194/198. My home address is 1000 Balmoral
Avenue, Kingston 10. I want fully comprehen-
sive.
```

C:

```
Insurance renewal form
Name of owner: ...................................
Address: ...............................................
Make of car: .........................................
Number: ................................................
Policy number: .....................................
Fully comprehensive:   YES      NO
Third party:           YES      NO
```

B: Listen to the conversation between C and A. Take notes and report back to C and A what you have heard. C and A: Check that B has reported all the information correctly.

PS: Proof-reading (2)

1

Reading for meaning and reading to find errors are two different kinds of reading. It is advisable to proof-read twice: once for errors in sense and again for typing errors.

Sometimes mistakes in meaning are made. The following is a transcription of a text taken down in shorthand. There are several errors such as the wrong word transcribed or a full stop put in the wrong place. Rewrite the text correcting the errors.

```
There are some men and women who live
much of their lives in a public gaze,
and through time to time they are held
up as people of principle who can be
relied at to say right thing at a right
time. They became known as people with
a firm view of what they believe in but
there is another side to them. For in
our private lives we are all prepared
to compromise in fact no man or woman.
Can exist for long in a family, without
giving as well as taking. He or she will
hold a certain view and find that it
need to be changed because the others in
the family looks at things in a differ-
ent way. For our family life we have to
be prepared to change our view from
time to time.
I believe this is good thing with us
all, because it helps which of us to
realise that we are only human, and
therefore we have to acknowledge that
other people can be just as right as we
think we are.
```

(*PEI* – Shorthand Speed Text, 90 wpm.)

The following business letter was typed with a number of mistakes. It has been retyped. Check that all the mistakes have been corrected. Type or write the second letter, correcting any mistakes you find.

Dear Sir

Thank you for your letter of 18 Nov.

We are enclosing samples of our Latest fabric designs plus a copy of our current pricelist

The desings are all original and I am sure you will agree that a length of this material could only enhance a room, weather it is a hotel lounge a foyer an office or a room in a private house.

From all prices we allow a Trade Discount of $33\frac{1}{3}$% on all orders recieved before 31/12/8-. under pressure of rising costs, we shall not find it possibel to extend this terms beyon that date, so why not take advantage of them now and send us an order imediately.

If specifcations are sent with the order we can make up items such as curtains table clothes serviettes cushions and etc.

We are offering   you goods of the very of the very highest quality on unusually generous terms & look forward to receivign your order.

Yours Faithfully

Dear sir

Thank you for your letter of 18 Nov.

We are enclosing samples of our latest fabric designs plus a copy of our current price-list

The designs are all original and I am sure you will agree that a length of this material could only enhance a room whether it is a hotel lounge a foyer an office or a room in a private house.

From all prices we allow a trade discount of $33\frac{1}{3}$% on all orders recieved before 31/12/8-. Under pressure of rising costs we shall not find it possible to extend this terms beyond that date, so why not take advantage of them now and send us an order immediately.

If specifications are sent with the order we can make up items such as table clothes, serviettes, cushions, etc.

We are offering you goods of the very highest quality on unusually generous terms & look forward to receiving your order.

Yours Faithfully

```
                                          OED no 916
                    ORDER

From
John Payne and Sons Limited    To
Office Equipment Division       Amalgamated Engineers Ltd.,
Bolton House                    Trading Estate,
Bolton Street                   Milltown, MN4 8OP.
Blanktown BN5 6RO
Telephone 07-1278963
Telegrams Payne Blanktown       Date  7th September 198-
```

Please Supply

Quantity	Description	Model	Price

Deliver to:

John Payne & Sons Ltd., Office Equipment Warehouse,
Green Lane, Blanktown.

signed .... (Buyer)

Petty Cash Voucher Folio_____ Date_____19⁻⁻

For what required	AMOUNT $	¢

Signature_____

Passed by_____

_____19__   _____19__   **70-19-85**

TECHNICAL BANK LIMITED

HOMETOWN

*Pay*_____ *or Order*

_____ $_____

_____

_____

$_____   _____

000331   "000331" 70 "1985": 4170736 5"

Miscellany

Exercise 1   *Pronouns (1)*

Avoid using the same word twice in one sentence unless the meaning is unclear.

Find the words in the following sentences that are used twice and change one of them either by using one of the words given below or by missing out words. You may have to change other parts of the sentences.

its, his, him, so, he, her, they, one, she, it, another's, their

1 Mary's typewriter needed servicing so Mary called the Service Engineer.
2 John is learning the new filing system and Agnes is learning the new filing system.
3 Emmanuel's mother visited Emmanuel last week and Emmanuel's mother decided to stay with Emmanuel for a month.
4 Harry should have been making the tea but Harry was not making the tea.
5 Mary prefers coffee and Peter prefers coffee.
6 I saw Lily typing without using a backing sheet and told Lily not to type without using a backing sheet.
7 Mr Finch composed the letter and Mr Finch's friends checked the letter for Mr Finch.
8 Ruth and Hilda wanted to work at the same place so Ruth and Hilda both applied for a job but only Ruth or only Hilda can get the job.
9 The manager has the small office and the secretarial staff have the big office.
10 Mr Saunders wanted Mr Saunders' arrival to coincide with Mr Saunders' secretary's.
11 The company has promised that the company's production will increase.
12 The students in the class corrected the students in the class's mistakes.
13 I was talking to my boss yesterday and remember my boss telling me of my boss's successful meeting.
14 Half of the staff working in the office had no training on any of the machines half the staff used.
15 Mr and Mrs Misebo decided that Mr and Mrs Misebo's shop was too small for the business that Mr and Mrs Misebo were doing.

In the following passages find the words that are used twice and decide whether to replace any of them:

16 There are two basic financial reports – the balance sheet and the income statement. These two reports are the keys to business planning. These two reports tell the management of the firm how much the firm owes, and how much the firm owns, and how much profit or loss resulted from the firm's activities.

17 This morning Jane Schuster, secretary to the General Manager, attended a meeting at which it was decided who would be the new office supervisor. The General Manager asked Jane Schuster to keep the decision confidential until an official announcement could be made. Bill Armstrong, a special friend of Jane Schuster's, took Jane Schuster out to lunch and asked, 'Please tell Bill Armstrong who got the job. Bill Armstrong promises not to tell anybody. Come on. It will be just between Jane Schuster and Bill Armstrong.'

18 Most stenographers prefer to use a pen for taking down shorthand notes. Stenographers who use a pencil always carry several pencils. Buy a plain pencil without an eraser and sharpen both ends of the pencil. You must have several of the pencils available at all times since the pencils lose their sharp points and are easily broken.

Exercise 2 *Word families*

Sort the following words into 10 word families.

Example: **absent, absence, absentee** and **absenteeism** belong to the same word family.

1 vary	*21* referred
2 suspect	*22* variety
3 fulfilling	*23* transfer
4 occurrence	*24* signify
5 sign	*25* fortunate
6 install	*26* transferred
7 technically	*27* variable
8 fortune	*28* technological
9 technicality	*29* transference
10 transferring	*30* refer
11 various	*31* fulfil
12 occur	*32* occurred
13 reference	*33* referring
14 technical	*34* unfortunately
15 fortunately	*35* signature
16 suspiciously	*36* installation
17 signatory	*37* occurring
18 fulfilment	*38* suspicion
19 technician	*39* fulfilled
20 instalment	*40* signet

Use a dictionary and add a total of five words to any one of the word families given.

Word families have the same *root word* – **nation** is the root word for **national**. Knowing the root word helps with spelling. In English the pronunciation changes but the spelling usually does not.

Use a dictionary to find out what the following suffixes mean:

Example: __ed added to a verb usually makes the past tense.

41 __ism	*46* __less
42 __er	*47* __a
43 __let	*48* __ly
44 __like	*49* __ian
45 __ess	*50* __ish

Make complete words using the word parts above.

In the following passage the root words have to be changed to their correct form:

Photocopying

There are several processes whereby an [51]**origin** document can be [52]**quick** reproduced. The copies may be made on plain paper, on sensitised paper, on transparencies, or on duplicating masters. A photocopy is complete and accurate, and may even be [53]**clear** than the original from which it is made.

In all[54]**case**, photocopying is more [55]**expense** than taking carbon copies, and should not be regarded as an [56]**alternate** to this method.

The cost of photocopying, allowing for [57]**depreciate** and [58]**maintain** of [59]**equip** and the [60]**consume** of paper, [61]**vary** according to the process.

Exercise 3 *Punctuation – semicolon (1)*

A clause is a sentence or part of a sentence which makes sense by itself:

Example: He corrected the manuscript is a clause and a simple sentence.
As a result of improved maintenance is not a clause, it is a phrase.

Clauses can be joined to make one complex sentence. List the words used to join the clauses in the following. Make sure that the words you have chosen join only clauses, not phrases.

1 It is useless to blame the listener if he does not understand what you are saying.
2 The reason for lack of understanding is either that the speaker has not chosen his words correctly or that he has not given sufficient explanation.
3 The person who does not understand has a duty to ask for an explanation.
4 Communication is always more difficult between strangers and formal correspondence between people who do not know each other can be time-consuming and expensive.

5 A telephone conversation between two people who understand each other quickly is effective and cheap and it is usually the quickest means of obtaining information.

When a sentence has two or more clauses of the same value, the clauses are called main clauses.

Example: The typewriter is the most commonly used office machine and it is the best known and as such it requires no general description.
The three main clauses are:
The typewriter is the most commonly used office machine.
It is the best known.
It requires no general description.

Find sentences with more than one main clause in the following:

6 The standard typewriter is designed for use in typing business documents and it is satisfactory for most general office work.

7 Most machines are fitted with a single type, usually roman, but a variety of other styles is available.

8 The basic standard machine can be modified in a number of different ways to meet special requirements.

9 Carriages are obtainable in a variety of sizes, but for exceptional widths it may be necessary to modify the typewriter.

10 On some typewriters, the carriage moves in relation to the type position and on others a type head moves along the length of the carriage.

11 Every typewriter is fitted with a device to enable the typist to stop the carriage or type head at predetermined positions, as an aid to setting out work accurately and quickly.

12 Portable typewriters, whether manual or electric, are of lighter construction than the standard typewriter and they are useful when one is travelling.

13 The electric typewriter can do more carbon copies, and typists can maintain a higher daily output but obviously they cost more than a manual typewriter.

14 There are typewriters which permit the use of a wide variety of styles and sizes of type.

15 Automatic typewriters of various kinds have been available for many decades and the term 'word processing' has been introduced to describe automatic typing processes which make use of electronic and magnetic equipment.

(*1–15* adapted from G Mills and O Standingford, *Office Organization and Method*, 6th edn, Pitman, 1978.)

Rule 1: If two main clauses have ideas that are linked, they can be joined by *and, but, or* or by a semicolon.

Put semicolons into sentences *6–15* above. Take out the linking words.

1

Example: All word processing machines have an electronic store or memory and for this reason they are sometimes called memory typewriters.

↓

All word processing machines have an electronic store or memory; for this reason they are sometimes called memory typewriters.

Rule 2: A semicolon is also used to separate items in a list, where commas have already been used in the items or the items are fairly long.

Example: Pitman's addresses include 6 Southampton Place, London; PO Box 46038, Kimathi Street, Nairobi; 495 Wellington Street West, Toronto; and 158 Bouverie Street, Carlton, Victoria.

Note: In this case the semicolon is used like a comma but it is also placed before the 'and' of the last item in the list.

From the following write two sentences using semicolons to separate the items in each list.

16 Start one sentence: The advantages of photocopying are __

17 Start the other: The disadvantages of photocopying are __

A	B
a copies easy to make	i) higher cost per copy than other duplicating machines
b copies can be made quickly	
c machines are easy to operate and require little training	ii) people tend to use machines for personal reasons
d no master needed – only a legible original	iii) there is a tendency towards making unnecessary copies
e pages from books can be copied for reference purposes	

Make up similar tables for yourself, eg the advantages and disadvantages of television, of large firms, of the telex, etc. Give your tables to a partner to produce sentences with semicolons.

Examination preparation: *Due to/Owing to*

Due to and **owing to** are frequently confused and eventually may be accepted as interchangeable. In the meantime, it can be important to know the difference, particularly in examinations.

DUE TO means 'caused by'.

Examples:

His resignation was *due to* his ill health. (= caused by his ill health)
Price rises *due to* increased costs were introduced last week. (= price rises were caused by increased costs)

OWING TO means 'because of'.

Examples:

Owing to ill health, he resigned. (= He resigned because of his ill health)
Price rises were introduced last week *owing to* increased costs. (= because of increased costs)

Complete each of the following sentences with either *due to* or *owing to*.

1 The train was late __ fog.
2 I missed the examination __ illness.
3 The accident was __ careless driving.
4 __ his unfortunate accident, the meeting was cancelled.
5 The cancellation of the meeting was __ his unfortunate accident
6 The programme was cancelled __ a technical fault.
7 __ a technical fault, the programme started late.
8 A technical fault __ poor maintenance delayed the start of the programme.
9 __ an electrical fault, there was a fire in the warehouse.
10 The fire in the warehouse was __ an electrical fault.

(*1, 2, 4, 7* from *PEI* – English for Office Skills)

All the sentences *11–20* are based on the table of tips for audio typists. Complete each one with either *due to* or *owing to*, and add the necessary information from the table.

11 __ the fact that she did not listen __, she did not type enough carbon copies.
12 His using the wrong size of paper was __ his not checking the indication slip to see __.
13 She didn't type the letter __ the fact that it did not make __ to her.
14 Errors __ poor spelling, __ should be checked.
15 Documents are frequently spoiled __ inaccurate __ and names.
16 He typed *there* instead of *their* __ his confusion because the two words __.
17 I am able to type continuously __ my ability to __ the dictating machine and not my typewriter.
18 She can remember long __, but my slowness is __ my poor memory.
19 Many errors of syllabication are __ not knowing __.
20 Poor presentation __ bad alignment of corrections is avoided by proof-reading material __.

TIPS FOR THE AUDIO TYPIST

Your ability to transcribe recorded material rapidly and accurately will be greatly improved if you remember the following points:

a Check the indication slip first and listen to any special instructions or corrections before you transcribe.
b Be sure your placement is correct. Check the indication slip for the length of the letter.
c Never type anything that does not make sense to you.
d Be alert for errors in spelling, grammar and punctuation.
e Check all addresses, figures, dates and names for accuracy.
f Do not confuse words which sound alike, such as *steak* and *stake*; *their* and *there*.
g Keep typing continuously. Stop and start the dictating machine – not the typewriter.
h Develop the ability to remember long phrases and avoid frequent replaying.
i Do not make errors of syllabication. Know the rules for word division and follow them.
j Proof-read all material before removing it from the typewriter.

(Adapted from G A Reid, *Modern Office Procedures*, 2nd edn, Pitman, Canada, 1978).

Unit 2

Summary: Summarising for telegrams and telexes

Exercise 1
1 *To reduce a phrase to a single word for inclusion in a telegram or telex*
2 *To recognise abbreviations commonly used in telegrams or telexes*
3 *To revise the use of compound words in telegraphic messages*

Telegrams must be kept short so that they can be sent as cheaply as possible. Replace each of the phrases below with words which can be used in telegraphic messages.

Example: throughout the world = WORLDWIDE

1 as soon as possible
2 for the time being
3 this is most important
4 I am sorry about
5 the least/cheapest possible
6 will not be able to/am not able to
7 is being sent as a follow-up to this telegram
8 at the latest
9 will be coming back on
10 has been despatched by air freight

Recognised abbreviations can also be used to shorten telegrams. Match the abbreviation on the left to the full form on the right.

11	ETA	a	my telegram
12	OK	b	as soon as possible
13	RETEL	c	cost, insurance and freight
14	MYTEL	d	referring to telegram/telex
15	COD	e	bill of exchange
16	CIF	f	cash on delivery
17	C/FWD	g	our letter
18	ASAP	h	agree
19	B/E	i	carried forward
20	URLET	j	estimated/expected time of arrival

Compound words (see PS on page 23) can be written as one word in telegrams.

Examples: twenty-one = TWENTYONE
up-to-date = UPTODATE

Write the following telegrams in complete sentences.
21 RETEL TWENTYSEVEN JULY STOP PLEASE FORWARD B/E SOONEST

22 INCREASE PRICE SILKSHEETS FIVEPERCENT IMMEDIATELY
23 REGRET DELAYED COPENHAGEN OWING FOG STOP ETA ROME TENTHIRTY FRIDAY
24 OWING DOCKSTRIKE SHIPMENT DELAYED TEMPORARILY STOP CIF QUOTED URLET THIRTYONE MAY UNCHANGED
25 URGENTLY REQUIRE PRICELIST AND SAMPLES NEXTYEARS RANGE STOP PLEASE QUOTE BEST DISCOUNT BULK ORDERS

Exercise 2 *To revise the distinction between **content** and **function** words, and to show how they are used in telegrams*

Another way of shortening telegraphic messages is to leave out all the unimportant words. But which words are unimportant? There are two kinds of word in English: *content* words and *function* words.

> FUNCTION words have very little meaning. They are used to relate words to each other to form sentences. The 50 most common words in English are all function words.
>
> Here are the 10 most common words in English:
>
> | | | | | |
> |---|---|---|---|---|
> | the | of | and | to | a/an |
> | in | is | I | it | that |
>
> We cannot create new function words.

> CONTENT words are the words which carry the meaning of the message. Content words are not as common as function words.
>
> Here are some examples of content words:
>
> | | | |
> |---|---|---|
> | number | people | write |
> | quickly | apply | green |
> | pencil | run | happy |
>
> We can create new content words – eg astronaut, Tanzania, television.

Separate the function words from the content words in the message below:

> The telegram service enables brief messages to be sent over long distances very rapidly.

Function words: the   to   be   over   very

Content words: telegram service enables brief messages sent long distances rapidly

The function words alone are nonsense. We can understand most messages quite clearly from the content words alone. Leaving out the function words is the best way to shorten a message when sending a telegram.

Work in pairs. Remove all the function words from the messages below. Use the word STOP in place of full stops.

1 The goods arrived on Saturday. I regret to have to inform you that three cartons were damaged.
2 Mark is ill. He has been rushed to hospital. You should return to Georgetown immediately. Dr Green has agreed to meet you at the airport.
3 Carroll's report has been delayed. We have therefore postponed tomorrow's meeting. I suggest we all meet on Thursday twenty-second to consider Carroll's recommendations.
4 Mrs Evans is unwell. Her doctor has advised her to stay at home. She hopes to return to the office on Monday. Please advise us if a replacement is necessary.
5 I have asked Caroline for 100 PB499 forms. She says only 10 are available. Please will you contact Printwell. You should place an order for 10 000 new forms. Please advise us of the approximate delivery date.

Exercise 3 *To use the necessary function words to make a telegraphic message clear*

Work in pairs. The function words have all been removed from the telegraphic messages on the left. Put back a *few* function words to avoid any confusion or ambiguity so that the messages on the left mean the same as the full messages on the right.

Exercise 4 *To write a series of telegrams using the techniques introduced in Exercises 1 to 3*

Write out the following messages as telegrams:

1 The goods which were despatched on 21 February arrived damaged. Please send replacements as soon as possible.
2 With reference to your telegram of 27 March, we are sorry that the goods arrived damaged. We sent replacements by air freight on 29 March. We have sent the documents to you by airmail.
3 We shall allow a discount of five per cent on all orders over 100 dollars and 10 per cent on all orders over 1 000 dollars.
4 We urgently require 400 XLC typewriters. Please quote your best price cost, insurance and freight to Hong Kong.
5 Unfortunately, we have only 200 XLC typewriters in stock at present. We are waiting for further deliveries from the manufacturer. We shall inform you when supplies are available.
6 Your telegram of 24 April did not give the quotation we requested. Please send us this quotation as soon as possible.
7 We are unsure what prices of XLC machines will be as we are expecting the manufacturers to raise the price in the new year.
8 Payment of your account is now long overdue. Please send $2 400 before 31 March to avoid the necessity for legal action to recover this sum.
9 If we do not hear from you before 4 April legal action will be initiated.
10 Mr Johnson has been delayed in Cairo because of illness. He now expects to arrive in Accra at 2300 on Saturday.

Example:

PRICE INCREASED ⸌TO⸍ THIRTY DOLLARS

The price has been increased to $30.

1 GOODS DESPATCHED SATURDAY DAMAGED STOP SEND REPLACEMENTS IMMEDIATELY STOP

The goods we despatched to you on Saturday were damaged. We will send replacements immediately.

2 DR GREEN TAKEN SON HOSPITAL STOP COMPLETE BUSINESS UNITED STATES STOP ADVISE RETURN BIRMINGHAM IMMEDIATELY STOP

Dr Green has taken your son to hospital. You should not complete your business in the United States. We advise you to return from Birmingham immediately.

3 CARROLLS REPORT DELAYED STOP MEETING POSTPONED THURSDAY THURSDAY STOP

Carroll's report has been delayed. The meeting has been postponed from this Thursday until next Thursday.

4 MISS JONES MRS EVANS ILL MONDAY STOP ADVISE RETURN OFFICE STOP

Miss Jones and Mrs Evans have both been ill since last Monday. We will advise you when they return to the office.

5 ORDER TEN THOUSAND NEW FORMS STOP ADVISE WHEN READY STOP

Order 10 000 new forms. Advise us when they will be ready.

Exercise 5 *To answer examination questions requiring telegrams*

1 Compose a telegram/telex message to be transmitted to Mr Black, your representative in Ibiza, informing him that your Tours Manager, Mr White, will be flying out to meet him on 24th June. Whilst there, he hopes to meet representatives of the builders – perhaps Mr Black could arrange a meeting on the 25th – he also hopes to inspect the hotels which are now to be used – Mr Black is to arrange this. Mr White will stay for three days.
(*LCCI* – Communications, Secretarial Studies Certificate)

2 Late yesterday afternoon a customer, Mr J C Piper, called at the warehouse of James Cameron Limited to place an order for 100 Rapid-Vu Display Books, RBV/A4/18, which appeared to be out of stock. As Mr Piper needed the books urgently, he said he would purchase them elsewhere, but soon after he left an assistant found that a new supply had been delivered but not unpacked.

Write a telegram in not more than 15 words informing the customer that the goods are available for immediate despatch if still required.
(*PEI* – English for Business Communications, Intermediate)

PS: Compound words

Compound words are those which are made up of two or more other words.

Example: Bedroom is a compound word.
Bedding is not.

Compound words can be:
a nouns – audio typist
b adjectives – part-time
c verbs – touch type

Compound words can be written:
a without a break – salesman
b hyphenated – mother-in-law
c as two words – shorthand typist

There are no rules on how to write compounds. If you are not sure, use a dictionary.

Decide which of the following are compound words. They have all been written without a break. Using a dictionary if necessary, decide how each compound word should be written.

1 witness	11 newspaper
2 soninlaw	12 document
3 stockholders	13 factoryworker
4 postscript	14 lumpsum
5 postdated	15 liquidation
6 solicitor	16 handwriting
7 lefthanded	17 addingmachine
8 business	18 insurance
9 officeworker	19 supplementary
10 downpayment	20 addressee

Copy the crossword below and use the clues to complete it:

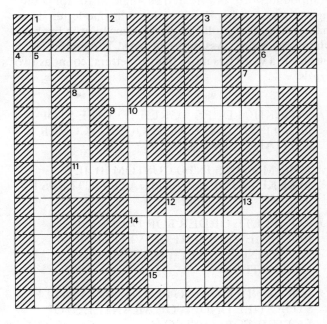

ACROSS

1 and 4. A description of a person who works in an office doing clerical, administrative or managerial work.

7 and 8 down. A person trained to make typewritten copies of manuscripts.

9 and 10 down. A paper cover for a letter, which is already addressed and the postage paid.

11 and 14. A member of a partnership who takes little active part in the running of the firm.

15 and 2 down. A person who is paid by the hour or week.

DOWN

2. See 15 across.
3. The percentage added to the cost of something when it is sold to customers.
5. Someone who holds a post or position corresponding to one's own or someone else's in another organisation.
6. The value of the popularity and reputation of a business.
8. See 7 across.
10. See 9 across.
12 and 13. The money made by a company after deduction of expenses but before taxes have been deducted.

Compound words are treated as single words for counting purposes. A hyphen is counted as one letter. How many words in the following telegrams? Put in hyphens where necessary. Assume one word is counted as 15 letters. If a word has more than 15 letters, count as two words.

1 STOCKHOLDERS AGREE TO SALE STOP SEND POST DATED CHEQUE TO COVER INITIAL PAYMENT

2 HHG MOVING INTO CUSTOM BUILT MARKET STOP INVESTIGATE OUTLETS IN JAPAN

3 COMPLETE ORDER FOR DRAWING EQUIPMENT NOT RECEIVED STOP AWAITING THIRTY TWO T SQUARES URGENTLY

4 AIR CONDITIONING PLANT NOT VIABLE STOP STILL UNDER GUARANTEE STOP LETTER FOLLOWING

5 JAY DELAYED STOP HIT AND RUN ACCIDENT STOP NOT SERIOUS STOP WILL ADVISE

Note: Associated words which are not usually hyphenated become hyphenated when used as an adjective before a noun.

Example: This timetable is out of date.
This out-of-date timetable is useless.

Sometimes a hyphen is needed to disambiguate a sentence.

Example: He is an old-car salesman.
He is an old car-salesman.

Put hyphens in the following where necessary:

6 The secretary was highly qualified.
7 The twenty four hour clock is now used internationally.
8 She had a full time job as a Personal Assistant.
9 The library has just obtained an up to date version of this book.
10 Well known makes of typewriter usually have better after sales service.
11 You will see the office on the left hand side of the road.
12 She is going on a three week refresher course.
13 To start the full time secretarial course you must be eighteen years old.
14 Every month there is a full scale four hour meeting.
15 Many businessmen rush hither and thither trying to live up to the image of the high flying, fast moving executive whose feet barely touch the ground.

Comprehension: Unfamiliar words

Exercise 1 *To show that a text can be understood even when some words are unknown to the reader*

Every eighth word has been missed out of the text below. Can you understand it?

> We are now living in a changing aaaaaa, and as science makes important new discoveries, bbbbbb researchers discover new methods and techniques, our cccccc of life is changing. Many of our dddddd are installing machinery and employing new methods eeeeee are bound to affect many people in ffffff working lives. Whilst some people may argue gggggg increasing mechanisation in industry, and in other hhhhhh too, will create greater unemployment, this is iiiiii necessarily so, and the reasons why will jjjjjj explained later in this chapter. Apart from kkkkkk changing industrial world, there have been other llllll. In many countries we now have many mmmmmm kinds of shops, all with one purpose nnnnnn view – to provide the consumer with the oooooo possible service. New developments such as the pppppp of self-service shops, supermarkets, and the qqqqqq use of automatic-machine vending, have given rrrrrr retail trade a new look. A whole ssssss of services (which are regarded as so tttttt to us in our everyday lives) are uuuuuu provided for us by our local town vvvvvv and the government.

You should have been able to understand nearly all of this text. How is this done?

1 Many words, especially function words, carry little meaning – it does not matter if we do not read them.
2 The position in the sentence and the context of the passage often provide clues which tell us what words are or what they mean.

See if you can use position and context to guess the missing words. Work by yourself and then compare answers with a partner. There will be more than one acceptable answer in many cases.

Exercise 2 *To identify the* **type** *of word required*

When we meet an unfamiliar word, it is important first to decide what *type* of word it is. Four suggestions are given for each of the difficult words in the following sentences. Only one could be right because it is the correct *type* of word. Which one?

Example: It would be useful to *conceptualise* the position of the senior secretary in a large international company.
a imagine   *c* imaginative
b imagination   *d* imaginary
Answer: a imagine (it is the only verb).

1 Someone coming to work in an office may at first find it difficult to establish a relationship *vis-à-vis* those already working there.

   a in relation to   *c* bearing little relation to
   b related to   *d* unrelated to

2 The introduction of typing pools and other shared facilities has led to a decrease in the traditional *dyadic* relationship between an executive and his personal secretary.

   a pairs   *c* in pairs
   b paired   *d* unpaired

3 A *holograph* will is one which is written entirely in handwriting by the person making it.

   a printer   *c* unprinted
   b print   *d* printing

4 One *caveat* to the general recommendation of the telex is that there is little security as messages may be read by anyone who has access to the machine.

   a advantage   *c* advantageously
   b advantageous   *d* disadvantage

5 A secretary who has worked for an organisation for many years may acquire a huge amount of *esoteric* information about the company. This information is especially valuable as it is not known to more senior personnel who have not been with the company for so long.

   a specialised   *c* specially
   b speciality   *d* specialise

Exercise 3   *To work out the meaning of unfamiliar words from their context*

Work in pairs. Try to agree on a meaning for the words underlined in the paragraphs below. In every case the context will give you the correct meaning. Do not use dictionaries.

1 Ink duplicating is also known as stencil duplicating or <u>mimeography</u> and is probably most useful for the small-to-medium sized firm where only one process is available.

2 Spirit duplicating is also known as <u>hectography</u> and is used for raising systems document sets (invoices, etc), memorandums and reports for internal distribution.

3 I heard of an old man who was going deaf and found it hard to hear the telephone bell, with the result that he missed a lot of calls. He explained this problem to the telephone company and they agreed to install a louder bell at no extra cost. The old man was delighted and asked when they would come to install it. The official said that he could not give a definite date but would phone the man when the engineers were ready. While this <u>anecdote</u> may seem amusing at first, it also shows how important it is for companies to understand the problems of their customers.

4 <u>Bürolandschaft</u> or the landscaped office, is a variation of the open-plan office designed to take account of the comings and goings of the staff and visitors and all aspects of communication within the organisation. It is of German origin. The space requirements of every employee are investigated, the equipment required, the area in which he (or she) needs to work and the access required to get to and from a desk. When all this information is available a chart is prepared which is translated into a plan for the available area.

5 The <u>virgule</u> is used to separate alternatives (Dear Sir/Madam) or to represent 'per' in certain abbreviations (90 km/hr).

6 The practitioner may be respected for his experience and probably his age, yet nevertheless despised for his lack of qualifications. <u>Ambivalence</u> of this sort is apparently widespread.

7 One might expect that training institutes would be at the forefront of change. Recent surveys and personal observations suggest that this is not so. In practice some training institutes, if not the majority, appear as conservative forces maintaining the <u>status quo</u> rather than acting as agents of change.

8 At such meetings, senior management, who in the ordinary way might not be approachable in the course of duty because they feel they might lose authority, become approachable and are prepared to discuss fairly trivial matters without <u>jettisoning</u> any of their authority.

(*4* and *8*, A Delgado, *The Enormous File*, Murray, 1978.)

9 It is essential that the senior secretary should be involved at all levels of decision-making by her boss. Without the knowledge and confidence brought by such an arrangement, she will be quite unable to act as her boss's <u>surrogate</u> when he is unavoidably absent or involved with other matters.

10 Training staff tend to be either theoreticians (the person employed to teach on the basis of his academic qualifications) or practitioners (the person who teaches a subject that he has learnt entirely through practice, through doing the job). Of course, there are those who have all the necessary academic or professional qualifications and are also experienced and skilled in doing the job for which they are training others. But such people, the <u>hybrids</u>, are rare.

(*6, 7* and *10*, adapted from W Reilly, *Training Administrators for Development*, Heinemann Educational Books, 1979.)

Check your answers in a dictionary when you have agreed on the meanings.

Exercise 4 *To interpret a text containing several totally unfamiliar words and work out the meanings of the unfamiliar words from their context*

It is very often possible to understand a lot about unfamiliar words by looking carefully at the contexts in which they are found. The passage below contains several unfamiliar words. Read the passage and then answer the comprehension questions underneath.

> The Royal Government of Bhutan, under its 25-year-old king Jigme Singye Wangchuck, has decided to change its monetary system, breaking away from the Indian rupee and substituting the ngultrum, which fortunately equals the rupee. As one would expect, the ngultrum is divided into 100 chhertums, while the major unit, the sertum, equals 1000 ngultrums.
> This Buddhist kingdom of 45,000 square kilometres and just over one million inhabitants lies sandwiched between the mountainous frontiers of Tibet and India.

(From an article in *The Sunday Telegraph*, 30 March 1980.)

1 What is Bhutan?
2 Where is Bhutan?
3 What is the main religion of Bhutan?
4 What is the area of Bhutan?
5 What is the population of Bhutan?
6 Do you think Bhutan is flat?
7 Who is Jigme Singye Wangchuck?
8 When was Jigme Singye Wangchuck born?
9 What is the ngultrum?
10 How much is the ngultrum worth in India?
11 What is the chhertum?
12 How much is the chhertum worth in India?
13 What is the sertum?
14 How many ngultrums are there in one sertum?
15 How many chhertums are there in one sertum?
16 How much would one sertum be worth in India?

PS: Writing formal definitions

Formal definitions are used in dictionaries, glossaries and some examination questions. They have three parts.

Example:

Look through the following definitions and find A, B and C in each one.

1 Compliments slips are small slips of paper printed '*with compliments*' of a department or company, for attaching to information copies of letters or to catalogues, etc when a letter is not required.
2 Golfball typewriters are electric typewriters which use small cylindrical heads containing all the usual characters instead of type bars.
3 Interliner is the small lever which is used to free the platen without losing the original typing line.
4 Landscape is the term used for the position of the paper when it is placed in the typewriter with the wider measurement across the page.
5 Letter-headings are the printed headings on business stationery.
6 Memorandums are written communications between branches or departments of an organisation.
7 Paper bail is the movable arm on which the paper grips are mounted.
8 Specifications are formal documents used by builders, designers, architects, etc to set out the exact measurements, details, materials and procedures to be used for a piece of work.
9 Touch control adjuster. This is a numbered selector for adapting the 'tension' of the typewriter to personal touch pressure.
10 Vari-typer is an electric machine which produces typewriting resembling printers' type.

(*1–10* adapted from S Burd, *The Typist's Desk Book*, 3rd edn, Pitman, 1974.)

Write a glossary (a list of definitions arranged in alphabetical order) for the following terms taken from the article in Exercise 1.
mechanisation
consumer
self-service shop
supermarket
automatic-machine vending

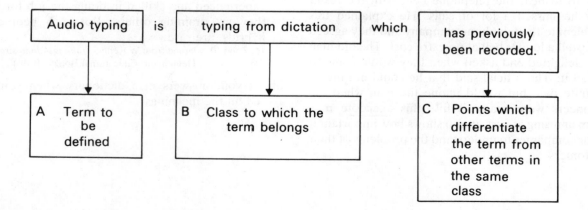

Composition: Organisation of a letter

Exercise 1 *To show understanding of the organisation of a letter*

The following are parts of two letters mixed up. One is a letter of enquiry and the other is the reply. Work in pairs and sort them out. Write or type each letter in blocked style. The letter-head for each letter has been given to help you.

2

1   Enquiry

> **KAMEKAWA IMPORT COMPANY**
> Kanda Building   4–4 Jimbocho   Kanda
> Chiyoda-Ku
> Tokyo
> JAPAN

a
> Mr Chew
> Purchasing Department
> Kamekawa Import Company
> Kanda Building
> 4–4 Jimbocho
> Kanda
> Chiyoda-Ku
> Tokyo
> Japan

b
> The Regional Sales Manager
> CI Fabrics Ltd
> Head Office
> 38 First Lokyong Road
> Jurong Town
> Singapore 22

c
> Dear Sir

d
> Chew Chong King
> Purchasing Dept

e
> Thank you for your letter of 18 February 198–.

f
> We are particularly interested in your range of denims and should appreciate having some samples.

g
> Enclosed are our latest catalogue and price-list as you requested.

h
> Yours faithfully

2   Reply

> **CI FABRICS LTD**
> (Head Office) 38 First Lokyong Road
> Jurong Town
> SINGAPORE 22

i
> Your representative called here about three months ago and left us your catalogue.

j
> 26 February 198–

k
> We are also sending under separate cover the samples of our full range of denims.

l
> Yours sincerely

m
> We have passed on your enquiry to Mr Charles, our Sales Representative in your area, and he will call on you should you have any further queries.

n
> Encs

o
> We were not in a position to place an order at the time; however we should now like to see your latest catalogue with an up-to-date price-list.

p
> Dear Mr Chew

q
> 18 February 198–

r
> E Lee
> Regional Sales Manager

s
> Goods can be delivered within two weeks of receipt of your order. Please note that we offer a trade discount of five per cent.

t
> Please forward details of delivery.

Exercise 2 *To match a letter and its reply to fill in missing information*

Letter A below is a letter of enquiry. Letter B is the reply. Type or write each letter filling in the missing information by matching corresponding parts of each letter. Supply your own information if either of the letters does not give it.

Letter A

ACACIA SAFARI LODGE

Kanda Kanda Park
P O Box 346   Kanda   Telephone 83302

1) _____

2) _____

The Sales Manager
Hotel Supplies Ltd
Renfrew Road
London   SW4
United Kingdom

Dear Sir

A colleague was visiting England last year and passed on your catalogue to me.

We are interested in replacing our china and should like to order
through your firm.   3) _____ and price-list and
tell me 4) _____ and delivery dates.

5) _____

P Phiri
Manager

Letter B

6)
_____

Renfrew Road

7)
_____

SW4
United Kingdom

14 July 198-

Mr P Phiri
8) _____
Acacia Safari Lodge
Kanda Kanda Park
P O Box 346
Kanda
Kenya

Dear 9) _____

Thank you for your letter of 4 July 198- asking for a catalogue and
price list.

I have pleasure in sending you 10) _____ which gives all prices,
and an order form. We give 15 per cent discount on orders of £200
or more, and payment must be made within 30 days of the invoice.

We send small orders 11) _____; larger orders can take 12) _____.
I hope these terms are agreeable and I look forward to 13) _____.

14) _____

A Jones
15) _____

Enc

Exercise 3 *To compose parts of letters from the matching parts in the enquiry or reply*

Column A has parts of different letters of enquiry. Column B has parts of replies. Write the corresponding part that is missing. The first one has been done for you.

A – Enquiries	B – Replies
1 12 December 198–	Thank you for your letter of 12 December 198–.
2 Yours faithfully *Paul Pham.* Paul Pham Import Manager	
3	Your ref: DA/NPR
4	We have pleasure in sending you our latest catalogue.
5 Would you please send details of the cabinets advertised in 'The Straits Times'.	
6	We can send the goods within a week of receiving your order.
7 I should like to book a single room from 22 May to 25 May inclusive.	
8	We are interested to hear that you saw our advertisement in 'The Office Machine News'.
9 I should appreciate a visit from your representative when he is next in the area.	
10	Our terms are 33⅓ per cent discount to approved accounts, with 2½ per cent for settlement within 15 days of the date of the invoice.

Exercise 4 *To use a reply to practise writing an enquiry.*

Write the letter of enquiry from the following reply:

Dear Mr Siung

Thank you for your letter of 16 March 198–.

We should be most pleased to arrange accommodation and facilities for your conference from 16 to 23 September 198–.

We have six hotels in Trinidad and Tobago and enclosed are details of the facilities and our price-list. Please note that there is a discount for parties of over 30 people.

We advise you to book at least two months in advance as there is a heavy demand in September, particularly for our conference rooms.

We look forward to hearing from you.

Yours sincerely

R. Bain.

R Bain
Manager

2

Exercise 5 *To write an enquiry from notes*

Use the following notes to write an enquiry from J W Lee, the Manager, Electrical Retailers, 9994 Aba Road, Ikeja, Lagos. The notes are not in any particular order.

catalogue – price-list – portable radios – delivery times – The Sales Manager, Technics Ltd, 20-24 Lock Road, Kowloon, Hong Kong – special terms for large orders.

PS: Vocabulary of business letters

Answer the following questions about parts of a letter by choosing the most suitable answer. (Use a reference book to look up any answers you do not know.)

1 *Yours faithfully* means:
   a You know the person you are writing to.
   b You have used *Dear Sir* to start the letter.
   c You are writing to a British firm.

2 *Enc* means:
   a There is a letter in the envelope.
   b There is a document with the letter.
   c There are at least three pieces of paper in the envelope.

3 *Dear Sir* means:
   a The person you are sending the letter to is a Member of the House of Lords in Britain.
   b The person has a better job than you have.
   c You are writing a formal letter.

4 *SW15* means:
   a An abbreviation for an American State
   b The typist's initials
   c An area in the south west of London

5 *January 1 198–* means:
   a The letter is from an American company.
   b The letter is from a country where New Year's Day is January 1.
   c The letter has been dated wrongly.

6 *cc* followed by a name means:
   a cubic centimetres
   b A copy of the letter has been sent to another person.
   c The person who wrote the letter was out of the office when it was signed.

7 *Esq* means:
   a The letter is from a man.
   b The letter is to a man.
   c The letter is to a very important man.

8 *Ms* followed by a name means:
   a You are not sure whether the woman you are writing to is married or not.
   b The person you are writing to is a campaigner for women's rights.
   c A manuscript

9 *Dear Sir or Madam* means:
   a The letter has been sent to many people.
   b The letter is addressed to a company, not a particular person.
   c The letter is to a husband and wife.

10 *Dear Sirs* means:
   a The letter is addressed to a company, not a particular person.
   b More than one person will read the letter.
   c There are two people in the company.

11 *Messrs* means:
   a The letter is to two men.
   b The letter is to a partnership.
   c An abbreviation for messengers.

12 *ADV/MP* means:
   a The typist is called Mary Phiri.
   b The letter was dictated.
   c The letter is filed under P.

13 *Dear Herr Schmidt* means:
   a The letter is to a foreign woman.
   b *Mr* has been left out.
   c The letter is to a German, a Norwegian or a Swede.

14 *cont/. . .* means:
   a The letter is not finished.
   b There is another sheet to the letter.
   c The letter is very long.

15 *Ref* means:
   a A filing reference will follow.
   b The letter is about a football match.
   c The letter must be shown to someone else.

The following letter has blanks in it. Choose items from the questions above to complete it.

D B BROWN & COMPANY
Travel Agents

58 Frederick Street, Port of Spain, Trinidad
Cable Address BROWNCO
Telephone 67-87 550/52

Your ref: 16) _____

Our ref: 643/AB/6

4 July 198–

The Manager
Hispaniola
Hastings
Barbados

Dear 17) _____

Would you please reserve 12 single rooms, full board for four nights from 20 May 198– starting with dinner.

A list of the full names of the guests is enclosed.

I should be grateful if you would confirm as soon as possible.

18) _____

M L P Thompson

M L P Thompson

19) ____ C Parsons
The Manager
Carib International
20) _____

30

Oral/Aural: Telephone calls

Exercise 1 *To be aware of the differences between face-to-face and telephone conversations*

Language changes when you cannot see the person you are talking to. Compare these two conversations:

Conversation 1
A: Hello.
B: Hello. Oh, you've got it. I was hoping it would be ready before lunch.
A: Well, I said I would. What's this then?

Conversation 2
A: Hello. A here.
B: Hello. This is B. Do you remember the report on Allied Chemicals I gave you to type yesterday? I just want to check to see if it will be ready before lunch.
A: It's ready now. Shall I bring it over?
B: Thanks. I've got another report that needs to be done by the end of the week.

Discuss the differences between Conversations 1 and 2. Decide what information is contained in each.

Exercise 2 *To invent a dialogue for a face-to-face conversation and convert it to a telephone conversation*

One half of a conversation is given below. Work in pairs and decide what the missing parts of the conversation could be:
A: ....
B: Yes, I've finished it.
A: ....
B: How many do you want?
A: ....
B: When for?
A: ....
B: All right.

In pairs, read out the complete conversations to the class. How many different situations are there? Do you always know what the conversation is about? In pairs, rewrite your conversation as it would be over the phone.

Again read out each conversation. The class can judge whether you have given sufficient information for a telephone call.

Exercise 3 *To sort out a mixed-up telephone call*

Before you make a telephone call, plan what you want to say. The following conversation is out of order. In pairs put it into the correct order:

1 B: 127 by 76 millimetres.
1 A: Good. I'm Julius Dawodu of Musa Business Enterprises and we are interested in purchasing index cards. Have you any in stock?
2 A: Well, what is the smallest size?
2 B: At 1700 hours.
3 B: 41 cents for a hundred.
3 A: Thanks. Goodbye.
4 B: Mr Salako speaking.
5 B: What sort are you interested in? We have ruled and plain, two sizes and a choice of colours.
4 A: And do you have those in white with lines?
5 A: How much are they?
6 A: Good morning. May I speak to Mr Salako please?
6 B: Yes, we have those too to go with the cards. They are 63 cents for a set and there are five colours to choose from.
7 B: Goodbye.
7 A: Good – and what about dividers to go with them?
8 B: Yes.
8 A: Thank you very much. Oh, what time do you close?

When you have sorted out the correct order, practise the conversation in pairs.

Imagine you are Julius Dawodu. Make notes about what you wanted to say before you made the above call.

Exercise 4 *To plan telephone calls*

If you are making an enquiry on the phone, what will you need to ask?

Example: If you were enquiring about first-aid kits, your notes for the call would be: Price, portable/attached to wall, what it is made of, how big, contents.

In pairs make notes about what you would need to ask about the following products:
1 Index card cabinets
2 Paper
3 Notice-boards
4 Scales
5 Envelopes
6 Erasers

Now study the following information from a catalogue to check if your notes cover all you need to ask about:

1 Index card cabinets

Ref No	No of drawers	Drawer size	Cabinet size	Price	
606	6	82 × 235 × 377 mm	699 × 281 × 406 mm	39·45	NL
609	10	50 × 235 × 377 mm	699 × 281 × 406 mm	46·01	NL
				52·25	L
605	15	50 × 235 × 377 mm	965 × 281 × 406 mm	60·12	NL
				65·87	L

NL = Non Lock   L = Lock

2 Paper

Type		Colour	Size	Price
Duplicator		White	A4	2·81 per ream
		Blue	,,	2·85 per ream
		Yellow	,,	2·85 per ream
Typewriting:	Bond	White	,,	0·48 per 50 sheets
	Copy	,,	,,	0·40 per 50 sheets

3 Notice-boards

Size	Aluminium frame Price	Wood frame Price
900 × 600 mm	14·40	14·10
1200 × 900 mm	23·40	19·39
1800 × 900 mm	33·30	32·40
1800 × 1200 mm	39·00	38·40

Price

Unframed: 600 × 300 mm − 4·20
               915 × 610 mm − 8·10

Notice-boards available in green, red, blue, brown, grey.

4 Scales

				Price
Model 25	Parcel Scale.	All metal.	10 kg × 50 g	42·00
Model 63	Letter and parcel.	0–1 kg × 10 g and 1–5 kg		
	Letter and parcel rates shown			16·50
Model 51	Letter scale.	Red plastic.	0–900 g × 5 g	
	Shows letter rates.			13·30

5 Envelopes

	Size	Price
Bankers	9 × 4	0·64 per 25
	12 × 5	0·78 per 25
	15 × 6	0·91 per 25
Pockets	4 × 9	0·76 per 25
	C6	0·81 per 25
	DL	0·82 per 25

6 Erasers

		Price
Ink/pencil	(box 20s)	3·23 per box
Eraser pencil	(box 10s)	1·85 per box
Pencil	(box 10s)	2·31 per box
	(box 20s)	2·46 per box

Exercise 5 *To practise making telephone enquiries*

Work in pairs. If possible sit back to back. A: Use your notes to make three telephone enquiries about:
1 Post scales
2 Index cabinets
3 Notice boards

B: Use the information from the catalogue to answer A's enquiries. Change over. B: Use the notes to help you make enquiries about:
1 Envelopes
2 Paper
3 Erasers

Exercise 6 *To find missing information in telephone messages*

The following messages have insufficient information. Work in pairs to identify what is missing.

1

TELEPHONE CALL

To *The Personnel Manager*

Time *1310 hrs*   Date *4/9/8—*

From *Paul Pham*

of *——*

Phone No.

MESSAGE *He can't manage the interview tomorrow. Would you phone him back to fix another time*

Operator *R. Sakala*

2

TELEPHONE CALL

To *R. S. Chin*

Time *15.20*   Date *9/11/8—*

From *Mr James*

of *Central Training*

Phone No. *Mufulira 63492*

MESSAGE *Mr James is arriving by train tomorrow. Will you arrange for him to be met?*

Operator *M. Banda*

3

TELEPHONE CALL

To *A. Igbokwe*

Time *1600 hrs*   Date *30 June 198—*

From *Frank*

of

Phone No. *43294*

MESSAGE *Cancel tomorrow's meeting. Let everyone know.*

Operator *C. Agodo*

4

TELEPHONE CALL

To *S. Tan*

Time *1400 hrs*   Date *22 May 198—*

From *International Travel*

of *2001 Bendemeer Rd*

Phone No.

MESSAGE *An order was placed three weeks ago. They haven't heard anything. Would you follow this up?*

Operator *Benny Ong*

Exercise 7 *To practise telephone conversations*

Sitting back to back if possible, work in pairs and reconstruct the conversation from each message in Exercise 6. You will have to make up some of the information, eg the name of the company you work for.

PS: Spelling *Helping your memory*

In the following list of words there are eight sets. Sort these out. Each set has something in common regarding spelling.

Example: embarrassed, marriage and *transferred* are words spelt with a double r.

1 achieved	*16* irreparable
2 anxiety	*17* maintenance
3 circumstance	*18* marriage
4 compatible	*19* negotiable
5 competence	*20* patient
6 correspondence	*21* permissible
7 embarrassed	*22* quiet
8 existence	*23* really
9 friend	*24* remittance
10 height	*25* their
11 illegible	*26* transferred
12 importance	*27* usually
13 independence	*28* valuable
14 indispensable	*29* weird
15 invisible	*30* woollen

Describe what is the same about each set.
Choose a word that you know how to spell that matches each set.

Example: **table** – indispens**able**, valu**able**.

Now make up a sentence for each set including as many of the words in the set as you can, as well as the word you know how to spell. The more bizarre the sentence, the better you will remember it.

Example: The golden *table* was *valuable* but very small and the wooden *table* was cheap and *indispensable* as everyone used it.

Build up a picture in your mind:

Miscellany

Exercise 1 *Paragraph division in business letters*

A paragraph usually contains a number of sentences dealing with one idea or topic. Modern business letters are often brief and contain fairly short paragraphs. Given below is a classification of the main types of paragraphs found in business letters (I–III) and also a list of typical statements (*1–25*). Match each of these (*1–25*) to one of the paragraph types (I–III).

I **Opening Paragraph.**
   It is common to have a short opening paragraph dealing with one of the following topics:
   a A reference to a previous letter
   b A reference to some other contact or document

II **Closing Paragraph.**
   It is also common to have a short closing paragraph dealing with one of the following topics:
   a The reply that you hope to receive
   b A reference to other letters or documents that will be sent
   c A conclusion drawn from the body of the letter
   d A greeting or message of appreciation

III **Middle Paragraph(s).**
   The body of the letter will contain at least one paragraph. Each paragraph should deal with a separate topic. Common topics in business letters include:
   a Asking for information
   b Giving information or prices
   c Acknowledging orders
   d Giving instructions

1 Our new price-list will be forwarded in September.
2 With reference to your letter of 22 May . . .
3 Will you please quote prices for the following . . .
4 Your order has been passed to the warehouse for despatch.
5 We should be glad to give you any further information you require.
6 Your name has been given to us by . . .
7 We look forward to your reply.
8 Our prices for the goods you are interested in are as follows:
9 With best wishes.
10 Thank you for your letter of 22 May.
11 Please ensure that the goods are sent by air.
12 We enclose our latest catalogue.
13 We should like to thank you for your co-operation.
14 We shall send further details as soon as they are available.
15 We confirm that the goods ordered are in stock and will be despatched as soon as possible.
16 In reply to your letter of . . .
17 We should be grateful if you would send us your catalogue.
18 A colleague has passed on your catalogue and . . .

19 We hope that the goods ordered will prove satisfactory.
20 Please notify our agents when you are ready to despatch our order.
21 Your letter has been passed on to the Sales Department, who will be in touch with you shortly.
22 We regret that we have been unable to help you on this occasion.
23 Further to my letter of . . .
24 Can you give us some indication of when our order will be ready?
25 We regret that the catalogue you ask for is not yet available.

Each of the letters below contains a salutation (Dear Sir, etc), a close (Yours sincerely, etc) and three paragraphs. Divide each letter into five parts.

26 Dear Mrs Brown Thank you for your letter of 22 February. This was passed on to me by our Eastern Region Office. I am pleased to say that we are able to supply the goods you require. The total cost, including postage and packing, will be $10·56. Please allow 28 days for delivery. Please note that the goods can be exchanged within 30 days. Yours sincerely T A Masters (Sales Assistant)

27 Dear Sirs I refer to your advertisement in today's 'Daily Tattle'. I should like to apply for the post of book-keeper. Will you please send me an application form at the above address. I look forward to your early reply. Yours faithfully S P Grey (Miss)

28 Dear Miss Grey Thank you for your recent letter in response to our advertisement in 'The Daily Tattle'. We have pleasure in enclosing an application form. We should be grateful if you would complete and return it as soon as possible. You should attach two passport-size photographs. Please ensure that we receive your returned application before 15 April. Yours sincerely W B Green (Personnel Manager)

29 Dear Miss Grey Your letter of 3 April with your returned application form has just been received. Unfortunately, your letter appears to have been incorrectly addressed and was consequently delayed. Regrettably, it was received too late for consideration. Interviews have already been held for this position. The company hopes to make an appointment in the near future. I regret that circumstances have prevented us from proceeding further with your application. Yours sincerely W B Green (Personnel Manager)

30 Dear Mrs White Reference is made to your recent application for a position with this company. I regret to inform you that your application has not been successful. The company has now filled this post. We should like to thank you for your interest in this position. Yours sincerely W B Green (Personnel Manager)

Exercise 2 *Abbreviations*

Some abbreviations we should know, many we can work out from the context in which they appear, and some we do not need to know at all as our understanding is not affected.

Decide whether we need to know what the abbreviations below stand for.

1 Applications should be sent to: Av. Alm. Reis 306.1⁰ E., Lisbon, Portugal.
2 ARRIVING ZAMBIA AIRWAYS FLIGHT QZ 463 THURSDAY TWENTYSECOND APRIL STOP PLEASE MEET
3 Please take a BPG up to Miss Clerk's office as soon as you can. She needs one urgently.
4 We need more paper. Please buy 100 reams of 297 mm × 210 mm.
5 Our ref WBG/jph (on a letter despatched).

Abbreviations can stand for different things according to the context. Use the context to decide what the abbreviations stand for in the following:

We type books, reports, etc. Any MS typed quickly and accurately. Reasonable rates. Phone 32704.

---

etc means:

6 *a* Eastern Trades Congress
  b Et Compagnie
  c etcetera (and so on)
  d European Trade Commission

MS means:

7 *a* Mississippi
  b female (marital status unknown)
  c manuscript
  d Master of Science
  e months after sight

MEMORANDUM
To: Branch Manager
From: Area Manager
cc: Company Accountant

---

cc means:

8 *a* cubic centimetres
  b carbon copy/circulation copy
  c centuries
  d continuance clause
  e County Council/City Council

Amount: ....
Cheque number: ....
A/C number: ....

A/C means:

9 *a* account   *c* aircraft
  b alternating current *d* accepted

Mr P K J Brown, c/o Mr L M Grey, 10 Paxton Street, Newtown

---

c/o means:

10 *a* commanding officer   *d* carried over
   b company   *e* cash order
   c county   *f* care of

Use the context to work out the meanings of the abbreviations in the following texts:

11 NCR paper is a type of paper coated with chemicals so that carbon paper is not required. It is available with three different kinds of coating – CB, CF, and CBF. If you want one copy, place a CB sheet on top of a CF sheet. When pressure is applied, the back of the top sheet is pressed against the front of the bottom sheet, producing a copy. If you want more than one copy, CFB is required. This has a coating on the front *and* the back so that it receives a copy from the CB sheet above it and passes it on to the CF sheet underneath.
12 Trainee mngt clk. Exc prosps. Phone 262 4761 or 742 7448 (evgs).
13 Tri-ling Sec French/German/English spkg requd. Phone Central Emp Agy 268 4871.
14 Telex/Tel/Rec for small friendly co. Sal $100 pw.
15 City Centre bkshop req typist sev morns a wk. Hrs and sal neg. Tel 892 5371.
16 Gen clk. Imm start. Tel 831 9119.
17 Copy typist reqd by lge city centre htl. Free meals, other benfts. Tel Personnel 533 5125.
18 Audio Secretary urg req for prpty co, 3-day wk or hrs by arrange. This is not a glam job but int wk and gd sal offered to someone prep to work hd for small friendly org. Tel Pat Brown 539 2823.
19 Jnr Audio Sec. West End Fin Co seeks young audio sec (knowledge of s/h advantageous). Exc prospects + exc co bens. Ring 632 1379.
20 Points to watch when changing a typewriter ribbon spool:
   a) Make sure the two spools are interchangeable because on some very old Imperial machines they are clearly marked LH and RH and if you throw away the wrong one, you may be unable to obtain a replacement.
   b) Make a quick sketch of the way the ribbon is wound round the spools. Draw two small circles to represent the left- and right-hand spools and then draw in the path of the ribbon.

Exercise 3 *Proof-reading (3)*

Match each of the following letters with the addressed envelope. Then check that the addressesses on the envelopes are correct. Identify any mistakes.

The letters are in pairs but mixed up. In each pair one letter is to and one letter is from a company or a person. The addresses on the letters are all correct.

1

TECHNICAL BOOKS LTD

P O Box 1613 Embala
CAIRO

9 November 198-

Herr R I Brusch
93 München 40
Neusser Strasse 3
West Germany

Dear Herr Brusch

2

Office Supplies Inc

P O Box 659   Nassau
Bahamas

21 June 198-

The Sales Manager
FTU Limited
P O Box 78
49 Melmac Avenue
Kingston 5
Jamaica

Dear Sir

3

641 Buccleuch Street
Edinburgh
EH3 9HS

17 August 198-

Dear Sirs

4

93 München 40
Neusser Strasse 3
West Germany

29 November 198-

Dear Sirs

5

TTM IMPORT CO LTD

6900 Broad St Harrisburg Pa   17105 7019

14 August 198-

Mr A Arumugam
East West Clothing Ltd
No 1004 Market Street
Singapore 1

Dear Mr Arumugam

6

FTU Limited, PO Box 78, 49 Melmac Avenue, Kingston 5, Jamaica

23 September 198-

Office Supplies Inc
P O Box 659
Nassau
Bahamas

Dear Sirs

7

East West Clothing Ltd, No 1004 Market St, Singapore 1

2 September 198-

TTM Import Co Ltd
6900 Broad Street
Harrisburg
Pa 171057019
USA

Dear Sirs

8

Av NS Copacabano 1259/1006
Rio de Janeiro
Brazil

23 June 198-

Evans Cycle Co Ltd
659-660 Maroondah Highway
Ringwood
Victoria 313
Australia

Dear Sirs

9

S R PHOTOGRAPHIC CO
16—19 Tsukiji 5 — chome Chuo-ku TOKYO

30 July 198-

Mr A Macarthur
641 Buccleuch Street
Edinburgh EH3 9HS
Scotland

Dear Mr Macarthur

10

EVANS CYCLE COMPANY
659–660 Maroondah Highway
Ringwood Victoria 313
Australia

21 July 198-

Ms A Celani
Av NS Copacabano 1259/1006
Rio de Janeiro
Brazil

Dear Ms Celani

a

Her R I Brush
93 Munchen 40
Neusser Strasse
Germany

f

Mr A Arumugun
East west Clothing
No 10004 Market Street
Singapore

b

The Sales Manager
FTU Ltd
P O Box 75
45 Melmar Avenue
Kington
Jamaica

g

Technical Books
P O Box 1316
Embaba
cairo
Egypt

c

Sales Dept
S R Photographic Co
16-19 Tsukji 5
choma
Cho-Ku
Tokyo
Japan

h

Evans Cycle Co Ltd
659-662 Maronda Highway
Ringwood
Victorai 313
Australia

d

R McArthur Esq
541 Bucleuk Street
Edinborough
Scotland

i

Mrs A Celana
AV NS Copacabana
1259-1006
Rio-de-Janeiro
Brazil

e

TTM Import Co Ltd
6800 Broad Street
Harisberg
Pa 17115
USA

j

The Manager
Office Suppliers Ltd
P O Box 659
Nasau
Bahamas

Examination preparation: *Only*

The word **only** can be put in a number of places in a sentence and the sentence will be grammatically correct. To make the meaning clear, put **only** in front of the word you want to add meaning to.

Example: **Only** Paul passed the exam.
(No one else passed.)
Paul **only** passed the exam.
(He did not get a distinction.)

Match the following sentences with the meanings given underneath:
1 Only John phoned Mary today.
2 John only phoned Mary today.
3 John phoned only Mary today.
4 John phoned Mary only today.

a John phoned Mary today but not at any other time.
b John phoned Mary but nobody else today.
c Nobody but John phoned Mary today.
d John phoned Mary today but didn't see her or write to her.

"SHE TYPES 40 WORDS A MINUTE, BUT ONLY 20 MAKE SENSE."

('Lucy'. From: *Girl About Town*, 2 June 1980)

5 Does the caption mean:
a She talks more quickly than she types.
b She types quickly but makes a lot of mistakes.
c She is the fastest typist in the office.

Rewrite: *She types at 40 words a minute* to mean the following by putting in **only**.
6 She and nobody else types at 40 wpm.
7 She can type at 40 wpm but does other things at a different speed.
8 She can type at 40 wpm. This is not very fast.

The following table shows three students' typing speeds when they were doing different tasks:

	Typing Task								
	Manuscript			Business Letter			Table		
	G	E	N	G	E	N	G	E	N
Student 1	40	9	31	30	3	27	25	2	23
Student 2	35	6	29	29	4	25	20	0	20
Student 3	30	0	30	25	1	24	20	3	17
G = Gross wpm		E = Number of errors			N = Net wpm				
Each task was timed for ten minutes of continuous typing.									

(Adapted from *Acquisition of Typewriting Skills* by Leonard J West, Copyright © 1969 by Pitman Publishing Corporation. Reprinted by permission of Pitman Learning, Inc., Belmont, California.)

Put **only** in the following sentences to match the meaning given in the brackets. Use the table to put in the missing information.
9 Student __ made one mistake in the business letter.
(ie not more than one mistake)
10 All the students typed at over __ wpm in the manuscript.
(ie not in the table or the business letter)
11 Student __ typed the table at 17 wpm.
(ie not faster than 17 wpm)
12 Student 2 made no mistakes in the __.
(ie no other student made no mistakes)
13 Each task was timed for __ minutes.
(ie the task wasn't timed for longer)
14 Student __ made a lot of mistakes.
(ie none of the others made as many mistakes)

15 Student 2 typed the table at __ wpm.
(ie she typed the letter and the manuscript more quickly)
16 Student 1 typed the business letter at __ wpm.
(ie the others typed the business letter more slowly)
17 Student __ can type at 31 wpm.
(ie no other student can type more quickly)
18 All the students typed the table at __ wpm or below.
(ie they typed the business letter and the manuscript more quickly)

Decide why the **only**'s are in the wrong places in the sentences below and rewrite them correctly:
19 She only died yesterday.
20 Please write the address only on this side.
21 Vegetarian food only served in this restaurant.
22 You only live once.

Summary: Relevant information in business documents

Situation

Forms and record cards provide summaries of information for companies or organisations. They enable important facts to be stored and recalled easily. All the exercises in this section are designed to practise summarising information in this way. They are based on the following situation.

You work as a clerk in the Personnel Department of Paramount Traders. You assist the Personnel Manager, Mrs W P Butt. It is part of your job to keep various records dealing with employees' attendance and discipline. You have just been handed the following telephone message by the switchboard operator:

Exercise 1 *To extract the relevant information from the telephone message to complete an attendance record*

An Attendance Record gives a day-by-day summary of an employee's attendance at work or the reasons for his/her absence. Use the information in the telephone message to decide how to fill in the Attendance Record below.

TELEPHONE CALL

To: *Personnel Department*

Time *09.25* .... Date *29 Feb 1980*

From *Ms J Brown (Clerk)* ....

of *Photocopying Dept* ....

Phone No. *56411 (Home)* ....

MESSAGE *Cannot come to work today as she must meet her mother at the railway station this afternoon. Back on Monday*

Operator *J A Solo*

ATTENDANCE RECORD

Employee's Name .... J. BROWN ....

Department .. PHOTOCOPYING & DUPLICATING

Date employed .... 2 JAN 1980 .... Year .... 1980 ......

	1	2	3	4	5	6	7	8	9	10	11	12	13	14	15	16	17	18	19	20	21	22	23	24	25	26	27	28	29	30	31
JAN	■	✓	✓	✓	■	■	X	✓	✓	✓	X	■	■	S	S	✓	✓	✓	■	■	✓	✓	✓	✓	X	■	■	SF	✓	✓	✓
FEB	X	■	■	X	✓	✓	✓	✓	■	■	S	✓	✓	✓	S	■	■	✓	✓	✓	✓	X	■	■	✓	✓	✓	✓	■		

Key:

A Accident

DF Death in family

H Holiday

B Away on company business

S Sick

SF Sickness in family

X Unauthorised absence

E Excused absence

Exercise 2 *To extract the relevant information to complete an Absence Summary*

The document shown is an Absence Summary. It summarises the information in the Attendance Record on p 41. Copy it and use the information in Exercise 1 to complete the Absence Summary for January and February 1980.

Exercise 3 *To extract the relevant information to complete an absence report*

An Absence Report summarises the details of an employee's absence from work. It must be completed each time an employee is absent. Copy out the Absence Report below and fill it in with information from this situation.

ABSENCE SUMMARY

Employee's name ....

Dept .... Year ....

	A	DF	H	B	S	SF	X	E
Jan								
Feb								
Mar								

Date ....

ABSENCE REPORT

(To be completed for each occasion on which an employee is absent from work)

Employee's name ....

Post ....

Department ....

Details of absence:

   Last day at work ....

   Date of expected return ....

   Absence reported to ....

   Absence reported by ....

   How reported ....

   Date reported ....

   Time reported ....

Reason for absence (tick):

   1 Accident at work ☐   6 Sickness ☐

   2 Accident elsewhere ☐   7 Family sickness ☐

   3 Suspension ☐   8 Death in family ☐

   4 Holiday ☐   9 Training ☐

   5 Industrial dispute ☐

   10 Other (give details and state whether absence authorised or not) ....

   ....

Exercise 4   *To extract relevant information to complete a Warning Record*

A Warning Record provides a written record of a warning given to an employee for disciplinary reasons. A warning may follow one serious offence or several minor ones. Your company's regulations require the Personnel Manager to give a warning if an employee is absent from work without adequate excuse three times or more in one month. Copy out the Warning Record below and fill it in with details of this situation. Do not sign it.

Exercise 5   *To extract relevant information to write a memorandum*

Send a memo to Mrs Butt about Ms Brown's absences from work. You should include the following information:

a Details of Ms Brown's absence today. Which documents are you attaching giving details of this?

b A detailed summary of Ms Brown's attendance record in February. Is this attendance record satisfactory? Which document are you therefore attaching for Mrs Butt's attention?

c A detailed summary of Ms Brown's attendance record since joining the company.

d A reminder that a warning must be given to Ms Brown because of her absences from work during February. Which document are you attaching because of this?

e A request that Mrs Butt should return the Warning Record to you for filing when she has stated what action has been taken and signed it.

3

WARNING RECORD   Date ....

(To be completed when an employee is given a disciplinary warning)

Employee's name ....

Post ....

Department ....

Date(s) of offence ....

Type of offence (tick):

1 Incompetence ☐   5 Disobedience ☐

2 Poor work ☐   6 Absenteeism ☐

3 Causing damage ☐   7 Poor time-keeping ☐

4 Causing accident ☐   8 Fighting ☐

9 Other (give details) ....

Details of offence ....

....

....

Signature ....

PS: Filing

Alphabetical Filing:
All files are arranged in alphabetical order according to the name of the client, customer, supplier, etc. State which drawer of the filing cabinet illustrated below you would file each of the following companies in.

Geographical Filing:
All files are arranged in alphabetical order according to the name of the town, area or country. State which drawer of the filing cabinet illustrated below you would file each of the following companies in (file each entry under the name of the country).

1 Zimba Pharmaceuticals, Zomba, Malawi.
2 Turners Trading Company, Runcorn, Cheshire, United Kingdom.
3 Lee & Sons, Singapore.
4 Zodiac Enterprises, Georgetown, Barbados.
5 Global Importers, Kano, Nigeria.
6 Jacksons Chemicals Incorporated, Atlanta, Georgia, USA.
7 IPM International, Paris, France.
8 North West Petroleum, Toronto, Canada.
9 McKendrick and Lewis, Sydney, Australia.
10 Transafrica, Mombasa, Kenya.

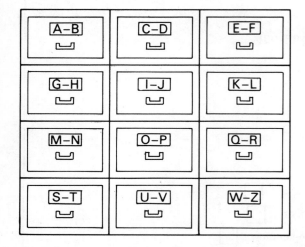

Comprehension: Diagrams in texts (1)

Exercise 1 *To match diagrams to the correct parts of the accompanying text*

Diagrams are used to help the reader understand the writer's message. This is done by telling readers to look at the diagram to help them understand the text.

Here is a set of instructions for changing a typewriter ribbon. The writer refers to the diagram throughout the instructions. Complete the instructions with the appropriate letters labelling the diagram.

> Lift the front cover by gripping it with both hands one either side of the space bar until it engages in its hinges. Wind the worn ribbon on to one of the two ribbon spools (1—). Move the ribbon control arm (2—) and remove the empty spool. Free the end of the ribbon from the hook in the spool centre (3—). Wind the remainder of the ribbon on to the full spool and lift the ribbon out of the ribbon carrier (4—). Now replace the spool holding the old ribbon with a new one. Put the free end of the ribbon on the projecting hook and press the hook into the spool centre. Now place the empty spool back on to the machine, taking care that the pick-up pin (5—) engages in one of the pick-up holes (6—). Thread the ribbon through both sides of the ribbon reversing arm (7—). Depress the shift lock key and take hold of the ribbon with both hands. Put the ribbon behind the ribbon carrier (8—) and insert it into the holding lugs (9—) as shown on the diagram. When using a two-coloured ribbon ensure that the red portion is facing downward.

(Adapted from *Operating Instructions for Olympia SM*, Olympia Werke AG.)

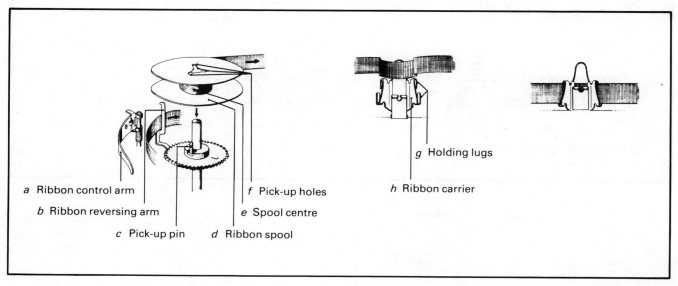

a Ribbon control arm
b Ribbon reversing arm
c Pick-up pin   *d* Ribbon spool
e Spool centre
f Pick-up holes
g Holding lugs
h Ribbon carrier

Exercise 2 *To match diagrams to the appropriate texts*

Underneath every diagram there should be a caption, which usually includes a title. Captions are particularly important where there are several similar diagrams on the same page or where diagrams and text are printed on different pages. The captions help the reader match the accompanying text to the correct diagram.

Here are three texts and three diagrams. They are all about folding letters and inserting them into envelopes. Match each text to the correct diagram.

> TEXT 1
>
> 1 Place the letter on the desk typed side down.
> 2 Fold the bottom of the letter up approximately one third of the way.
> 3 Fold the letter once more.
> 4 Insert the letter in the envelope so that the name and address show clearly in the window.
>
> TEXT 2
>
> The letter must be folded in three approximately equal parts.
> 1 Place the letter on the desk typed side up.
> 2 Turn the bottom edge up and fold one third of the way from the bottom.
> 3 Fold up once more. Try to leave about 5 mm of paper showing at the top.
> 4 Insert the folded edge of the letter in the envelope.
>
> TEXT 3
>
> The letter must be folded twice.
> 1 Place the letter on the desk typed side up.
> 2 Fold the bottom up to within 5 mm of the top.
> 3 Turn the folded letter counter-clockwise so that the short edge is toward you.
> 4 Fold the bottom up about half way from the bottom of the page, leaving about 5 mm of paper showing at the top.
> 5 Insert the folded edge of the letter in the envelope.

(Adapted from G A Reid, *Modern Office Procedures*, Pitman, Canada, 2nd edn, 1978.)

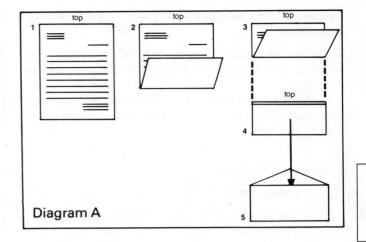

Diagram A

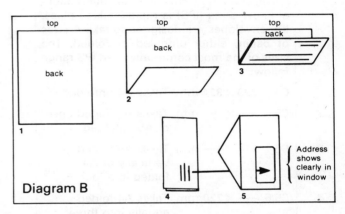

Diagram B

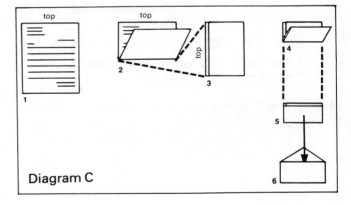

Diagram C

Here are three titles:
a) Folding and inserting a letter in a large (C5/6) envelope.
b) Folding and inserting a letter in a window envelope.
c) Folding and inserting a letter in a small (C6) envelope.

Give each text a title and each diagram a caption using these three titles.

3

Exercise 3 *To scan texts and diagrams to supply missing information*

Texts and diagrams support each other: information which is unclear (or even missing) in one is clearer in the other.

Both the text and the diagrams shown have information missing. Use information from one to complete the gaps in the other.

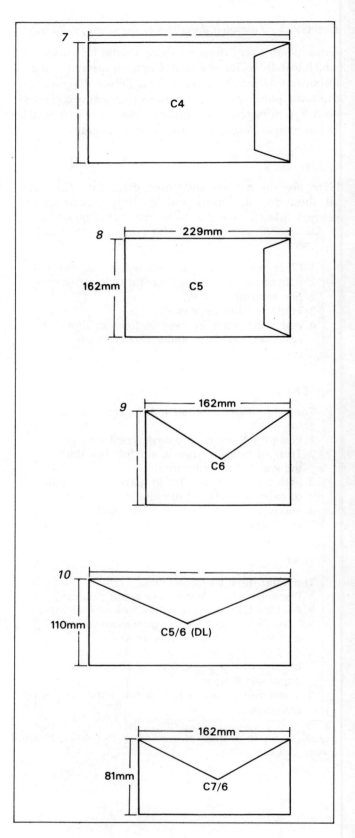

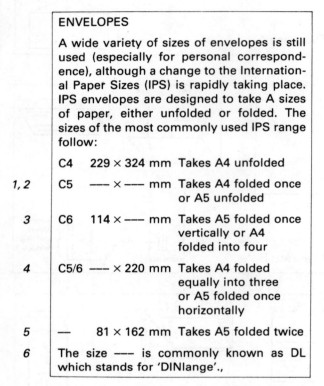

ENVELOPES

A wide variety of sizes of envelopes is still used (especially for personal correspondence), although a change to the International Paper Sizes (IPS) is rapidly taking place. IPS envelopes are designed to take A sizes of paper, either unfolded or folded. The sizes of the most commonly used IPS range follow:

C4   229 × 324 mm Takes A4 unfolded

1, 2 C5   —— × —— mm Takes A4 folded once or A5 unfolded

3 C6   114 × —— mm Takes A5 folded once vertically or A4 folded into four

4 C5/6 —— × 220 mm Takes A4 folded equally into three or A5 folded once horizontally

5 —— 81 × 162 mm Takes A5 folded twice

6 The size —— is commonly known as DL which stands for 'DINlange'.,

(Adapted from E Mackay, *The Typewriting Dictionary*, Pitman, 1977.)

46

Exercise 4 *To use information from a text to complete a set of diagrams*

The diagrams in column A below show which paper sizes can be inserted into the most common IPS envelopes. The diagrams are not finished. Use information from the text in Exercise 3 to complete column A with items from column B.

A

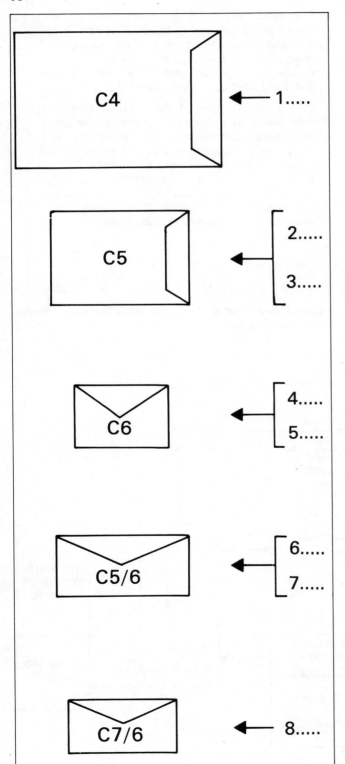

B

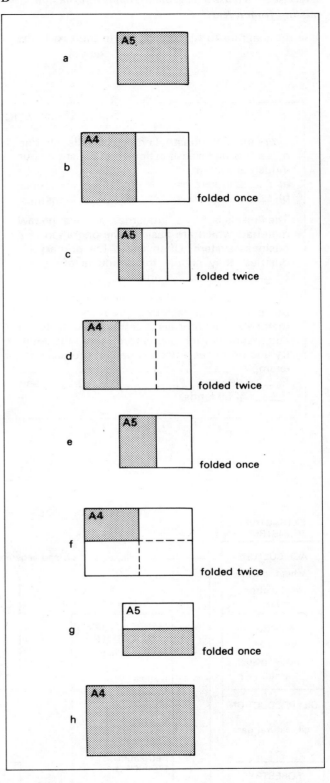

(From F G Holliday (ed), *The Manual of Stationery, Office Machines and Equipment*, The British Stationery and Office Products Federation.)

Exercise 5 *To use a diagram to supply information missing from a text*

Use the diagram to fill in the gaps in the text below.

THE CLASSIFICATION OF BUSINESS ACTIVITY

Every form of industrial enterprise falls into one of [1]_____ broad classifications that constitute our industrial system:

a) [2]_____ industries   c) [4]_____ industries
b) [3]_____ industries   d) [5]_____ industries

The first class, [6]_____ industries, provide the raw materials which are basic to the operation of a business system. Often called the primary industries, they supply the products of [7]_____, [8]_____, [9]_____, [10]_____ and [11]_____.

[12]_____ industries are all those engaged in the process of manufacturing products from raw materials. This process is carried on in factories and manufacturing plants throughout the country and produces a wide variety of products, for example [13]_____, [14]_____, [15]_____, [16]_____, [17]_____, [18]_____, [19]_____, [20]_____, [21]_____ and [22]_____ of all kinds.

The third category, [23]_____ industries, are engaged in the process of distributing raw materials and manufactured goods. They move goods from producer to producer, and from producer to the ultimate consumer. They perform the functions of [24]_____, [25]_____ and [26]_____.

Finally, [27]_____ are all those businesses and individuals which provide service to the other processes. The number of individuals and businesses engaged in these industries is very large. Their activities range from the [28]_____ such as doctors and accountants, to large [29]_____ (for example, banks), [30]_____ (telephone and telegraph companies), [31]_____ (gas, water and electricity suppliers) and government departments.

(Adapted from G A Reid, *Modern Office Procedures*, Pitman, Canada, 2nd edn, 1978.)

THE FLOW OF GOODS AND SERVICES IN THE MODERN ECONOMY

EXTRACTIVE INDUSTRIES

AGRICULTURE wheat, meat, wool, cotton etc.

MINING iron, coal, nickel, gold etc.

OIL PRODUCTION oil, natural gas

FORESTRY lumber, plywood etc.

FISHING seafood, freshwater fish etc.

milk, eggs, fruit and vegetables

MANUFACTURING INDUSTRIES
Food products
Clothing and textiles
Wood and paper
Furniture
Plastics
Chemicals
Petroleum products
Iron and steel
Rubber
Machinery

SERVICE INDUSTRIES
Financial institutions
Communications
Professions
Government departments
Utilities

DISTRIBUTIVE INDUSTRIES
Transportation
Storage
Marketing

RETAIL TRADE

ULTIMATE CONSUMER – HOME

– ABROAD (EXPORTS)

fresh fish

PS: Spelling *Problems with double letters*

The following words all have at least two sets of double letters. Use the definitions on the right to fill in the blanks with the correctly spelled word.

Example:

MISSPELL ED   written incorrectly

1	AC .... LE	able to be reached or approached
2	AC .... LY	not deliberately
3	AC .... TE	to give someone a place to live
4	AD .... EE	the person to whom a letter is sent
5	AS .... IN	a political murderer
6	BO .... ER	a person who keeps financial records
7	CO .... EE	a small group of people dealing with matters on behalf of a larger group
8	CO .... UR	an expert judge of something
9	EM .... NT	feeling of shame or discomfort
10	MA .... SS	a stuffed bag on which one sleeps
11	OC .... LY	sometimes
12	OC .... CE	something that has happened
13	OP .... ON	cruel and unjust treatment; tyranny
14	PO .... ON	ownership; something that is owned
15	PR .... LY	opposite of amateurishly
16	SU .... UL	having the desired result
17	SU .... ES	prevents something from being known
18	UN .... RY	not needed

There are several pairs of words in English which are spelt alike except that one has a double letter and the other does not. There are two rules which can be of some help when trying to remember which is which:

A double vowel is always longer than a single one.
Examples: met   meet
shot   shoot

A double consonant shortens the preceding vowel.
Examples: siting   sitting
taping   tapping

Each of the questions below contains two words which are spelt alike except for the doubled letter. Decide which word goes in which space.

Example: He was a *taping*........ the music as he was
b *tapping*.... on his drum. (taping/tapping)

19 When you have finished *a* __ in that form, please finish *b* __ those papers. (filing/filling)
20 The *a* __ reached $100 before the article was finally sold.
I'm *b* __ my time: I'll ask for a pay rise when the right opportunity turns up. (biding/bidding)
21 That screw is *a* __; you will *b* __ the top if you don't tighten it up. (lose/loose)
22 They are *a* __ the new store outside town on the North Road.
Stop *b* __ there – do something! (siting/sitting)
23 I *a* __ over this morning but I *b* __ fine now. (fell/feel)
24 The wires should be *a* __ before being connected to the plug. All windows should be securely *b* __. (bared/barred)
25 It is *a* __ hot *b* __ work. (to/too)
26 There is no ice-cream for *a* __ in the *b* __: it would melt! (desert/dessert)
27 The *a* __ ate her *b* __ in the restaurant. (diner/dinner)
28 One *a* __ the workmen fell *b* __ the roof. (of/off)
29 He *a* __ off his *b* __ shirt before taking a bath. (striped/stripped)
30 All the paint should be *a* __ off before you repaint. This car is going to be *b* __: we're buying a new one. (scraped/scrapped)
31 We're *a* __ ourselves of this problem once and for all.
We're going *b* __ this afternoon. (riding/ridding)
32 We're *a* __ to go away this weekend.
The door won't close properly: it needs *b* __. (planing/planning)

3

Composition: Replies to letters

Exercise 1 *To decide what information is essential in a letter*

Read the following letter of complaint. Type or write the letter leaving out any inessential information:

1

> Dear Sirs
>
> Order No 594/BJS
>
> We received the above order for 75 shirts on 16 August 198–. It was a national holiday here. Unfortunately 50 of the shirts do not match the sample of those we ordered. Although the weather is very nice here several have poor stitching. Just a minute the phone is ringing. Sorry about that. Where was I? Oh yes. We cannot accept these goods at the price agreed. My wife already thinks I spend too much money on going to the cinema never mind paying for poor quality goods. We can accept the shirts only on condition that you reduce the price; otherwise we should expect you to replace the order. By the way I bought a new car the other day at a really good price. I must finish now – I'm going to play golf. Please let me know what you wish to do about either replacement or a price reduction. Do you play golf? Perhaps we could get together some time for a game. Our agent, who does not play golf – tennis is his thing – can bring a sample of the order should you wish to inspect it.
>
> Yours faithfully

Read the following letter of enquiry:

2

> Dear Sirs
>
> We have recently seen an article in 'Office Machinery News' about your visible file system. We are interested in introducing this system into one of our branches.
> Please send us your catalogue and price-list.
>
> Yours faithfully

The next letter is the reply. Type or write out the letter leaving only the essential information:

3

> Dear Mr Dwyer
>
> Thank you for your letter of 18 October 198– enquiring about the visible file system.
> I am sorry it has taken so long to reply to your letter but we have had so many enquiries since the article appeared in 'Office Machinery News'. Also my wife has been ill in hospital so I have had to take some time off work. This meant that we were short-staffed in the office and my mail was not dealt with until I got back.
> Enclosed are our latest catalogue and price-list. The catalogue has 15 pages.
> We look forward to hearing from you and receiving your order.
> We promise you that your order will be dealt with promptly as we are advertising for another clerk. Business is so good that we can afford to employ someone else in the office. We'll probably get a clerk typist as we don't need anyone to do shorthand. If you hear of someone suitable we should be most grateful if you would let us know.
>
> Yours sincerely

4 Decide whether the following statements are true or false:
  a Business letters must give as much information as possible.
  b Business letters should be brief but polite.
  c Business letters should use long words.
  d Business letters should not include any unnecessary information.
  e It is not necessary to plan the points you make in a letter.

Exercise 2 *To practise planning a letter by listing the points to be made*

The following points were planned for letter *3* in Exercise 1. Decide which five points should have been included in that letter:

1 Their order has been received.
2 Hope they give us an order.
3 Ask for a catalogue and price-list.
4 Order 500 files.
5 Tell them catalogue and price-list enclosed.
6 Refer to what they enquired about.
7 Refer to original letter.
8 Give the reason for the complaint.
9 Ask when they would like the order.
10 Explain and apologise for the delay.

Now use letter *1* in Exercise 1 to make a list of points that would be made before that letter was written.

Exercise 3 *To complete a reply to a letter*

The following letter is a reply to letter *1* in Exercise 1. Choose the best way to complete the letter from the choices given.

Dear Sir

1)_____ .

We are sorry to hear that the 75 shirts you ordered were not of the quality you expected.

We have looked into the matter and have found that your order was not up to our usual standard 2)_____ .

We have arranged for 3)_____ to be sent immediately. Our agent will collect the original order within the next two weeks.

4)_____ and will take all possible steps to make sure 5)_____ .

Yours faithfully

---

1 a We got your letter on 27 August 198–.
  b Thank you for your letter of 18 August 198–.
  c Your letter of complaint arrived today.
  d Your letter of 18 August arrived today and we are very sorry.
2 a because our machines are really old.
  b because Mr Chin did not notice.
  c because of a fault in one of our machines.
  d because we have a new machine operator.
3 a money
  b a replacement order
  c an order of 75 shirts which are the best we have got
  d a repeat of your order for 75 shirts but this time everything is all right
4 a I do not know how to say how sorry I am that this has happened
  b We are very sorry for any inconvenience caused
  c We humbly ask your forgiveness for any trouble we have caused
  d We are sorry

5 a we do not repeat this mistake which has given you so many problems.
  b you will still order your goods from us.
  c Mr Chin does not make the same mistake again. In fact he is fairly old and will retire soon.
  d such a mistake is not made again.
6 Choose a suitable subject heading for this letter.

Exercise 4 *To write a reply from points given*

Write a reply to the following letter. Use the points given below the letter.

Dear Sirs

Order No XC 19948

We have received the above order and appreciate the prompt delivery. Everything seems to be correct apart from the contents of case 7. Unfortunately, when this case was checked we found articles which we had not ordered. We can only assume that a mistake has been made and that this case has been delivered to the wrong address.

We enclose a list of the contents of case 7 which you can check against the invoice. We shall keep the case until you tell us what you wish us to do.

Would you please arrange for the missing goods to be sent immediately.

Yours faithfully

---

1 Thank you for letter of 30 July.
2 Apologise about case 7.
3 Explain mistake made in delivery.
4 The right goods have been sent.
5 Keep case 7 – we shall collect.
6 Apologise again.

3

PS: Word puzzles

In the puzzle, find words that mean the same as the definitions given below it. The words can go in any direction, such as up, down, forward, backward and diagonally. Some letters can be used twice. The initial letter of each word has been given.

Q	T	W	E	R	T	Y	U	I	O	Y	O	P	O	A
S	D	W	O	O	L	L	E	N	F	L	G	H	F	J
K	L	Z	E	S	X	C	X	V	B	L	M	N	E	Q
W	E	O	R	L	T	I	I	Y	N	A	U	I	B	S
I	M	O	M	P	F	A	T	E	I	U	Q	S	R	D
Y	D	A	F	E	G	T	H	R	E	S	J	O	U	K
A	L	Z	R	X	M	C	H	T	C	U	S	V	A	B
D	N	P	M	G	Q	W	E	N	E	S	R	T	R	Y
O	U	I	O	P	I	A	S	E	I	D	F	G	Y	H
T	N	A	N	O	S	N	O	C	C	U	R	R	J	K
L	Z	X	C	V	B	N	S	M	Q	W	E	R	T	Y

1 Spaces allowed along the right- and left-hand sides of a letter. M..........
2 Not a vowel. C..........
3 Day after yesterday. T..........
4 Word, or part of a word, added to the beginning of another word to change the meaning. P..........

5 Inter-office written communication. M..........
6 A middle point. C..........
7 Used for cutting paper, fabric, etc. S..........
8 Not noisy. Q..........
9 Before the thirteenth. T..........
10 My sister's daughter. N..........
11 Way out. E..........
12 Made of the hair of a sheep. W..........
13 The second month of the year. F..........
14 Normally. U..........
15 Happen. O..........

If any of the following words contain a prefix or a suffix, write down the first letter of the root word. The letters make a word. Write down the word the letters spell out:

16 acknowledge	*21* dictate	*26* quiet
17 noticeable	*22* finance	*27* definitely
18 decide	*23* losing	*28* guardian
19 omitted	*24* among	*29* centre
20 rewrite	*25* equipment	*30* extremely

There is an extra letter in some of the following words. Write down each extra letter to make a new word.

31 beginning	*36* really	*41* possesses
32 occassion	*37* sccissors	*42* nieece
33 analysiis	*38* quieet	*43* fullfilled
34 install	*39* marriage	*44* psyychology
35 innoculate	*40* harrassed	*45* planning

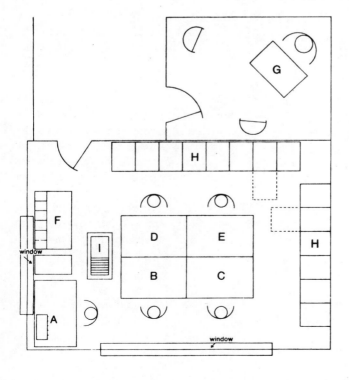

Scale plan of office

Locations:

A Telephonist
B Filing clerk
C Typist
D Invoicing clerk
E Junior/messenger
F Post trays and sorting table
G Office manager
H Filing cabinets (4 drawer)
I Sorting desk

(From *Guidelines for the Smaller Business*, No 10, British Institute of Management.)

Oral/Aural: Problem solving

Exercise 1 *To state problems and to give advice*

Give different ways of stating a problem other than those below:
a) I can't . . .
b) My problem is that . . .
c) The difficulty is that . . .

Choose three students (or however many can write at the chalkboard at one time). Give them all the problems you have about work to write on the board.

Example: I can't get to class on time.

If you have no problems, make them up.
Check that the students have recorded the problems correctly.

Give different ways of offering advice other than those below:
a) If I were you . . .
b) I suggest you . . .
c) It might be a good idea if you . . .

Offer advice for all the problems written on the board.

Exercise 2 *To use group discussion to solve a problem*

Imagine that you work in the office shown on p 52 where the problem is a great shortage of space. You have to make changes in the office to solve that problem.
  Work in groups of six. Each person in the group should choose to be one of the following:

Telephonist	Invoicing Clerk
Filing Clerk	Junior/messenger
Typist	Office Manager

As a group discuss the changes that can save space. Remember there is no extra space in the rest of the building and that the company cannot afford to move.
  List the group's suggestions and note what would be needed to make any changes. If necessary make cutouts of the furniture in the office.

Each person should spend a few minutes studying the information about his or her job and then use it in a discussion about what changes to make in the office.

A *Telephonist*
   Your job is to operate the small switchboard, which can be easily moved. Most of the calls you deal with are from customers requiring details of their invoices. This means you have to get up from your desk and check information in the filing cabinets. If the order was made less than a week ago, you have to check with the Invoicing Clerk. This means you have to get up and go to his desk.
   Your problem is that you have to walk round the sorting table to see the invoice clerk and you have to walk round all the desks to get at the filing cabinets. You want your desk moved so that you are next to the Invoicing Clerk and nearer the filing cabinets.

B *Filing Clerk*
   You are in charge of the filing. Anything to be filed is put on the sorting desk. You collect it from there to file. You also have to make several trips a day to the Office Manager's office as he asks to see certain files. You want to be nearer the door and nearer the filing cabinets. Also you know from the office you worked in before that lateral files take up half the space needed for vertical files. Your idea is to replace the vertical filing system with cabinets for lateral files.

C *Typist*
   Your job is to type statements, invoices and general correspondence. When you have finished typing any document you take it to the post table where the messenger collects it and takes it to the right department for posting. You want to be nearer the post table.

D *Invoicing Clerk*
   Your main job is to prepare invoices making sure that the prices are up to date. You have to deal with the Telephonist's queries. You also have to take invoices, etc to the Typist which means walking all round the desks. You would like to be nearer the Telephonist and nearer the Typist.

E *Junior/messenger*
   Your main job is to sort all the incoming and outgoing mail. This means you spend most of your time at the table with the post trays (F). You do other general duties like taking documents to the duplicating room, but helping the Filing Clerk takes much of the rest of your time. You would like to be nearer the post table and also nearer the filing cabinets.

G *Office Manager*
   You are in charge of the meeting. Your aim in holding it is to arrive at an agreed solution to the problem which makes everyone happy. You think the solution is to get rid of some of the filing cabinets as they take up too much space. You have in fact checked that only 60 per cent of the space in the cabinets is being used at present. This means that you could remove six of them and perhaps sell them or ask if any of the other offices need them and then arrange for all the correspondence to be put in the remaining nine cabinets.

Discuss your solutions as a class and decide which is the best solution that solves everybody's problem. If necessary, draw an office plan to show what changes your group has decided on.

3

PS: Two-word verbs

For this exercise you will need a dictionary. Work in groups of three. Half the groups in the class use list A and the other half use list B. For each verb in your list use a dictionary to write a true definition. Then write two false definitions.

Example: TO GET RID OF (something)

True definition:
TO GET RID OF means to remove something. For example, 'The office manager got rid of the filing cabinets' means he arranged for them to be moved out of the office.

False definition:
TO GET RID OF means to remove the top from a container. For example, 'He couldn't open the jar of jam so he soaked it in water to get rid of it.'

False definition:
TO GET RID OF means to remove a horse rider. For example, 'The horse swerved suddenly and got rid of me.'

A

to count on (somebody)
to catch up with (something)
to deal with (something)
to arrive at (something)
to use up (something)
to pay attention to (somebody)
to try out (something)
to note down (something)
to look up (something)
to call off (something)

B

to talk over (something)
to hold back (something)
to mess up (something)
to close down (something)
to own up to (something)
to pad out (something)
to play down (something)
to sort out (something)
to switch over to (something)
to sound out (somebody)

Each group of three from one half of the class should find a group of three from the other half to work with. Take it in turns to give your definitions. The winners are the teams who guess the most correct definitions.

Miscellany

Exercise 1 *Homophones*

Homophones are words which sound the same but are spelt differently (there/their, hear/here, rite/right/write, cite/site/sight, etc). They cause one of the most common types of spelling mistake. Here is a list of the most commonly confused pairs of homophones and some sentences which may help you remember the differences. Can you think of some more sentences to help you?

affect/effect	
counsel/council	
dependant/dependent	'Auntie Amy and Uncle Arthur Are my dependAnts.'
ensure/insure	
except/accept	
fare/fair	
for/four	'The number **four** has **four** letters.'
formally/formerly	
heard/herd	
knew/new	
passed/past	
peace/piece	'Would you like a **pie**ce of **pie**?'
practice/practise	
principal/principle	'The princi**pal** is my **pal**.'
stationary/stationery	'L**E**tters and **E**nvelopes are station**E**ry.'
their/there	'Come **here**! **Where**? **There**!'
two/too	
weather/whether	

The passage below has a number of gaps in it. After each gap are pairs of homophones. Choose the correct homophone to fill each gap.

At a meeting of the Town [1] __ (Council/Counsel) last [2] __ (knight/night) it was decided to [3] __ (altar/alter) the [4] __ (way/weigh) in [5] __ (witch/which) bills are [6] __ (cent/sent) out to [7] __ (residence/residents).

In the [8] __ (passed/past) all bills were posted with a stamped addressed envelope enclosed. This [9] __ (ensured/insured) that people returned [10] __ (their/there) bills quickly, because they did not have to [11] __ (right/write) the address on the envelope or [12] __ (by/bye/buy) a stamp. However, this [13] __ (practice/practise) will cease at the end of the [14] __ (currant/current) year. [15] __ (Their/There) are [16] __ (to/too/two) [17] __ (principal/principle) reasons for changing: the ever-increasing cost of postage and the expense of printing special [18] __ (stationary/stationery). It is claimed that the [19] __ (knew/new) scheme will save a lot of [20] __ (waist/waste) because most people do not [21] __ (male/mail) bills – they prefer to call at the accounts department and pay in person.

Exercise 2 *The apostrophe with letters and figures*

The apostrophe has three main uses:

1) To show possession.

> *Examples:* My mother's hat. = The hat of my
> mother.
> The boss's desk. = The desk of my boss.

2) To show contractions.

> *Examples:* I'm = I am
> can't = cannot
> o'clock = of the clock

3) With the plurals of letters and figures.

> *Examples:* There are two m's in accommodation.
> You should dot your i's and cross your
> t's.
> His 1's look like his 7's.
> 4's can be written in two ways.

> *Note:* Apostrophes are not normally used for the
> plurals of numbers above 9.

> *Examples:* More students learnt shorthand in the
> 1970s than in the 1960s.
> The company bought two Fotorapid
> 249s.

Punctuate each of the following sentences with apostrophes where necessary.

1 Many of our staff are now in their late 50s or early 60s and we should like to replace them with younger people in their 20s or 30s.

2 Please may I have three 5 cent stamps and twenty 6s?

3 How many ps are there in accompany?

4 Scottish Airways have ordered two Boeing 747s.

5 To call the police, dial three 9s.

6 Production of all Mark 3s came to an end in 1977.

7 We need 10 462s and one 442.

8 Four 7s are 28.

9 We've run out of P6s and we'll soon need some more T9s.

10 Us are not used on licence plates as they look like Vs.

Rewrite the words and numbers underlined in the following passage, putting in apostrophes where necessary. The passage includes all the uses of the apostrophe.

The first practical 11)typewriters were invented in the 12)1860s. Many of the early 13)inventors were 14)printers and so based their 15)keyboards on the letter arrangement of a 16)printers type frame. The first commercial typewriter was produced in America in the 17)1870s. 18)Its keyboard arrangement was as 19)follows:

```
2 3 4 5 6 7 8 9 - ,  _
Q W E R T Y U I O P :
; A S D F G H J K L M
& Z C X V B N ? ; . '
```

It can be seen that this keyboard (patented by Christopher Sholes) 20)wasnt very different from 21)todays. 22)Sholess typewriter typed only in 23)capitals and, like some modern 24)machines, had only eight 25)numerals - capital 26)is had to be used instead of 27)1s and capital 28)os used as the keyboard 29)hadnt got a zero. This keyboard - the universal keyboard, as 30)its now known - has several 31)disadvantages. Research was carried out in the 32)1920s by a Dr Hoke into the comparative frequency of the 33)letters of the alphabet. Dr 34)Hokes 35)results showed that the six most common 36)letters are used more frequently than the other twenty together. Several other 37)investigators 38)findings have confirmed 39)Hokes 40)conclusions and have also shown that the left hand (most 41)peoples weaker hand) 42)performs 57 per cent of all key striking while the right 43)hands responsible for only 43 per cent. 44)Its been said, quite rightly, that 45)were using a left-handed typewriter in a right-handed world.

(Adapted from E Mackay, *The Typewriting Dictionary*, Pitman, 1977.)

3

Exercise 3 *Spelling – One word or two?*

There are many pairs of words that are spelt alike except for their division.

Examples: a head/ahead
    some thing/something
    every body/everybody

Note: all right ⎱
     no one ⎰ must never be written as one word.

Fill in the blanks in the following passage with the correct form of the words in brackets.

On 14 April 1912 the *Titanic*, the largest and most luxurious passenger ship [1] __ (a float), ran [2] __ (in to) thick fog off the coast of Newfoundland. [3] __ (In spite of) the danger of icebergs, the ship's speed was not reduced as [4] __ (every body) believed she was unsinkable. Sixteen watertight compartments were constructed [5] __ (in side) her double hull and the ship would float even if four of these were full of water.

Shortly before midnight there was [6] __ (a loud) noise: *Titanic* had struck an iceberg which tore a hole [7] __ (all most) 100 metres [8] __ (a long) her side. Five of the compartments [9] __ (all together) on the same side of the ship filled with water and there was [10] __ (no thing) that [11] __ (any body) could do to prevent her from sinking. [12] __ (Every body) tried to climb [13] __ (in to) the lifeboats but there were not enough for [14] __ (every one). The women and children were able to get [15] __ (a way) and distress signals were sent to any ship which was [16] __ (near by). The nearest ship was only 30 kilometres from the *Titanic* but her radio operator had [17] __ (all ready) gone off duty. There was little hope for [18] __ (any one) if they were not picked up by [19] __ (an other) ship. [20] __ (Never the less), [21] __ (a lot) jumped [22] __ (overboard) [23] __ (in to) the icy sea. [24] __ (All most) [25] __ (every one) of them was drowned. Two and a half hours after the accident the ship sank and all those left [26] __ (a board) went down with her. [27] __ (All together) 1 500 people died in the disaster and it was never possible to recover [28] __ (every body).

One result of the disaster was that an international ice patrol was set up, [29] __ (all ways) ready to warn ships of dangerous ice that [30] __ (may be) [31] __ (a head) of them. Warnings are sent out [32] __ (every day) of the year and [33] __ (no one) now faces the same dangers as the passengers on the *Titanic*.

Examination preparation: *Some, any* and *no*

Use **any** for questions.

Example: Do you want **any** new forms?

Use **any** for negatives.

Example: They do not want **any** new forms.

Use **some** for positive statements.

Example: They want **some** new forms.

Decide whether **some** or **any** should complete the following:

1 Have we had ...?
2 We have had ... .
3 We haven't had ... .
4 I've brought ...thing for you.
5 He wasn't speaking to ...one.
6 He didn't write to ...body.
7 I haven't brought ...thing for you.
8 He was speaking to ...one.
9 Did he write to ...one?
10 We shall have a meeting about this ... time.
11 He wrote to ...body.
12 Was he speaking to ...body?
13 Have you brought ...thing for me?

Use **no** for negatives in formal writing.

Example: They want **no** new forms.

Do not put two negatives together.

Example: They don't want no new forms.

This can be corrected in two ways:

a They **don't** want **any** new forms.
b They **want no** new forms.

Correct the following in two ways:

14 We haven't had no lunch.
15 He wasn't speaking to no one.
16 We haven't had no time.
17 There hasn't been no post today.
18 I haven't discussed this with nobody.
19 We didn't buy nothing for the office.
20 There didn't seem to be nothing wrong.

Correct the following:

21 We didn't buy nothing in the gift shop.
22 If you let me down, you will not be given no more chances.
23 Hasn't the new scheme made no difference to you?
24 It wouldn't do him no harm to do some hard work.
25 As far as I could see, there didn't seem to be nothing wrong.

(21–25, PEI – English for Office Skills.)

Unit 4

Summary: Summaries of business documents

Exercise 1 *To choose suitable headings for various business documents*

Many business documents – letters, memorandums, notices – have a heading which indicates the subject of the document. This subject heading has several uses:

a) It helps with the sorting of the mail.
b) It helps the reader understand the purpose of the document.
c) It helps when the document is filed.

Choose the most suitable heading for each of the following documents from the four choices given under each one. Work individually and then compare your answers with a partner. Discuss the answers you disagree about.

1

RIVERSIDE CHAMBER OF COMMERCE

The monthly Committee meeting will be held on Monday 27 June at 2000 hours in the regional offices of the Chamber.

The Honorary Treasurer will present his report for the first half of the year. Other items for inclusion on the agenda should be submitted not later than 20 June.

Signed: *W P Williams*

Honorary Secretary

---

a Riverside Chamber of Commerce Committee
b Notice of Monthly Committee Meeting
c Agenda of the Next Monthly Committee Meeting
d Invitation to the Monthly Committee Meeting of the Riverside Chamber of Commerce

2

MEMORANDUM

To: Sales Representatives   *Date:* 13 May 198–

From: Area Sales Manager

Subject: _____

There will be a meeting of all Sales Representatives in my office in Oldtown on 25 May 198– at 1000 hours.

The main subject for discussion will be sales planning for the next half year, including the introduction of new products, promotion campaigns and sales forecasts.

Please confirm your attendance and give details of transport arrangements.

---

a Introduction of new products
b Sales forecasts for next half year
c Sales planning meeting
d Notice of May meeting

3

Dear Sirs

We are pleased to announce the introduction of our new ZPX Heavy Duty Circulation Pump.

This new product is an important addition at the top end of our popular range of industrial pumps and we are sure that it will prove popular with your customers with large factories, warehouses, office blocks or other installations. Technical specifications of the ZPX are enclosed on a separate sheet. Our Sales Representative will be pleased to demonstrate the ZPX and discuss possible applications when he next calls on you.

---

a ZPX Heavy Duty Circulation Pump
b Industrial Pumps
c Product Information
d Visit of Salesman to demonstrate ZPX Pump

4

Dear Sirs

Further to our letter of 22 January, we now regret to inform you that there will be a delay in the despatch of your order of 4 January.

This delay has been caused by the recently-introduced government restrictions on the export of certain items. These new regulations require us to apply for an export licence before shipping your order. We expect this procedure to cause a delay of approximately one month.

We are glad to say, however, that the new regulations apply only to this particular order and that your other orders with us are unaffected.

a Order D6788544 – 4 January 198–
b Bad news
c New government regulations
d Delays in shipping orders

5

Dear Mr Lee

The Group Managing Director, Mr W M Khan, will be making a tour of the Group's factories in the eastern division during October.

Full details of his itinerary will be sent to you when they have been finalised. In the meantime we can tell you that he plans to visit your factory in the third week of the month. He would like you, as Manager, to arrange an inspection tour of the plant on the morning of Monday 22 October with a meeting of all Heads of Department on the afternoon of the same day. Please set aside the following day for discussion with yourself and the Head of Accounts. It is usual to arrange a meeting with local dignitaries (Mayor, Chief of Police, etc) on the Wednesday afternoon as part of our campaign to improve our relations with the community.

Please go ahead with these arrangements and inform Head Office when they are complete.

a Mr Khan's tour, 198–
b Visit of the Managing Director, October 198–
c Inspection tour by the Managing Director, 22 October 198–
d Managing Director's itinerary, October 198–

Exercise 2 *To write memorandums in response to the documents in Exercise 1*

Memorandums contain the essential information required for a number of purposes:

a) To inform someone of decisions, action taken, etc.
b) To request someone to take action, decisions, etc.
c) To invite or require someone to attend meetings.
d) To remind someone of a meeting, action, etc.

Memorandums should be short and contain only essential information. The summarising skills required when writing memos are those of extracting the relevant information and presenting it in a concise form.

Use the documents in Exercise 1 to write the following memorandums. Make sure you use appropriate memorandum headings for each one.

1 A memo to your secretary, Miss Banda, asking her to write a short letter to the Hon Secretary of the Riverside Chamber of Commerce. The letter should confirm your attendance at the meeting and suggest that 'Fund-raising activities for the next year' should be included on the agenda.
2 You are Mr Yong, Sales Representative at the Newtown office. Write a memo to Mr Lim, the Group Transport Officer, asking him to arrange for a car to take you to the meeting of sales representatives. The journey to the Area Sales Manager's office takes approximately 90 minutes. You expect the meeting to end at about 1630.
3 A memo to Mr King, Technical Sales Manager, enclosing the specifications of the ZPX heavy duty circulation pump and asking if he thinks there is a demand for such a pump among local customers. If so, ask him to meet the Sales Representative when he calls.
4 A memo to the Site Manager, Port Antonio Project, telling him that the order for the refrigeration unit has been delayed. Tell him briefly why the order has been delayed and when he can now expect it. Ask him how this delay will affect the progress of the project.
5 A memo to Mr Chan, Head of the Accounts Department. Give details of the meetings he will have to attend with the Group's Managing Director. You know that Mr Chan had planned a holiday for that week. Ask him to discuss alternative dates for his holiday with you.

Exercise 3   *To produce business documents summarising the situations in Exercises 1 and 2*

Use the information in the documents in Exercises 1 and 2 to complete the documents below.

1

```
┌─────────────────────────────────────────────┐
│      RIVERSIDE CHAMBER OF COMMERCE          │
│                  AGENDA                      │
│                                              │
│   for a)_____ meeting to be held on│
│                                              │
│   b)_____ in c)_____ at d)_____  │
│                                              │
│   (i)    Apologies for absence               │
│   (ii)   Minutes of last meeting             │
│   (iii)  Matters arising                     │
│   (iv)   e)_____'s Report                 │
│   (v)    Proposal of new member – J T        │
│          Engineering Ltd                     │
│   (vi)   f)_____  │
│   (vii)  Any other business                  │
│                                              │
│   W P Williams                               │
│                                              │
│   g)_____                          │
└─────────────────────────────────────────────┘
```

2

```
┌─────────────────────────────────────────────┐
│  TELEPHONE MESSAGE                          │
│                                              │
│  To: Mr J Langton a) (_____)            │
│  While you were out Mr Yong, b)_____    │
│  from the Newtown office phoned.             │
│                                              │
│  Message: He confirms c)_____ to attend │
│  the d)_____ to be held in e)_____ │
│  on f)_____. He will be travelling g)___ │
│  _____.                                 │
└─────────────────────────────────────────────┘
```

3

```
┌─────────────────────────────────────────────┐
│  Dear Sirs                                   │
│                                              │
│  Earlier this month we announced the introduc-│
│  tion of our new Heavy Duty Circulation Pump,│
│  the a)_____ . This pump is designed for│
│  customers b)_____│
│                                              │
│  Mr T T Gillette, our c)_____ , will be  │
│  calling on you on 29 November 198–. The pur-│
│  poses of his visit are d)_____ and to   │
│  discuss e)_____                        │
└─────────────────────────────────────────────┘
```

4

```
┌─────────────────────────────────────────────┐
│  RE YOUR a)_____ NUMBER b)_____    │
│  OF c)_____ STOP REGRET DELAY IN        │
│  d)_____ DUE NEW e)_____ STOP      │
│  EXPECT DELAY OF f)_____ DAYS STOP      │
│  YOUR OTHER ORDERS g)_____ STOP         │
│  LETTER h)_____                         │
└─────────────────────────────────────────────┘
```

4

5

DIARY			
Date	Time	Place	Business
Monday a)_____	0900	Kuala Lumpur Factory	b)_____
	1230		Lunch with Mr c)_____ , Factory Manager.
	1430		Meeting with d)_____
e)_____	0900	f)_____	Meeting with g)_____ and h)_____
i)_____	0900		Tour of city
	1500	Eastern Empress Hotel	j)_____

PS: Filing and indexing

The way in which documents are filed has already been practised. Here are the conventions for filing and indexing more difficult items:

A When a business name includes a person's name, the first filing unit is the person's surname or family name (ie ignore titles, first or given names and initials).

Examples:

William P Jones & Partners	is filed under	Jo
Sir Isaac Pitman & Sons Ltd	is filed under	Pi
R T Solo Office Equipment	is filed under	So

B Function words are not counted as filing units and so are not used when filing or indexing.

Examples:

The British Steel Corporation	is filed under	Br
The North Shipping Line	is filed under	No

C Prefixes to family and business names are included as part of the name for filing purposes.

Examples:

Sean O'Reilly & Sons	is filed under	Or
T van de Rotte	is filed under	Va
MacDonald Fashions Ltd	is filed under	Ma
L'Estrange Chocolate Co.	is filed under	Le

D Numbers are either filed as if spelt out (ie alphabetically) or filed separately at the beginning of the file (ie numerically).

Examples:

The 1990 Club	is filed under	Ni or 1990
3M West Africa Ltd	is filed under	Th or 3
1–2–3 Supermarkets	is filed under	On or 1

E Abbreviations are filed as if they were spelt in full if we know what they stand for.

Examples:

St Margaret's Hospital	is filed under	Sa
N W Water Authority	is filed under	No

Business names which contain initials as an essential part of the name are usually filed separately at the beginning of the letter if it is not known what they stand for.

Examples:

N P Auto Repairers	is filed under NP	⎫ All are
N G Exporters Ltd	is filed under NG	⎬ filed
N & J Consultants	is filed under NJ	⎭ before Na

Put the following business names in correct alphabetical order for filing in the cabinet shown below. File numerical names in alphabetical order.

a T W Ogbara & Sons
b K F Yeo Importers
c AAA Taxi Company
d Kamaruddin Traders Inc.
e 101 Cleaning Products Ltd
f St Vincent Transporters
g E L M'Boyo Associates
h The Bank of Ghana
i TV and Radio Repairs Ltd
j Dr Kumar & Partners
k Tichner & Webb Typewriters
l Charles Lee & Company
m East African Shipping Lines
n 14th National Bank of Chicago
o The Hong Kong Printing Corp.
p F P Yong (Publishers)
q Henry Higgens & Sons
r The Accident & General Insurance Company
s North Eastern Transport
t TPC Corporation

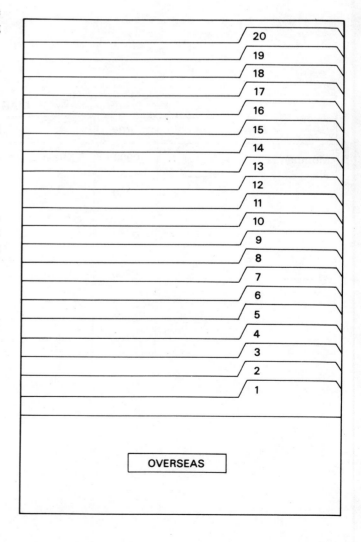

OVERSEAS

Comprehension: Diagrams in texts (2)

Exercise 1 *To use a text to supply information missing from a diagram*

Diagrams are a very useful method of displaying information clearly and effectively. One diagram may contain all the important information in quite a long text.

Use this text to complete the diagram.

PROCESSING THE OFFICE MAIL

In large offices all mail is received and sent out from a central mailing room. This room is responsible for opening, sorting, date-stamping and distributing the mail to various departments of the firm. Some of the major departments receiving mail include:

a) *Purchasing Department* Every company must purchase supplies, equipment or material in order to carry on its business. Most large companies have a separate purchasing department for this purpose. A good purchasing agent keeps in touch with many sources of supply, and knows all the different firms that manufacture a particular item, their prices and the quality of their products.

b) *Production Department* The production department may vary in size from a small one-room workshop to the large-scale manufacturing facilities of a modern corporation. Once the decision to begin production has been made, the production department issues a production order and the manufacturing plant begins work. During the process of manufacture, materials must be requisitioned from the stockroom, orders for materials which are not in stock must be made out and passed to the Purchasing Department, and various time and labour records must be kept.

---

c) *Sales Department* The sales department is responsible for maintaining and increasing sales of a company's product. A large company will have a separate sales department responsible for the planning for sales; market research and analysis; advertising and product promotion campaigns; direction of the activities of salespersons; the handling of enquiries and orders; the shipping of approved orders, and the servicing of the product after it has been sold. Correspondence plays a major part in the sale of goods. Many firms prefer to place an order by mail because a copy of the letter or purchase order, kept on file in their own office, acts as a record of the transmission in case of dispute.

d) *Accounts Department* The accounts department has four main responsibilities. It handles all the money received by the firm. Money is received by the company in various ways: cheques, money orders and cash are received, recorded and deposited each day. It also handles all money paid by the firm. Firms pay their outstanding debts by cheque. When an invoice is received it is checked for accuracy, approved for payment and a cheque is issued to pay the amount owing. Thirdly, the accounts department is responsible for the company's payroll: paying out the salaries and wages of the employees. Lastly, the department is responsible for keeping a complete record of all financial transactions and operations of the business.

e) *Personnel Department* The personnel department is responsible for the recruitment and discharge of all personnel, the negotiation of salaries, and all matters pertaining to labour relations, the health, training, safety and welfare of employees, and any other services that the company may provide for its employees.

(Diagram and text adapted from G A Reid, *Modern Office Procedures*, Pitman, Canada, 2nd edn, 1978.)

4

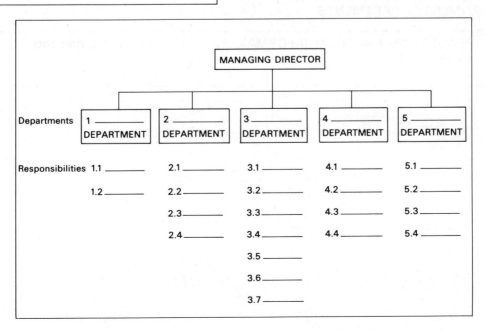

Exercise 2 *To draw conclusions from a text and a diagram*

The table below lists ten of the most common types of correspondence received by the mail room of a large company:

It is one of the major jobs of the mail room to sort all incoming mail and distribute it. To which department should each of the 10 types of correspondence listed below be sent? Use the text and diagram in Exercise 1 to answer this question. Work in pairs and try to reach agreement on your answers. One department has no incoming mail. Which one? Can you think why this is so?

FROM SUPPLIERS

1	ENCLOSING PRODUCT INFORMATION	catalogues, price lists, samples
2	DELIVERY INFORMATION	advice notes, despatch notes, consignment notes
3	REQUESTING PAYMENT	bills, invoices, statements
4	ACKNOWLEDGING PAYMENT	receipts

FROM CUSTOMERS

5	REQUESTING PRODUCT INFORMATION	requesting catalogues, price lists, quotations
6	ORDERING	order forms, purchase orders
7	ENCLOSING PAYMENT	cheques, money orders
8	QUERIES/COMPLAINTS	concerning quality, orders, delivery dates

FROM POTENTIAL EMPLOYEES

9	REQUESTING EMPLOYMENT	job applications

FROM GOVERNMENT DEPARTMENTS

10	REQUESTING FINANCIAL INFORMATION/ PAYMENTS	tax forms, demands

Exercise 3 *To express the answers to Exercise 2 in the form of a diagram*

Copy out the following diagram. Then use your answers to Exercise 2 to complete it by filling in the gaps labelled 1–13.

(Diagram based on J Harrison, *First Steps in Business Training,* Pitman, 1975.)

An arrow has been drawn from the box labelled 'Enclosing product information' to the box labelled 'Purchasing Department'. This arrow shows that catalogues, price-lists, samples, etc, are sent from the Mailing Room to the Purchasing Department. Draw arrows from boxes 5–13 to the appropriate department boxes. Your answers to Exercise 1 will give you the information to draw these arrows.

Give the diagram a title.

MAILING ROOM	PURCHASING DEPARTMENT	1 _____ DEPARTMENT	2 _____ DEPARTMENT	3 _____ DEPARTMENT	4 _____ DEPARTMENT
Enclosing product information	→				
5 _____ _____					
6 _____ _____					
7 _____ _____					
8 _____ _____ _____					
INCOMING MAIL ► 9 _____					
10 _____ _____					
11 _____ _____					
12 _____ _____					
13 _____ _____ _____ _____					

4

Exercise 4   *To apply the answers to Exercise 3*

The letters below have been received and opened by the Mailing Room of Igwilo's Building Supplies. Work in pairs and use the information in Exercises 1–3 to decide which department each letter should be sent to.

1

Dear Sirs

We were very interested in your latest catalogue.

We should be glad to receive a quotation for the following items in the quantities indicated:
1 000 B456 Shelf brackets with side lips
1 000 B590 Shelf brackets (concealed fixing)
1 000 B494 Extending guard rails for shelves
Please give all prices cif Kano, Nigeria.

We look forward to receiving your quotation.

Yours faithfully

A I Ahmed

A I Ahmed
Buying Dept

2

Dear Sirs

We thank you for your cheque for $293.72 in payment of order ref no D72397. We enclose our receipt for this amount.

The amount shown on the invoice sent out in connection with this order was in fact $392.72. We can only assume that your cheque was incorrectly made out as the result of a slip.

We should be grateful to receive the balance of $99 as soon as possible.

Yours faithfully

T P Chin

T P Chin
for A P B Products Ltd

3

Dear Sirs

We are importers and distributors of builders' supplies. At present we are expanding our operations throughout the area and are looking for alternative suppliers.

Will you please send us your latest catalogues and price-lists for your complete range of products, as well as details of trade discounts normally offered.

Yours faithfully

AM

Western Construction Supplies Ltd

4

Dear Sirs

We have pleasure in enclosing our latest trade catalogues and price-lists.

We are particularly proud to announce the introduction of our Aphrodite porcelain enamelled luxury bath range in ten exotic colours with slimline plated fittings and trim.

We look forward to further business with your company and assure you of prompt service at all times.

Yours faithfully

SM

Bathing Beauties Incorporated

5

Dear Sirs

We enclose our cheque for $15 276.74 in settlement of your invoice number FZ27307 of 27 August 198–.

This clears our account with you.

Yours faithfully

Wambert

Chief Accountant

6

Dear Sirs

I saw your advertisement for an Assistant Storesman in 'The Daily Nation'.

I should like to apply for this post and enclose details of my education and previous experience on a separate sheet.

Yours faithfully

J K Jere

J K Jere

7

Dear Sirs

Please refer to our order P98981S of 23 March 198–.

We are concerned that we have received no acknowledgement of this order. Will you please confirm that it has been received and when you will supply the items ordered.

Please cable your immediate reply.

Yours faithfully

P. Togo

TP Togo and Sons

8

> Dear Sirs
>
> Your consignment of 2 000 plated lever furniture handles (concealed fixing) in fulfilment of our order no 944666 arrived recently.
>
> On unpacking this consignment we discovered that the plating on approximately 200 handles is faulty and these we are returning to you. We trust that under the terms of our agreement these can be replaced.
>
> Yours faithfully
>
> *AH*
>
> Albert Brothers (Builders) Ltd

9

> Dear Sirs
>
> We are pleased to inform you that the goods ordered by you on 24 April 198– (ref 877351) will be despatched by air freight on 15 June 198–. Bills for air freight charges will be forwarded as soon as the goods have been despatched.
>
> Yours faithfully
>
> *ML*
>
> Eastern Building Products Ltd

10

> From the Inspector of Taxes, Eastern Area
>
> The enclosed taxation forms for the quarter ending 30 June 198– should be completed and returned to this office not later than 1 July 198–.
>
> Signed
>
> *AM*
>
> Inspector of Taxes

PS: Spelling   *Irregular spelling patterns*

English, like many other languages, expands its vocabulary by adding prefixes and suffixes to existing words. For instance, many verbs can be turned into nouns simply by adding -ation. There is no change in the spelling otherwise:

alter	+ -ation	= alteration
consider	+ -ation	= consideration
expect	+ -ation	= expectation

However, in several words there is an unexpected change of spelling:

despair	+ -ation	= desperation
pronounce	+ -ation	= pronunciation
explain	+ -ation	= explanation
reveal	+ -ation	= revelation

The following passage contains many words which are frequently misspelt because we draw false conclusions about their spelling. Fill in the gaps in the passage with the correct form of the words in brackets.

Care of typewriters

To assist with the [1] __ (success + full) [2] __ (produce + ion) of first class work it is [3] __ (essence + ial) that a typewriter is kept in good working order. It is the typist's [4] __ (responsible + ity) to keep her typewriter as clean as possible. The following [5] __ (proceed + -ure) is recommended:

a The typewriter should [6] __ (all + ways) be covered at the end of the day.

b The typist should remove the front cover and give all [7] __ (access + able) parts of the typewriter a [8] __ (care + full) brushing with a soft brush [9] __ (day + -ly).

c The type faces of all [10] __ (four + -ty)-six keys should be regularly cleaned with a stiff-bristled brush, preferably at the [11] __ (begin + -ing) of each day.

d Every [12] __ (eight + -th) or [13] __ (nine + -th) day the typist should wipe the carriage rails with a lightly oiled duster.

e When erasing, the typist should move the carriage to the side so that rubber particles will not fall into the type basket. The [14] __ (explain + -ation) for this is that most [15] __ (circle + -ar) erasers contain powdered glass particles which damage metal.

f A typewriter should never be left near an [16] __ (enter + -ance) or in any other position where a clumsy passer-by could knock it off the [17] __ (furnish + -ure).

g The typist should never pull the paper out of her machine when she is [18] __ (anger + -y).

h When using an electric typewriter, the typist should take care to ensure that there are no trailing cables or [19] __ (extent + ion) leads, which could cause harm to both passer-by and typewriter.

i If any part of the typewriter [20] __ (machine + -ism) is not working properly, the typewriter should not be used until a [21] __ (skill + full) [22] __ (machine + -ic) has repaired the fault. Regular [23] __ (maintain + -ance) is [24] __ (desire + able) for all typewriters in frequent use. Following the [25] __ (occur + -ence) of any fault, the typist should look out for any [26] __ (appear + -ent) [27] __ (repeat + -ition) of the fault.

j Make sure that all electric typewriters are switched off at night. Failure to do this can be [28] __ (disaster + -ous): a machine left on overnight is a [29] __ (substance + -ial) fire risk.

A typewriter is a [30] __ (value + able) and indispensable piece of equipment in any office and if the above points are observed by the typist the working life of the machine will be considerably prolonged.

(Adapted from E Mackay, *The Typewriting Dictionary*, Pitman, 1977.)

4

Composition: Business letters in examination questions

Exercise 1 *To choose the most appropriate extracts of letters written in answer to examination questions*

Situation A

Write a letter of 150–200 words for your company, Discrecord Ltd. (Wheatley House, Wheatley Road, London, K18 4RF) to L Wallace, Sales Manager of Record Distributors Ltd. (1984 Bude Avenue, New York, USA), informing him that the last two consignments of gramophone records that were ordered from his company have not arrived and that this is causing a shortage in the shops run by your company. Ask him to do something about this matter very quickly.
(*LCCI* – English for Commerce, Intermediate)

1 The inside address should be:
   a L Wallace, (Sales Manager)
     Record Distributors Ltd
     (1984 Bude Avenue, New York, USA)
   b Mr L Wallace
     Sales Manager
     Record Distributors Ltd
     1984 Bude Avenue
     New York
     USA
   c The Sales Manager
     Record Distributors Ltd
     1984 Bude Ave
     NY
     USA

2 The most appropriate opening sentence would be:
   a The last two consignments of gramophone records that were ordered from his company have not arrived.
   b This matter is very urgent.
   c We ordered two consignments of gramophone records from you on 30 July, 198–. These have not yet arrived.

3 The best explanation of the problem caused would be:
   a The delay in receiving these goods means that there is a shortage of records in our shops.
   b This is causing a shortage in the shops run by your company.
   c We are terribly sorry to tell you that the delay is causing a shortage in the shops run by our company.

4 The most appropriate closing sentence would be:
   a Do something about this matter very quickly.
   b We look forward to receiving the records in the very near future.
   c Please cancel our order.

5 The best complimentary close is:
   a Yours faithfully
     DISCRECORD LIMITED

     a. N. Other

     Your name
   b Yours Faithfully
     pp DISCRECORD LTD

     A. N. Author.
     Your name
   c Yours sincerely

     Purchasing Manager

Situation B

Write a circular letter to the customers of your company announcing the transfer of the company house to new and convenient premises. State other services that are available for the customers at the new premises.
(Nigerian *FME* – English, Confidential Secretary III)

1 The inside name and address would be:
   a To whom it may concern
   b (No inside name and address required.)
   c All customers

2 The salutation should be:
   a Dear Customers
   b Dear Customer
   c Dear Sirs

3 The most appropriate opening sentence should be:
   a We are happy to announce that we shall soon be moving to new premises.
   b We are announcing the transfer of the company house to new and convenient premises.
   c This circular letter is to make an announcement we are sure you will like.

4 The most appropriate statement of other services would be:
   a There are other services available for the customers at the new premises.
   b We are sure the other services will be available for the customers at the new premises.
   c We are sure you will find the new premises more convenient as the building is nearer the town centre. In addition, all our departments will be in the same building making our whole operation more efficient.

5 The most appropriate closing sentence would be:
   a We are looking forward to welcoming you to our new premises.
   b We sincerely hope you will come and visit us when we move.
   c Please do not stop doing business with us just because we have moved.

Situation C

As a Purchasing Manager of a firm selling household utensils, write a reminder to Messrs M. Maduna & Sons, who appear to have failed to settle their account which is now overdue.

1 A suitable name for your company would be:
  a Messrs Maduna and Sons
  b Household Suppliers Ltd
  c Utensils Ltd

2 The salutation would be:
  a Dear Messrs Maduna
  b Dear Sirs
  c Dear Sir

3 The most appropriate opening sentence would be:
  a You haven't paid for your household stores.
  b We have been checking our records, and it appears your account is now overdue.
  c You have failed to settle your account.

4 The most appropriate request for payment would be:
  a You had better pay or we shall put the matter in the hands of our solicitors.
  b We are really sorry to have to ask you but would it be too inconvenient to pay this outstanding amount as soon as possible?
  c We should be grateful if you would forward the amount owed as soon as possible.

5 The complimentary close should be:
  a Yours faithfully

  a. N. Other

  Your name
  Purchasing Manager

  b Yours sincerely
  Purchasing Manager

  A. N. Author.

  Your name

  c Yours faithfully

Situation D

As assistant to the Personnel Officer of Grayson Components Ltd, York, write to the Fourstar Bureau. Your firm needs a temporary shorthand-typist to cover staff holidays for six weeks from the 8th of next month. Give details of work involved, hours, pay.
(*PEI* – English for Business Communications, Intermediate)

1 The most suitable inside address would be:
  a The Personnel Officer
    Grayson Components Ltd
    York
  b Fourstar Bureau
    York
  c Fourstar Bureau
    15 Cathedral Street
    York
    YK1 CS4

2 The best salutation would be:
  a Dear Sirs
  b Dear Mr Fourstar
  c Dear Bureau

3 The most suitable subject heading would be:
  a Temporary Shorthand Typist
  b Staff Holidays
  c Six weeks' work

4 The most suitable statement of your requirements would be:
  a The normal hours of work will be involved and pay will depend on age.
  b Our hours of work are 0830–1600 hours and temporary workers are paid by the hour. The rate of pay will depend on age and experience.
  c The details of work involved, hours and pay are enclosed.

5 Suitable details of the work involved would be:
  a The work involves some filing and receiving visitors as well as dictation and typing business correspondence.
  b The work involved is not too difficult.
  c The work involved is nice and Mr Grayson is not very busy at the moment.

4

Exercise 2   *To compose a letter from given headings*

Type or write a letter based on the last situation in Exercise 1. Make sure you include the following:

1 Letterhead
2 Today's date
3 Inside name and address
4 Salutation
5 Subject heading
6 Body of the letter:
  a What you require
  b When
  c Details of duties, hours, salary, etc
  d Closing sentence
7 Complimentary close
8 Your signature and name
9 Designation

Exercise 3   *To complete letters from given situations in examination questions*

Type or write the letters for situations A, B and C in Exercise 1. Use your answers to the questions in Exercise 1 as a guide.

Exercise 4   *To answer an examination question without any guidelines given*

Answer the following examination question:

Write a letter of between 150 and 200 words on behalf of your company, ABC Exports, Bank Lane, London E26 4LM, England, to the Sales Manager, World Stores, Accra, Ghana, West Africa, informing him that your company has just appointed a new African representative, Mr. K. Myers, who will be in Ghana next month and will be calling at World Stores to discuss future trading with the Sales Manager. Point out that Mr Myers has a wide knowledge of Africa and has spent fifteen years in the exporting business and that his appointment as African representative should mean more business and greater profits to World Stores. Lay out your letter correctly.

(*LCCI* – English for Commerce, Intermediate)

PS: Appropriate vocabulary for business letters

In the following list, find pairs of words that are similar in meaning:

1	error	*17*	pass
2	correct	*18*	rectify
3	discern	*19*	read
4	remit	*20*	anticipate
5	commence	*21*	end
6	expect	*22*	notice
7	agree	*23*	buy
8	keep	*24*	maintain
9	communication	*25*	letter
10	purchase	*26*	elapse
11	terminate	*27*	begin
12	despatch	*28*	assent
13	peruse	*29*	help
14	utilise	*30*	use
15	assist	*31*	send
16	send	*32*	mistake

Business does not need a special language except for a few technical terms which have to be learned, eg fob. The rule for writing business letters is always use the most common suitable word which best expresses the meaning.

33 Choose the more common words from each pair you have listed.

34 Rewrite or type out the following letter making the vocabulary simple and straightforward. Some words will have to be changed and some will have to be missed out.

Dear Sir

Thank you for your communication of 22 May 198–.

We were sorry to hear that an error was made pertaining to your order. We have investigated the cause and have discovered that the error, which should have been rectified in our packing room, was not discerned before the order was remitted.

We have despatched a repeat order which should arrive soon.

Please accept our apologies for the inconvenience you have been caused.

Yours faithfully

Oral/Aural: Statistics

Exercise 1 *To understand a graph through asking questions.*

1 In order to understand the following graph, what questions do you want answered? Work in pairs and discuss what you need to know.

2 Some information has now been added. Do you now understand the graph? Which of your questions have been answered and which have not?

—— with knowledge of score

······ without knowledge of score

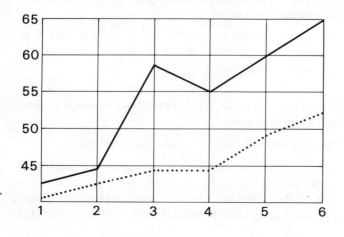

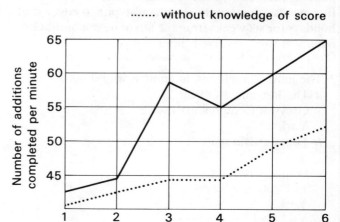

3 The graph below is complete. Is there still anything you do not understand?

The influence of knowledge of score on students' performance

 —— with knowledge of score

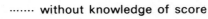 ······ without knowledge of score

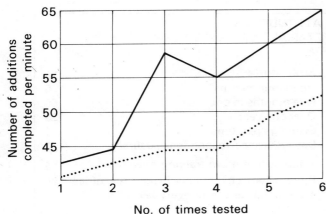

No. of times tested

4 Work in pairs and decide whether the following statements are true, false or not known according to the graph:

a Six students did a test.

b The test was done six times.

c Those students who were not told their scores on each test did better than those students who were told their scores.

d The dotted line shows the scores of students who were not told their score.

e On the sixth test one group did 65 additions in one minute.

f The results show that it is better to tell students the results of tests.

g Giving someone results is called 'feedback'.

h In typewriting you know quickly whether you have made a mistake or not.

i The graph shows the average number of additions in a minute made by a group of students.

j If no knowledge of results is given, then no improvement is possible.

Use the following passage to help you understand the graph better. Can you decide whether *all* the statements above are true or false after reading the passage?

The graph shows the average number of additions done in a minute by two groups of students. One group, shown by the solid line, were allowed to count up how many additions they had done after each test. The other group were not allowed to do this so they did not know what their score was. The importance of feedback, ie giving results, is most important in learning a physical skill such as typewriting. Usually in typewriting a student knows quickly when he has made a mistake, but if the student was not allowed to see what he had typed then improvement would be slow.

Exercise 2 *To plan an experiment similar to that used to make the graph in Exercise 1*

Work in pairs to plan an experiment. Plan:
a) What you would say to the participants;
b) What instructions you would give;
c) How you would show your results.

Description of the experiment:	
Instructions for Group A:	Instructions for Group B:
Tell them to draw a line five centimetres long without using a ruler. Tell them to do this six times. Each line should be covered up after it is drawn so that it cannot be copied. Tell them after each attempt by how much each line is too long or short.	Give the same instructions as for Group A but do *not* tell them how accurate each line is.

Work in pairs with the class divided into two halves. One half: Give instructions to your partners who are *not* told how accurate their lines are. The other half: Give instructions to your partners who are told their results.

As a class work out the graph showing the results.

4

Exercise 3 *To ask questions to complete a survey*

Use the following survey results as a guide to making
the same survey in your own college. Plan:
1 What you are going to ask. (Do you need more
  headings than those given?)
2 How you will record the results.
3 When and how you will interview people.
4 How you will present the results.

A SURVEY OF THE ATTITUDES AND AMBITIONS OF SECRETARIAL STUDENTS IN 1978

The students:
The sample comprised 970 girls (98%) and 19
boys (2%) currently undergoing training in colleges of technology and further education and at
private secretarial colleges throughout the country.

Age	%
16 or 17	35
18 or 19	36
20 to 23	16
over 23	13

Qualifications	%
'O' Levels	49
'A' Levels	31
Further education qualifications	32
Degree	7

These percentages exceed 100 owing to the fact
that students can sit for any number of these
qualifications.

Why become a secretary?	%
Secretarial work was chosen career	35
Stepping stone to different career	20
Earning potential	15
Parental pressure	8
Changing from another field of work	4
Advice from careers officer	3
Status of secretarial work	1
Other reasons	14

Important qualities	%
Accuracy and presentation	33
Initiative	24
Ability to deal with people	15
Personality	7
Discretion	6
Loyalty	5
Spelling and grammar	4
General knowledge	4
High speeds	2

Ideal course	%
Up to four months	6
Five months to one year	69
Over one year	23
Evenings/part time	1
Day release/correspondence courses	1

Areas where more training needed	%
Practical work experience in an actual office	56
More practical use of everyday office machinery	49
Talks by employers of successful senior secretaries	34
Instruction on interview techniques	26
Telephone techniques	20
Instruction in specialist terminology (eg Medicine)	15
Filing techniques	8

Favourite subjects

	Most Interesting %	Least Interesting %
Typing	74	11
Shorthand	72	17
Business practice (Commerce/Law etc)	29	33
English	27	26
Office routine	25	49
Languages	15	20
Grooming and etiquette	10	14
Accounts	10	45

Most important subjects	Votes
Shorthand/typing	404
Office practice	352
Typing	142
Shorthand/audio	56
Languages	22
English	19

(Adapted from: *Tomorrow's Secretaries*, Alfred Marks Survey, July
1978)

PS: Words of comparison in interpreting a graph

Use the graph and the passage to complete the sentences given.

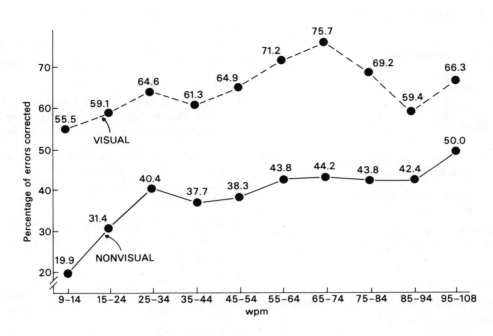

Number in each group:

  9–14   wpm – 24 typists
15–24 wpm – 64 typists
25–34 wpm – 27 typists
35–44 wpm – 23 typists
45–54 wpm – 31 typists
55–64 wpm – 28 typists
65–74 wpm – 27 typists
75–84 wpm – 21 typists
85–94 wpm – 11 typists
95–108 wpm – 10 typists

In this experiment there were 266 typists ranging in skill from 9 to 108 gross wpm as measured in a 12-minute straight copy-typing test. First they were told to copy-type under normal conditions, but asked to retype a word as soon as they knew they had made a mistake.

They were then asked to do the same thing but this time they each wore a shield which entirely blocked the typist's view of the typewriter and the typescript.

Results
The beginner who is not allowed to see the typewriter and the copy does not know just by touch whether he has made a mistake. The skilled typist may *think* he nearly always knows when he has made a mistake without looking. The results of the experiment show that he does not. Although there was no great reduction in speed between the two tests, there was an enormous effect on errors. Beginners more than doubled their errors when they could not see what they were doing.

From *Acquisition of Typewriting Skills* by Leonard J West Copyright © 1969 by Pitman Publishing Corporation. Reprinted by permission of Pitman Learning Inc, Belmont, California.

The following words can be used to complete the sentences below. Choose the correct word for each sentence:

fewer, more, than, lowest

1 __ typists could type at 15–24 wpm than at any other speed.
2 __ typists in the experiment could type at 95–108 wpm than at 75–84 wpm.
3 Typists made __ mistakes which they did not notice when they could see the typewriter and the typescript.
4 The __ percentage of mistakes corrected was by the typists who could not see what they were doing.
5 __ mistakes were corrected when the typists could see the typewriter and the typescript.
6 Typists at 55–64 wpm who could not see the typewriter and typescript corrected __ mistakes __ the typists at 45–54 wpm.
7 Beginners made __ mistakes when they could not see what they were doing.
8 Typists at 95–108 wpm corrected 16·3% __ of their errors when they could see what they were doing.
9 Typists made __ mistakes that they did not correct when they could see the typewriter and the typescript.
10 Typists made __ mistakes that they did not correct when they could not see the typewriter and the typescript.

4

Miscellany

Exercise 1   *Spelling – Suffixes*

A suffix is added to the *end* of a word to change its meaning.

Example:

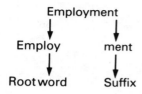

Employment

Employ   ment

Root word   Suffix

Match each of the following descriptions with one of the words given in brackets:

1 A word with a soft j sound spelt **ge**.
(*a*) gear *b*) target *c*) gauge)

2 A word (without a suffix) ending in two consonants.
(*a*) comfortably *b*) lazy *c*) quiet)

3 A word (without a suffix) ending in **e**.
(*a*) subtle *b*) movable *c*) knowledge)

4 A word of one syllable with two vowels together.
(*a*) wool *b*) foolish *c*) marriage)

5 A word ending in a soft s spelt **ce**.
(*a*) cause *b*) niece *c*) certain)

6 A word ending in **le** without a suffix.
(*a*) acceptable *b*) desirable *c*) subtle)

7 A word in which the suffix begins with a consonant.
(*a*) comfortably *b*) fulfilment *c*) independent)

8 A word of one syllable ending in a vowel followed by a consonant.
(*a*) but *b*) hypothesis *c*) chaos)

9 A word (without a suffix) ending in a consonant followed by **y**.
(*a*) completely *b*) cursory *c*) analysis)

10 A word with the suffix **able**.
(*a*) indispensable *b*) cable *c*) probable)

11 A word with an **ly** suffix.
(*a*) ally *b*) lying *c*) occasionally)

12 A word with the suffix **ous**.
(*a*) enormous *b*) dangerous *c*) unconscious)

Decide which words are needed to complete the following rules:

A Words ending in a single __ drop the __ when adding a suffix beginning with a vowel, eg move/movable, accommodate/ __.

B Words ending in a single **e**, keep it when the suffix begins with a __, eg complete/completely, immediate/immediately.

C Words ending with **ce/ge** which make a soft s/j sound keep the **e** before the suffixes **ous** and __, eg advantage/advantageous, notice/noticeable.

D In words of one __ that end in a single vowel followed by a single consonant, double the __ when adding a suffix beginning with a vowel, eg plan/planning, fit/ __.

E In words of one syllable that end in two __, do __ double the final __ when adding a suffix, eg wield/ __, guard/guardian.

F In words of one syllable with two vowels together followed by a consonant, do __ double the __ when adding a suffix, eg brief/briefly, view/ __.

G Words ending in __ drop the __ when adding the suffix __, eg incredible/incredibly, __ /ably.

H Words ending in **y** preceded by a consonant change the **y** into __ before any suffix except **ing** eg busy/business, hungry/ __.

Look at the following list of words and decide which of the rules they follow:

13 aggravation
14 appropriately
15 begging
16 changeable
17 coming
18 definitely
19 fashionably
20 favourably
21 helped
22 looking
23 losing
24 necessarily
25 psychological
26 putting
27 replaceable

Exercise 2 *Verbosity*

The shorter a sentence, the easier it is to understand. Think of shorter ways to say the following. The first one has been done for you.

1 In view of the fact that ..as....
2 At present ....
3 In the near future ....
4 During the course of ....
5 With a view to ....
6 At that time ....
7 In the first place ....
8 Because of the fact that ....
9 At this point in time ....
10 It is apparent that ....

Find the phrases and clauses in the following letter which can be replaced with something shorter. Type or write out the letter making it easier to understand.

> Dear Mr Chin
>
> Account No 654314
>
> Thank you for your letter of 10 July 198– about the above account.
>
> In view of the fact that you have made an application to extend your credit, I should like you to make arrangements to have a meeting with us sometime during the course of the next month.
>
> I am sure you are aware of the fact that our interest rates could be going up in the near future. I should like to point out that it would be advisable to take into consideration the length of time you will require to repay the amount you wish to borrow.
>
> We look forward to seeing you at the earliest opportunity.
>
> Yours sincerely

Exercise 3 *Tautology*

Tautology is the repetition of the same idea in one sentence.

Example:
a) This year's losses follow after five years of profits.

This sentence is tautologous because 'after' repeats the idea of 'follow'. Many cases of tautology arise because two sentences are confused, in this case:

b) This year's losses follow five years of profits.
   and
c) This year's losses come after five years of profits.

In each of the following sets of sentences, sentence *a*) is tautologous. It is tautologous because two correct sentences have been confused. Sentence *b*) is *one* of the correct sentences that has led to the confusion. Can you find the *other* sentence, sentence *c*)?

1 a Our stocks of paper are quite adequate enough. Don't buy any more.
   b We have quite enough paper. Don't buy any more.
   c --
2 a We need to discuss about next year's production targets.
   b We need to discuss next year's production targets.
   c --
3 a I hope we can co-operate together on this matter.
   b I hope we can co-operate on this matter.
   c --
4 a She descended down the stairs so quickly that she tripped and broke her ankle.
   b She descended the stairs so quickly that she tripped and broke her ankle.
   c --
5 a The reason that electric typewriters are less fatiguing is because the motor does 95 per cent of the striking action.
   b The reason that electric typewriters are less fatiguing is that the motor does 95 per cent of the striking action.
   c --
6 a There's a lot of work to be done when June returns back from her holiday.
   b There's a lot of work to be done when June returns from her holiday.
   c --
7 a He hasn't repaid back the money I lent him at the end of last year.
   b He hasn't repaid the money I lent him at the end of last year.
   c --
8 a Two copies of the agreement are enclosed herewith.
   b Two copies of the agreement are enclosed.
   c --
9 a Please endorse this cheque on the back.
   b Please endorse this cheque.
   c --
10 a The subject of this meeting is about the price rises recently introduced by some of our suppliers.
   b The subject of this meeting is the price rises recently introduced by some of our suppliers.
   c --

4

Examination preparation: *Defining business terms*

Formal definitions are the most basic type of examination question. They are included not only in some English Language examinations, but also in many papers in other commercial subjects.

Column A contains examination questions which require formal definitions as answers. First, decide what the term requiring definition is. Then use the words in columns B and C to write your definitions. The first one is shown here as an example:

1 'By hand' is /*m*) a delivery instruction /*vii*) indicating that a letter is to be transmitted by messenger.

A	B	C
(Term requiring definition)	*(The class to which the term belongs)*	*(Points which differentiate the term from other terms in the same class)*

A *(Term requiring definition)*

1 What does 'By hand' mean on an envelope?
2 Your office manager asked you to telephone a hotel for a tariff. What did he want?
3 What is registered post?
4 What is meant by sending a letter recorded delivery?
5 In what way do Yellow Pages differ from a standard telephone directory?
6 Your firm will refund out-of-pocket expenses. What does this mean?
7 What is prepaid postage?
8 What is a night safe at a bank?
9 A National Savings Certificate receives compound interest. What does this mean?
10 If your customer is 'in credit' at the bank, what would this mean to you?
11 If an address on a letter contains the word FREEPOST what does this mean?
12 Some firms will grant credit only to a householder. What does this mean?
13 What is meant by a typing pool?
14 What is meant by a telegraphic address?
15 What is meant by cash on delivery (COD)?
16 What is meant by the drawer of a cheque?
17 What is meant by a crossed cheque?
18 What is meant by a telex?
19 What is meant by an insurance premium?
20 Gross wages are ....

B *(The class to which the term belongs)*

a a telephone directory or section of a telephone directory
b an annual payment
c an abbreviated address
d a person
e a cheque
f a postal service
g a list
h expenses
i an office
j a safe
k wages
l a postal service
m a delivery instruction
n a postal service
o interest
p the person or firm
q a postal service
r a banking term
s a communication system
t a postal service

C *(Points which differentiate the term from other terms in the same class)*

i) who makes out the cheque.
ii) which allows postage to be paid in advance on large quantities of mail.
iii) from which deductions have to be made.
iv) who owns or rents a house.
v) which allows goods to be paid for when they are delivered by the Post Office.
vi) listing businesses under relevant trades or professions.
vii) indicating that a letter is to be transmitted by messenger.
viii) which is paid on the principal and on the interest which is earned.
ix) in which a number of typists work for many different members of a firm.
x) which many business firms have for use on telegrams.
xi) which are actually incurred by the employee while on company business.
xii) which is set into the outside wall of a bank so that customers can deposit cash and cheques when the bank is closed.
xiii) showing that a customer has a positive balance in an account.
xiv) which cannot be exchanged for cash at a bank but must be paid into the recipient's bank account.
xv) of prices charged for various services.
xvi) enabling letters to be posted without a stamp, postage being paid by the addressee.
xvii) which provides a rapid typewritten link between subscribers.
xviii) which is used for sending items of value.
xix) made for insurance cover.
xx) which provides proof that the item has been delivered to the addressee.

Unit 5

Summary: Using charts and tables

Various documents used in business show the progression of time. These vary from simple documents such as diaries and calendars to more complex ones such as itineraries, timetables and some types of graph.

Exercise 1 *To extract information from a timetable*

Timetables are a very concise way of showing the times at which things happen. They are common in schools and colleges to show lessons or lectures, and in transport systems to show times of departure and arrival.

The following timetable shows Zambia Airways' flights from Ndola to the towns of the Northern Province, including the popular resort of Kasaba Bay. Use the timetable to answer the questions underneath.

Day	1	4 & 6	5		Routing To/From		1	4 & 6	5
Flight number	QZ480	QZ482	QZ484				QZ481	QZ483	QZ485
	10.05	10.05	13.00	d	Ndola ↑	a	18.10	18.10	18.10
	10.45	10.45	13.40	a	Mansa	d	17.30	17.30	17.30
	11.15	11.15	14.10	d	Mansa	a	17.00	17.00	17.00
	12.05	12.05	15.00	a	Kasama	d	16.10	16.10	16.10
	12.35	12.35		d	Kasama	a	15.40	15.40	
		13.10		a	Mbala	d	15.05		
		13.40		d	Mbala	a	14.35		
	13.15	14.00		a ↓	Kasaba Bay	d	14.15	15.00	

Key: 1 = Monday 2 = Tuesday 3 = Wednesday 4 = Thursday 5 = Friday
6 = Saturday 7 = Sunday a = arrive d = depart

The questions below ask for *specific* information – days, times or numbers.

1 How many flights are there each week from Ndola to Kasaba Bay?
2 How many flights are there each week from Kasama to Ndola?
3 How many flights are there each week from Mansa to Kasaba Bay?
4 Is there a flight from Mbala to Ndola on Fridays?
5 On which days of the week do planes fly from Kasama to Kasaba Bay?
6 How long does the flight take from Mansa to Ndola?
7 How long does it take to fly from Mbala to Kasama?
8 How long does Monday's flight from Ndola to Kasaba Bay take?
9 How long do Thursday's and Saturday's flights from Ndola to Kasaba Bay take?
10 How long do planes stop at Mansa?
11 How long do planes stop at Kasaba Bay before returning to Ndola?
12 How much longer does the flight from Kasaba Bay to Ndola take on Thursday and Saturday than on Monday?

Exercise 2 *To extract information from a timetable to construct an itinerary*

Use the information in the timetable in Exercise 1 to complete the following itinerary. The itinerary summarises details of a long weekend (ie Thursday–Monday) trip from the industrial city of Ndola to the resort of Kasạba Bay.

```
         T R A V E L   I T I N E R A R Y
        Weekend visit to Kasaba Bay, Zambia
                12-15 August, 198-


Day    Time                     Place
a)     0930         dep  President Hotel, Ndola
       0945         arr  Ndola Airport
b)                  dep  Ndola Airport
c)                  arr  Kasaba Bay Airstrip
      _____
d)     1330         dep  Twiga Lodge, Kasaba Bay
       1350         arr  Kasaba Bay Airstrip
e)                  dep  f) _____
g)                  arr  Ndola Airport
```

Exercise 3 *To extract information from a table*

In Exercise 1 all the questions required answers which gave *specific* information. It is possible to make specific statements about the table below.

Example: In 1931 there were 1 426 000 clerical workers in Britain. In 1961 there were 3 066 000 clerical workers in Britain.

It is also possible to make *general* statements using the same information.

Example: The number of clerical workers in Britain doubled between 1931 and 1961.

Note that general statements do not include particular numerical information.

Complete each of the following sentences with *general* statements using information from the table.

1 In 1921 there were __ than female clerical workers.
2 Between 1921 and 1931 the number of male clerical workers __ and the number of female clerical workers __.
3 Between 1921 and 1931 the total number of clerical workers __.
4 In 1966 there were __ male clerical workers.
5 The percentage of male clerical workers __ between 1921 and 1951.

Use information from the table to make *general* statements based on the following notes.

6 No m clerical wkrs 1921 - 71

7 % m clrcl wkrs '21 - 71

8 No f clrcl wkrs '21 - 71

9 % f clrcl wkrs '21 - 71

10 Total no clrcl wkrs '21 - 71

11 No m clrcl wkrs cp no f clrcl wkrs '21 - 71

12 % m clrcl wkrs cp   "

The following table shows the numbers of clerical workers in Britain during the period 1921–71.

Year	Total (thousand)	No males (thousand)	% of total	No females (thousand)	% of total
1921	1 073	581	54·1	492	45·9
1931	1 426	778	54·6	648	45·4
1951	2 341	932	39·8	1 409	60·2
1961	3 066	1 120	36·5	1 945	63·5
1966	3 339	1 093	32·7	2 246	67·3
1971	3 492	1 043	29·9	2 449	70·1

(*Source:* British Labour Statistics – Historical Abstracts 1886–1968, Year Book 1974, HMSO)

Exercise 4 *To interpret information presented in the form of graphs*

Below are seven graphs based on the information presented in the table in Exercise 3. Identify the information that is shown in each graph by comparing it with the table. Then label the axes (a and b) in each graph and the keys in graphs 4 and 7. Write a brief title for each graph using your answers to Exercise 3.

1

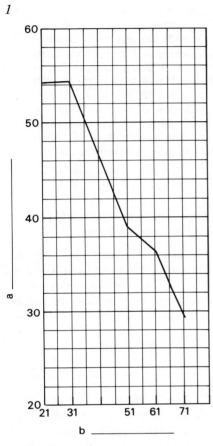

2

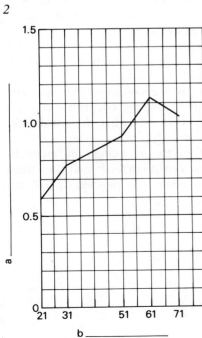

4 Key

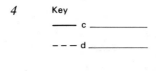

3

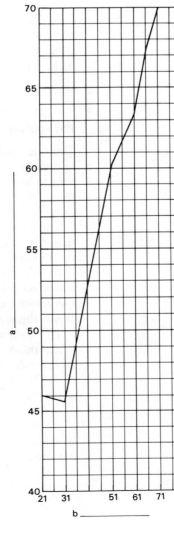

5

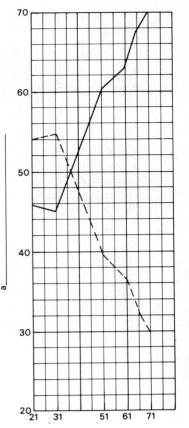

5

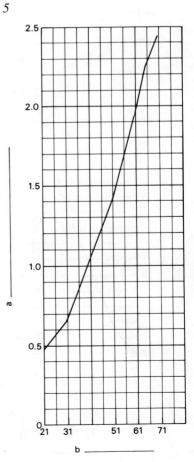

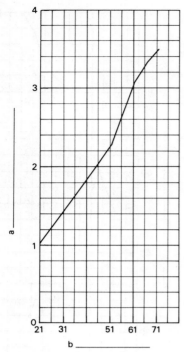

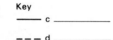

6

7

Key

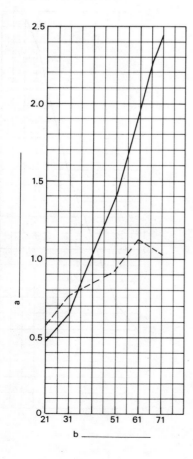

Exercise 5 *To construct a timetable from a written text*

Work in pairs. Construct a timetable using the information in the following paragraph. Use the airways timetable in Exercise 1 as a model to help you.

> Air Tanzania is now operating two Boeing 720 flights a week between Dar es Salaam and London's Gatwick airport. An outbound flight (TC612) leaves Dar at 2235 on Thursdays, serving Kilimanjaro (0035), Athens (0730) and Zurich (0905), arriving in London at 1045, while the inbound service (TC613) departs from Gatwick at 1700 on Fridays, calling at Rome (2020), Cairo (0030) and Kilimanjaro (0750), landing at Dar at 0945. A Sunday flight (TC610) leaves Dar at 2200 and stops at Kilimanjaro (2355), Cairo (0515), Rome (0945) and London Gatwick (1110). The reverse flight (TC611) departs from London at 1700 on Monday evenings, with stops at Zurich (1855), Athens (0010) and Kilimanjaro (0710), getting to Dar at 0905.

Exercise 6 *To use information from the timetable constructed in Exercise 5 to write a telegram*

Your local manager in Dar es Salaam has to go to London for a week's business. He must be in London by lunch-time on Monday 26 May. Write a telegram to be sent to the London office saying when, where and on what flight he will arrive, and asking for someone to meet him.

PS: Spelling – telex code

The telex service is like the telephone service but uses teleprinters instead of telephones. Messages can be sent to and received from most other telex machines in the world. Messages can be recorded on a perforated tape and transmitted automatically.

The series of holes corresponds to the symbols on a teleprinter keyboard, which is a simplified version of the typewriter keyboard.

The diagram represents five words on telex tape. The words have been misspelt. Use the teleprinter code on the following page to work out what the words are. Write the words out correctly.

The following five words are commonly misspelt. Write them in code, two spelt correctly and the others incorrectly. Give your code to a partner to find the misspelt words and correct them.

a privilege
b opinion
c piece
d wield
e weird

Teleprinter alphabet code

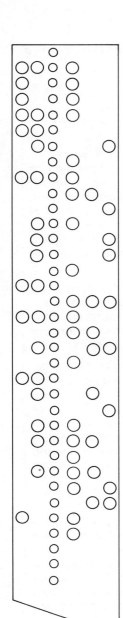

In alphabetical order

Letters	1	2	Feed	3	4	5
A	●	●	•	○	○	○
B	●	○	•	○	●	●
C	○	●	•	●	●	○
D	●	○	•	○	●	○
E	●	○	•	○	○	○
F	●	○	•	●	●	○
G	○	●	•	○	●	●
H	○	○	•	●	○	●
I	○	●	•	●	○	○
J	●	●	•	○	●	○
K	●	●	•	●	●	○
L	○	●	•	○	○	●
M	○	○	•	●	●	●
N	○	○	•	●	●	○
O	○	○	•	○	●	●
P	○	●	•	●	○	●
Q	●	●	•	●	○	●
R	○	●	•	○	●	○
S	●	○	•	●	○	○
T	○	○	•	○	○	●
U	●	●	•	●	○	○
V	○	●	•	●	●	●
W	●	●	•	○	○	●
X	●	○	•	●	●	●
Y	●	○	•	●	○	●
Z	●	○	•	○	○	●
CARRIAGE RETURN	○	○	•	○	●	○
LINE FEED	○	●	•	○	○	○
LETTERS	●	●	•	●	●	●
FIGURES	●	●	•	○	●	●
SPACE	○	○	•	●	○	○
NOT USED	○	○	•	○	○	○

In code order

Letters	1	2	Feed	3	4	5
X	●	○	•	●	●	●
F	●	○	•	●	●	○
B	●	○	•	○	●	●
Y	●	○	•	●	○	●
S	●	○	•	●	○	○
D	●	○	•	○	●	○
Z	●	○	•	○	○	●
E	●	○	•	○	○	○
LETTERS	●	●	•	●	●	●
K	●	●	•	●	●	○
FIGURES	●	●	•	○	●	●
Q	●	●	•	●	○	●
U	●	●	•	●	○	○
J	●	●	•	○	●	○
W	●	●	•	○	○	●
A	●	●	•	○	○	○
V	○	●	•	●	●	●
C	○	●	•	●	●	○
G	○	●	•	○	●	●
P	○	●	•	●	○	●
I	○	●	•	●	○	○
R	○	●	•	○	●	○
L	○	●	•	○	○	●
LINE FEED	○	●	•	○	○	○
M	○	○	•	●	●	●
N	○	○	•	●	●	○
0	○	○	•	○	●	●
H	○	○	•	●	○	●
SPACE	○	○	•	●	○	○
CARRIAGE RETURN	○	○	•	○	●	○
T	○	○	•	○	○	●
NOT USED	○	○	•	○	○	○

5

Comprehension: Written directions

Directions are explanations or instructions telling you how to do something or how to go somewhere.

All the exercises in this section ask you to follow written directions. In each exercise the end result will show whether you have followed them correctly.

Exercise 1 *To use a set of written directions to complete a pair of diagrams*

Read the following set of directions and then use them to number the boxes underneath.

COLLATION OF DOCUMENTS

There are several ways of collating documents, two of which are described here.

Method 1:

If, for example, a 10-page document is to be collated, the copies of each page should be stacked in neat piles along a table, the piles containing pages 1 to 10 consecutively. The clerk should then walk along the side of the table and collect one sheet from each pile, starting with page 10 and finishing with page 1.

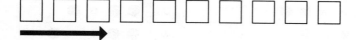

Method 2:

The second method of collating documents is both quicker and less tiring. The copies are again stacked in piles, but this time in two rows – four pages in the top row and six in the bottom. They are then collected from the table with both hands, again starting from page 10 and working through to page 1. Start at the two ends of the bottom row and work towards the centre, picking up the even pages with the right hand and the odd pages with the left hand. Pages 1 to 4 are stacked in the top row. Again work from the ends of the row towards the centre, picking up pages 4 and then 2 with the right hand and pages 3 and then 1 with the left. As each sheet is picked up from its pile it is placed on the desk in front of the clerk and as a result there is less movement and both hands are fully employed.

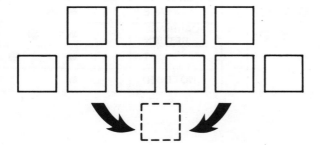

Exercise 2 *To use a set of written directions to draw a diagram*

Use the following directions to draw a Business Reply Card.

BUSINESS REPLY SERVICE

Under this service a person who wishes to obtain a reply from a client without putting him to the expense of paying postage may enclose in his communication an unstamped reply card, letter card, envelope, folder or gummed label of special design. The client can post the card, etc, in the ordinary way, but without a stamp, and the addressee will pay the charges on all the replies he receives.

Complete printed proofs of the cards, envelopes, folders or gummed labels which the licensee intends to use must be approved by the Director-General and their design must conform to the following pattern and regulations:

1 The design must be 10 cm long by 7 cm wide.
2 A panel 4 cm long and 1 cm wide containing the words 'Business Reply Service' on the top line and including the Licence number (for example 'Licence No. 123456') on the second line must appear in the centre of the card. A space of 3 cm must be left between the top edge of the card, etc, and the top of the 'Licence Number' panel.
3 The name and full postal address of the licensee (for example 'Jambo Motors, P O Box 1234, Nairobi') must be printed parallel to the length of the card, etc, and below the panel containing the licence number.
4 The words 'No postage stamp necessary if posted for delivery within East Africa' must be printed in a box in the top right-hand corner. The box must measure 2½ cm by 2½ cm and should touch the edges of the card.
5 The words 'Postage will be paid by the Licensee' must be printed in a box in the top left-hand corner. The box must measure 2½ cm by 2½ cm and should touch the edges of the card.
6 There must be two vertical lines ½ cm wide and 4½ cm long underneath the 'No postage' box. The lines should start ½ cm from the right-hand edge of the card and should be ½ cm apart.

Exercise 3 *To follow sets of written directions on a map*

1 a Come out of the railway station on the east side. Turn right into Railway Street.
   b Walk down Railway Street and take the first turning on the left, and then the second turning on the right.
   c Take the first left again and then the first right.
   d It is on the left. What is it?

2 a Come out of the bus station into Upperhead Row.
   b Go down Half Moon Street; turn right into Westgate and take the third turning on the left.
   c Go down this street, taking the third turning on the right.
   d You will see the Empire on the corner. What is the Empire?

3 a As you enter the town from the south east you come to a roundabout.
   b Go across the roundabout and up King Street.
   c Go to the T junction at the top and turn left.
   d Take the first turning on your right.
   e You will see it at the top of the road. What is it?

Exercise 4 *To give directions to be followed on a map*

Work in pairs. Each write down a set of directions using the map in Exercise 3. Each set of directions should explain how to get from one place in the town to another. Then give your set of written directions to your partner. Can your partner follow the directions correctly?

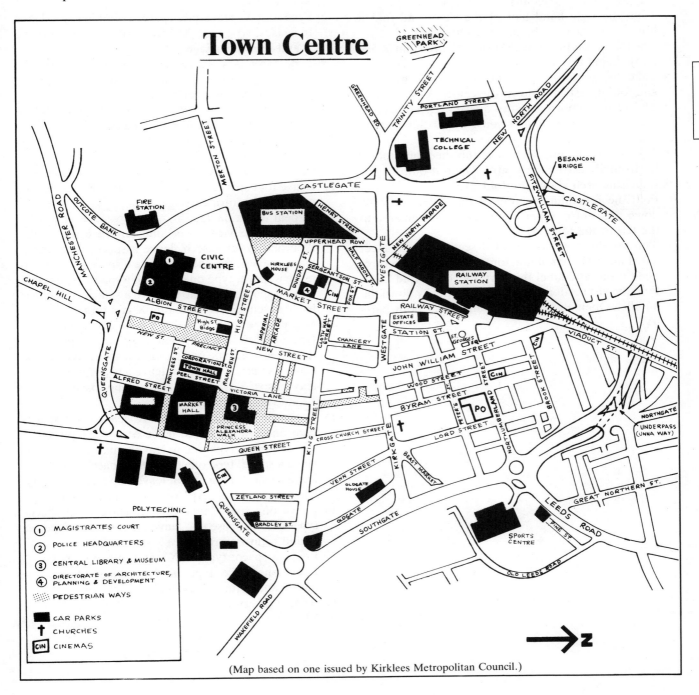

(Map based on one issued by Kirklees Metropolitan Council.)

Exercise 5 *To use a set of written directions to carry out a practical task*

The following set of directions illustrates the relationship between the different International Standards Organisation (ISO) paper sizes. You will need one sheet of A4 (210 mm × 297 mm). By the end the sheet of paper should be correctly folded and labelled.

Each paper size is achieved by folding the next largest size into two equal parts.

1 Take a sheet of A4 paper and place it landscape on a flat surface.
2 Fold the sheet vertically down the middle. Open it out.
3 The area on the left of the fold represents ISO size A1 (594 mm × 841 mm). Label this area 'A1'.
4 Take the right-hand half of the sheet and fold it horizontally across the middle. Open it out.
5 The top half represents ISO size A2 (420 mm × 594 mm). Label this area 'A2'.
6 Take the bottom right-hand quarter of the sheet and fold it vertically down the centre. Open it out.
7 The left-hand portion of this quarter represents ISO size A3 (297 mm × 420 mm). Label this portion 'A3'.
8 Take the remaining section of the sheet and fold it horizontally across the centre. Open it out.
9 Label the area above the fold 'A4'.
10 Fold the remaining section of the sheet vertically down the centre. Open it out and label the area to the left of the fold 'A5'.
11 You should now have a small section of the sheet left. Fold this section horizontally across the centre, open it out and label the part above the fold 'A6'.
12 Fold the last section of the paper vertically down the middle. Open the paper out and label both parts 'A7'.

PS: Instructions at the typewriter

This exercise is intended to be done on a typewriter, but it can be done using squared paper and a pen if a typewriter is not available.

The directions below show you how to draw a picture on a typewriter. Follow the directions using a sheet of A4 or A5 paper. Leave a left-hand margin of 30 spaces and use single spacing.

1 Leave 10 spaces, type 18 capital X's, return carriage.
2 Leave 10 spaces, type one X, leave 16 spaces, type one X and return carriage.
3 Repeat direction 2.
4 Repeat direction 2.
5 Repeat direction 2.
6 Type one X, leave one space, type nine X's, leave 16 spaces, type nine X's, leave one space, type one X and return carriage.
7 Type three X's, leave seven spaces, type one X, leave 16 spaces, type one X, leave seven spaces, type three X's and return carriage.
8 Type one X, leave one space, type 34 X's, leave one space, type one X and return carriage.
9 Leave five spaces, type one X, leave 26 spaces, type one X and return carriage.
10 Leave four spaces, type 30 X's and return carriage.
11 Leave four spaces, type one X, leave 28 spaces, type one X and return carriage.
12 Repeat direction 11.
13 Leave four spaces, type one X, leave six spaces, type one lower case o, leave a space, type one o, leave a space, type one o, leave a space, type one o, leave a space, type one o, leave a space, type one o, leave a space, type one o, leave a space, type one o, leave seven spaces, type one X and return carriage.
14 Leave three spaces, type one X, leave eight spaces, type one lower case o, leave a space, type one o, leave a space, type one o, leave a space, type one o, leave a space, type one o, leave a space, type one o, leave a space, type one o, leave nine spaces, type an X and return carriage.
15 Leave two spaces, type one X, leave eight spaces, type one lower case o, leave a space, type one o, leave a space, type one o, leave a space, type one o, leave a space, type one o, leave a space, type one o, leave a space, type one o, leave nine spaces, type one X and return carriage.
16 Leave one space, type one X, leave eight spaces, type 18 lower case o's, leave eight spaces, type one X and return carriage.
17 Leave a space, type 36 X's and return carriage.
18 Leave one space, type one X, leave 34 spaces, type one X and return carriage.
19 Repeat direction 17.
20 What do you have a picture of?

Composition: Using statistics

Exercise 1 *To construct a bar graph to understand fully what the graph represents*

One of your jobs as Office Manager is to organise staff holidays. You do not want any of your staff to take their holiday at a busy time. You decide to make a graph to show how the work is distributed throughout the year.

The following are the records of the number of accounts processed. Organise the information to draw a bar graph.

NO OF ACCOUNTS	PROCESSED BY	DATE	SIGNED	NO OF ACCOUNTS	PROCESSED BY	DATE	SIGNED
51	B. YEO	4/1/8–	S. Chee.	62	B. Yeo	4/7/8–	F. Wang
49	A. Tan	11/1/8–	F. Wang	68	A. Tan	11/7/8–	F. Wang
53	A. TAN	18/1/8–	S. Chee.	65	B. YEO	18/7/8–	S. Chee
47	B. Yeo	25/1/8–	F. Wang	59	P. LIM	25/7/8–	S. Chee
33	C. SIM	8/2/8–	F. Wang	16	C. SIM	8/8/8–	F. Wang
30	B. Yeo	15/2/8–	F. Wang	19	P. LIM	15/8/8–	S. Chee
34	A. TAN	22/2/8–	S. Chee	12	L. CHONG	22/8/8–	S. Chee
31	L. CHONG	26/2/8–	S. Chee	21	L. CHONG	29/8/8–	S. Chee
41	P. LIM	7/3/8–	S. Chee	28	B. YEO	5/9/8–	F. Wang
43	B. YEO	14/3/8–	S. Chee	19	P. LIM	12/9/8–	F. Wang
36	P. LIM	21/3/8–	F. Wang	14	C. SIM	18/9/8–	F. Wang
24	B. YEO	29/3/8–	S. Chee	17	A. TAN	26/9/8–	S. Chee
74	S. YEO	11/4/8–	F. Wang	11	L. CHONG	3/10/8–	F. Wang
79	A. TAN	18/4/8–	S. Chee	17	C. SIM	10/10/8–	F. Wang
68	A. TAN	20/4/8–	S. Chee	19	A. TAN	17/10/8–	S. Chee
79	C. SIM	25/4/8–	S. Chee	25	A. Tan	24/10/8–	F. Wang
22	P. LIM	2/5/8–	S. Chee	14	A. TAN	7/11/8–	S. Chee
23	L. CHONG	9/5/8–	S. Chee	25	L. CHONG	14/11/8–	F. Wang
24	C. SIM	16/5/8–	S. Chee	23	B. Yeo	21/11/8–	F. Wang
31	B. Yeo	23/5/8–	F. Wang	29	L. CHONG	28/11/8–	S. Chee
19	P. LIM	6/6/8–	F. Wang	26	L. CHONG	5/12/8–	F. Wang
37	C. SIM	13/6/8–	F. Wang	31	P. LIM	12/12/8–	F. Wang
31	B. Yeo	20/6/8–	F. Wang	24	L. CHONG	17/12/8–	S. Chee
36	C. SIM	27/6/8–	S. Chee	25	B. YEO	30/12/8–	F. Wang

Exercise 2 *To complete sentences using some of the words used to describe graphs*

Complete the following sentences using the graph you have drawn and the words given below:

1 The __ month was April.
2 There was __ work in August than in any other month.
3 There were __ as many accounts processed in May as in January.
4 There was almost __ the number of accounts processed in July as in February.
5 There were __ as many accounts processed in March as in October.

6 After July the number of accounts processed went __.
7 The __ number of accounts processed in the year was 1664.
8 A __ number of accounts was processed in December than in November.
9 There was a sharp __ in the number of accounts processed in April.
10 There was a sharp __ in the number of accounts processed in August.

down, greater, twice, total, less, half, double, busiest, decrease, increase

Exercise 3 *To write a comparison of two bar graphs*

The following bar graph shows the number of accounts processed in the previous year. Write 10 sentences comparing this graph with the one you drew in Exercise 1.

Exercise 4 *To use statistical information to make a decision given in the form of a memo*

Write to all your staff to tell them when the heaviest work load is and when, therefore, they should avoid taking their holidays. Type or write your message in the form of a memo.

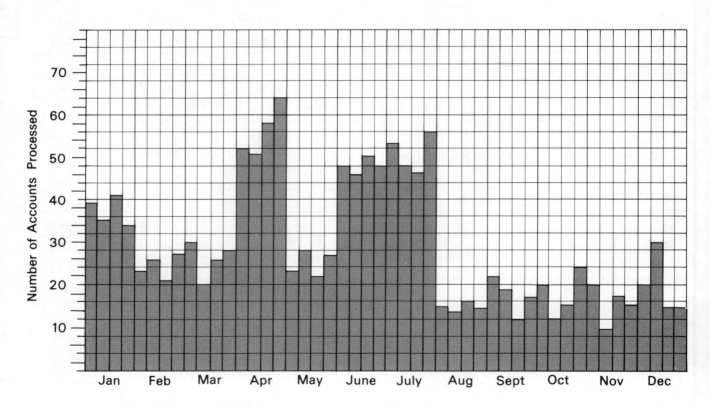

PS: Vocabulary of statistics

The following graph shows the orders a company received each month in one year:

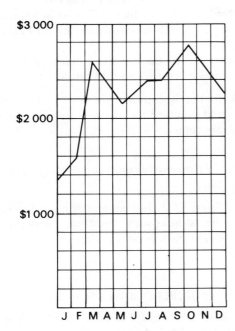

The company sells motoring products: first-aid kits, foot pumps, tyre gauges, petrol cans, tool kits and tow ropes. The following pie chart shows the relative number of sales in one month:

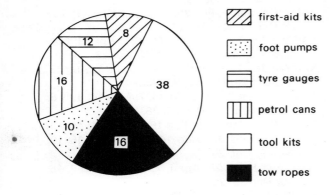

first-aid kits

foot pumps

tyre gauges

petrol cans

tool kits

tow ropes

The following histogram or bar chart compares the home sales with the export sales:

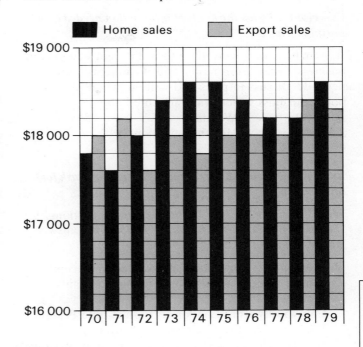

Home sales   Export sales

Complete the following sentences using the statistics given:

1 The __ shows that the sale of tool kits made up 38 per cent of one month's sales.
2 The horizontal axis of the histogram shows __.
3 The histogram shows __.
4 The __ shows the value of orders received each month of one year.
5 The vertical __ of the graphs shows __.
6 Foot pumps made up 10 __ of the sales in one month.
7 Home sales __ export sales in 1974.
8 The __ value of orders was received in October.
9 In February orders worth approximately __ were received.
10 The orders received __ after October 198–.
11 The company sold more __ than any other product in one month.
12 __ was a good year for exports.
13 Sales were lowest in the month of __.
14 In 1975 the __ sales were worth $36 000.
15 The __ value of sales in one month was $1 275.

5

Oral/Aural: Sources of information

Exercise 1   *To list the kinds of information needed on a business trip*

If your boss were travelling to a different country on business, what information and documents would be needed? Discuss in pairs and write down all the questions your boss would want answered about:

1 Travel   3 Weather   5 Visas
2 Money   4 Health regulations

Exercise 2   *To use different sources to give and ask for information.*

Work in pairs. A: Ask B the following questions. B: Use the information on pages 86–9 to find the answers. Do this exercise as quickly as possible.

1 What is the temperature in Kingston in December?
2 Which three countries have a public holiday on January 29?
3 Can you fly from London to Lusaka on a Friday?
4 What is the official language of Kuwait?
5 If it is 1530 hours GMT, what time is it in Hong Kong?
6 Where is the Cedi used as currency?
7 In which month is the heaviest rainfall in Hong Kong?
8 How many passenger flights are there from London to Hong Kong each week?
9 What nationality are the people from Banjul?
10 Where is Malay a national language?

Now change over. B: Ask A the following:

11 What is the capital of Malawi?
12 If you fly to Kingston, which country are you visiting?
13 Which month is the hottest in Hong Kong?
14 How many national holidays are there per year in Ghana?
15 If it is 1420 hours GMT, what time is it in Bermuda?
16 What is the currency of Sierra Leone?
17 What time does the Monday flight to Lagos leave London?
18 What is the official language in Port of Spain?
19 Of what country is Gaborone the capital?
20 Which is the driest month in Mombasa?

Now make up your own questions to ask a partner.

Exercise 3   *To answer questions for a particular business trip*

Work in pairs. Imagine your boss lives in London and is going to Tokyo on business. Use the information on pages 86–9 to answer the following:

1 How many flights are there each week to Tokyo?
2 Is there a flight on Tuesdays?
3 If so, what time does it leave?

4 Can your boss travel first class?
5 What time is it in London when he arrives in Tokyo if he leaves on Friday?
6 What is the currency used in Tokyo?
7 What is the weather like in Tokyo in September?
8 Can he arrange a business meeting on February 11 in Tokyo?
9 Do most people understand English in Tokyo?
10 What kind of clothes should he take for his trip?

Go back to the questions you wrote in Exercise 1. Where would you find the answers to these questions? Find answers relevant to Tokyo.

Exercise 4   *To invent and answer questions about one particular place*

Work in pairs. Use the information given on pages 86–9 to write 10 questions about one particular place. Find a different partner and ask him your questions.

PUBLIC HOLIDAYS FOR 198–

GAMBIA, THE: Jan 1; Feb 2, 18; Apr 4, 7; May 1; Aug 12, 13; Oct 19; Dec 25.

GHANA: Jan 1, 13; Mar 6; Apr 3, 7; July 1; Dec 25, 26.

HONG KONG: Jan 1; Feb 16, 18, 19; Mar 31; Apr 4, 5, 7, 21; June 17; July 1; Aug 4, 25; Sep 24; Oct 17; Dec 25, 26.

JAMAICA: Jan 1; Feb 20; Apr 4, 7; May 23; Aug 4; Oct 13; Dec 25, 26.

JAPAN: Jan 1, 15; Feb 11; Mar 21; Apr 29; May 3, 5; Sep 15, 23; Oct 10; Nov 3, 23.

KENYA: Jan 1; Apr 4, 7; May 1; June 1; Aug 13, 14; Oct 20; Dec 12, 25, 26.

MALAWI: Jan 1; Mar 3; Apr 4, 7; May 14; July 6; Aug 4; Oct 18; Dec 25, 26.

MALAYSIA: Jan 1, 29; Feb 16, 17; Apr 4; May 1, 10; June 6, 16; Aug 14, 15, 31; Oct 16–19; Nov 9; Dec 25.

NIGERIA: Jan 1, 29; Apr 4, 7; Aug 12; Oct 1, 16, 19; Dec 25, 26.

SIERRA LEONE: Jan 1, 29; Apr 4, 7; Aug 12, 13; Oct 16–19; Nov 9; Dec 25, 26.

SINGAPORE: Jan 1; Feb 16–19; Apr 4; May 1; Aug 9; Dec 25.

TANZANIA: Jan 12; Feb 5; Apr 4, 7, 26; May 1; July 7; Aug 12; Oct 16–19; Dec 9, 25.

THAILAND: Jan 1; Feb 16–19; Apr 6, 13; May 5; Aug 13; Oct 23; Dec 10, 25, 31.

TRINIDAD AND TOBAGO: Jan 1; Feb 18, 19; Apr 4, 7; May 26; June 5; Aug 4, 31; Sep 24; Oct 16; Dec 25, 26.

ZAMBIA: Jan 1; Mar 8; Apr 4, 5; May 1, 26; Jul 7, 8; Aug 4; Oct 24; Dec 25.

(From: *Philips' Modern College Atlas for Africa*, George Philip and Son Ltd, 1980.) ▶

COUNTRY	CAPITAL	NATIONALITY	OFFICIAL LANGUAGE
Bahamas	Nassau	Bahamian	English
Barbados	Bridgetown	Barbadian	English
Bermuda	Hamilton	Bermudan	English
Botswana	Gaborone	Batswana	English
Gambia	Banjul	Gambian	English
Ghana	Accra	Ghanaian	English
Guyana	Georgetown	Guyanese	English
Hong Kong	—	from Hong Kong	English
Jamaica	Kingston	Jamaican	English
Japan	Tokyo	Japanese	Japanese
Kenya	Nairobi	Kenyan	English/Swahili
Kuwait	Kuwait	Kuwaiti	Arabic
Malawi	Lilongwe	Malawian	English/Nyanja (or Chichewa)
Malaysia	Kuala Lumpur	Malaysian	Malay
Nigeria	Lagos	Nigerian	English
Sierra Leone	Freetown	Sierra Leonean	English
Singapore	—	Singaporean	Chinese/English/ Tamil/Malay
Tanzania	Dar es Salaam	Tanzanian	English/Swahili
Thailand	Bangkok	Thai	Thai
Trinidad and Tobago	Port of Spain	Trinidadian Tobagonian	English
Uganda	Kampala	Ugandan	English/Swahili

5

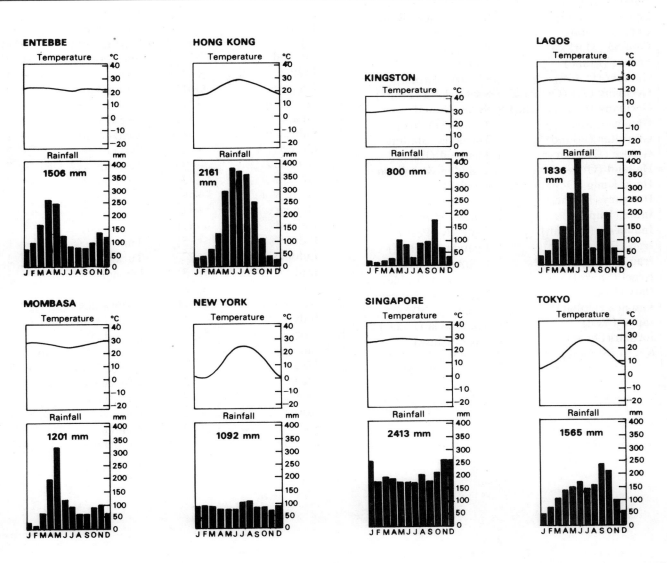

ENTEBBE — Temperature °C — Rainfall 1506 mm — J F M A M J J A S O N D

HONG KONG — Temperature °C — Rainfall 2161 mm — J F M A M J J A S O N D

KINGSTON — Temperature °C — Rainfall 800 mm — J F M A M J J A S O N D

LAGOS — Temperature °C — Rainfall 1836 mm — J F M A M J J A S O N D

MOMBASA — Temperature °C — Rainfall 1201 mm — J F M A M J J A S O N D

NEW YORK — Temperature °C — Rainfall 1092 mm — J F M A M J J A S O N D

SINGAPORE — Temperature °C — Rainfall 2413 mm — J F M A M J J A S O N D

TOKYO — Temperature °C — Rainfall 1565 mm — J F M A M J J A S O N D

CURRENCY

Country	Country
Afghanistan (Afghani)	**Korea** (Won)
Algeria (Dinar)	**Kuwait** (Dinar)
Argentina (Peso)	**Lebanon** (Livre)
Australia (Dollar)	**Libya** (Dinar)
Austria (Schilling)	**Luxembourg** (Franc)
Bahamas (Dollar)	**Malaysia** (Dollar)
Bahrain (Dinar)	**Malta** (Pound)
Belgium (Franc)	**Mexico** (Peso)
Bermuda (Dollar)	**Morocco** (Dirham)
Bolivia (Peso)	**New Zealand** (Dollar)
Botswana (Pula)	**Nigeria** (Naira)
Brazil (Cruzeiro)	**Norway** (Krone)
Brunei (Dollar)	**Oman** (Rial)
Bulgaria (Lev)	**Pakistan** (Rupee)
Canada (Dollar)	**Peru** (Sol)
Chile (Peso)	**Philippines** (Peso)
Colombia (Peso)	**Poland** (Zloty)
Costa Rica (Colon)	**Portugal** (Escudo)
Cyprus (Pound)	**Qatar** (Rial)
Czechoslovakia (Koruna)	**Romania** (Leu)
Denmark (Krone)	**Saudi Arabia** (Rial)
Dominican Rep. (Peso)	**Sierra Leone** (Leone)
Ecuador (Sucre)	**Singapore** (Dollar)
Egypt (Pound)	**South Africa** (Rand)
Finland (Markka)	**Spain** (Peseta)
France (Franc)	**Sri Lanka** (Rupee)
Gambia (Dalasi)	**Sudan** (Pound)
Germany (E.) (Ostmark)	**Sweden** (Krona)
Germany (W.) (D. Mark)	**Switzerland** (Franc)
Ghana (Cedi)	**Syria** (Pound)
Gibraltar (Pound)	**Taiwan** (Dollar)
Greece (Drachma)	**Tanzania** (Shilling)
Holland (Guilder)	**Thailand** (Baht)
Hong Kong (Dollar)	**Trinidad & Tobago** (Dollar)
Hungary (Forint)	**Tunisia** (Dinar)
India (Rupee)	**Turkey** (Lira)
Indonesia (Rupiah)	**Uruguay** (Peso)
Iran (Rial)	**Uganda** (Shilling)
Iraq (Dinar)	**U.S.A.** (Dollar)
Israel (Shekel)	**U.S.S.R.** (Rouble)
Italy (Lire)	**Venezuela** (Bolivar)
Jamaica (Dollar)	**Yemen** (Rial)
Japan (Yen)	**Yugoslavia** (Dinar)
Jordan (Dinar)	**Zaire** (Zaire)
Kenya (Shilling)	**Zambia** (Kwacha)

TIME + OR − HOURS GMT

Country	Hours	Country	Hours
Algeria	GMT	Liberia	GMT
Argentina	− 3	Libya	+ 2
Australia	+8 to +10	Liechtenstein	+ 1
Austria	+ 1	Luxembourg	+ 1
Bahamas	− 5	Malawi	+ 2
Bahrain	+ 3	Malaysia	+ 7
Bangladesh	+ 6	Malta	+ 1
Barbados	− 4	Mexico	− 6
Belgium	+ 1	Morocco	GMT
Bermuda	− 4	Mozambique	+ 2
Bolivia	− 4	Netherlands	+ 1
Botswana	+ 2	New Zealand	+12
Brazil	−3 to − 4	Nigeria	+ 1
Bulgaria	+ 2	Norway	+ 1
Burma	+ $6\frac{1}{2}$	Pakistan	+ 5
Canada	−$3\frac{1}{2}$ to − 8	Panama	− 5
Chile	− 4	Papua New Guinea	+10
China	+ 8	Paraguay	− 4
Colombia	− 5	Peru	− 5
Congo	+ 1	Philippines	+ 8
Cuba	− 5	Poland	+ 1
Cyprus	+ 2	Portugal	GMT
Czechoslovakia	+ 1	Puerto Rico	− 4
Denmark	+ 1	Romania	+ 2
Ecuador	− 5	Saudi Arabia	+ 3
Egypt	+ 2	Sierra Leone	GMT
Fiji	+12	Singapore	+ $7\frac{1}{2}$
Finland	+ 2	Spain	+ 1
France	+ 1	Sri Lanka	+ $5\frac{1}{2}$
Gambia	GMT	Sudan	+ 2
Germany	+ 1	Sweden	+ 1
Ghana	GMT	Switzerland	+ 1
Gibraltar	+ 1	Syria	+ 2
Greece	+ 2	Taiwan	+ 8
Grenada	− 4	Tanzania	+ 3
Guyana	− 3	Thailand	+ 7
Hong Kong	+ 8	Trinidad & Tobago	− 4
Hungary	+ 1	Tunisia	+ 1
Iceland	GMT	Turkey	+ 2
India	+ $5\frac{1}{2}$	Uganda	+ 3
Indonesia	+ 7	United Arab Emirates	+ 4
Iran	+ $3\frac{1}{2}$	United Kingdom	GMT
Iraq	+ 3	United States	−5 to −11
Ireland	GMT	USSR: Moscow	+ 3
Italy	+ 1	Venezuela	− 4
Ivory Coast	GMT	Yugoslavia	+ 1
Jamaica	− 5	Zaire	+ 1
Japan	+ 9	Zambia	+ 2
Jordan	+ 2	Zimbabwe	+ 2
Kenya	+ 3		
Korea	+ 9		
Kuwait	+ 3		
Lebanon	+ 2		

Depart	Day	Flight No	Class	Arrive
London → Hong Kong				
1000	7	BA 003	FY	0940*
1130	3	BA 003	FY	0950*
1215	4	BA 307	C	1210*
1550	1	BA 601	C	1400*
1600	1	BA 003	FY	1420*
London → Kano				
1315	6	WT 915	FY	2135
2300	1	WT 801	FY	0435*
2300	2	WT 803	FY	0435*
2300	3	WT 805	FY	0435*
London → Kingston				
0950	6	JM 002	FY	1600
1220	3	BA 267	FY	1825
1245	4	BA 265	FY	1850
1320	4	JM 102	FY	2100
London → Kuala Lumpur				
1400	5	BA 033	FY	1320*
1425	7	BA 013	FY	1355*
1445	3	BA 012	FY	1340*
1745	1	MH 001	FY	1730*
London → Lagos				
1315	6	WT 915	FY	2340
1600	4	WT 917	FY	2220
2300	1	WT 801	FY	0655*
2300	2	WT 803	FY	0655*
London → Lusaka				
1900	2	QZ 703	FY	0700*
1900	4	QZ 705	FY	0700*
1900	6	QZ 701	FY	0700*
1900	7	QZ 039	FY	0700*
London → Tokyo				
0845	3	SU 072	FY	1745*
1010	4	JL 073	FY	2015*
1350	2	JL 463	FY	1540*
1520	5	JL 465	FY	1710*

All times local   * – next day
1–Mon   2–Tues   3–Wed   4–Thurs
5–Fri   6–Sat   7–Sun
F–First Class   Y–Economy Class   C–Cargo

PS: Reference books

Match the descriptions of the contents of various reference books with the titles given (a–t):

1 Details of postal facilities, inland and overseas postal rates, methods of posting different types of material, etc.
2 Definitions and explanations of commercial terms and phrases. A special section listing the most frequently used abbreviations.
3 Maps of different countries of the world, population tables, national resources, climate, etc.
4 Languages that are spoken in different countries, surveys of weather conditions throughout the year, clothing appropriate for local conditions, working hours for government and business offices, hotels and restaurants, lists of public holidays.
5 Information about every branch of knowledge, in alphabetical order.
6 Names, initials, addresses, occupations, telephone numbers.
7 Names of streets and the occupiers of each house, office, shop and flat. These are arranged under headings of streets in alphabetical order. Trades and professions are also listed.
8 Correct pronunciation and spelling of common words in use in business, forms of address, typing display, etc.
9 Collections of words or phrases grouped together according to similarities in meaning.
10 Information on companies, securities, investments, etc.
11 News, advertisements, radio and TV programmes, local weather, exchange rates, etc.
12 Climate, population, social services, public health, housing, crime, education, labour, trade, transport, finance, etc.
13 Meanings of words, pronunciation, parts of speech, weights and measures, abbreviations, etc.
14 City to city air timetables, flight data, transfer connections, tariffs, etc.
15 List of telex subscribers, addresses, telex numbers codes and call charges.
16 Shorthand outlines and definitions of words.
17 Topics on typing, the typewriter, layout, typing for duplicating and all aspects of typing.
18 Report on the proceedings of parliament with verbatim record of all debates.
19 Lists of names, departments, posts and extension numbers.
20 List of a company's products, prices, reference numbers, specifications and ordering procedures.

a Catalogue
b Business terms, phrases and abbreviations
c Typewriting Dictionary
d Travel Guide
e World Airways Guide
f Dictionary of English and Shorthand
g Newspaper
h Atlas
i Statistical Year Book
j Telex Directory
k Stock Exchange Official Year Book
l Telephone Directory
m Hansard
n Thesaurus
o Encyclopedia
p Post Office Guide
q Street Directory
r Internal telephone directory
s Typist's Deskbook
t Dictionary

5

Match the following extracts from reference books with their titles (a–g below): *24*

a *The Typewriting Dictionary*, E Mackay, Pitman
b *The Pitman Dictionary of English and Shorthand*, Pitman
c *Fowler's Modern English Usage*, Oxford University Press
d *Heinemann English Dictionary*
e *Business Terms, Phrases and Abbreviations*, Ed D W Fiddes, Pitman
f *Business Punctuation*, J W Owen and J Davies, Pitman
g *Roget's Thesaurus of English Words and Phrases*, Longman

21

Deld.	Delivered
Dep.	Departs
Dept.	Department
D/f	Dead freight
Dft.	Draft
Diam.	Diameter
Diff.	Difference
Dis.	Discount
Dist.	District, discount
Div.	Dividend, division
Dk	Dock, deck
D.L.O.	Dead Letter Office
D/N	Debit Note
D.N.	Dispatch Note
D/O	Delivery Order
do.	Ditto, the same
Dols.	Dollars

22

2. The second purpose of hyphens is to form compound words that are to be used as one, eg
a foot-in-the-door salesman
an out-of-date issue of Punch
a happy-go-lucky girl

23 **B: Table** – *continued*

Word part or rootword	English example	Literal meaning	Further reference
aurum, Latin = gold	*auri*ferous	*gold*-bearing	
autos, Greek = self	*auto*biography	a *self*-written life story	*auto*mobile (moves by *itself*)
bene, Latin = well	*bene*volent	*well*-wishing	Compare *male, eu-*
bi, bin-, Latin = two	*bi*cycle	*two* wheel	*bin*oculars
biblios, Greek = a book	*biblio*graphy	a *book*-list	Compare *liber, libri*
bios, Greek = life	*bio*logy	the study of *life*	*bio*graphy, aero*bic*

24

diffu′sively, *adv.,* extensively; widely.
diffu′siveness, *n.,* the character of being diffusive.
dig, *v.t.,* to open and turn up with a spade; *v.i.,* to work with a spade or similar implement.
dig′amist, *n.,* a person second time married.
digam′ma, *n.,* a lost Greek letter, probably equivalent to *v* or *f.*
dig′amy, *n.,* a second marriage.
digas′tric, *adj.,* double bellied.
di′gest, *n.,* a collection of Roman laws, arranged by the Emperor Justinian; any similar collection of summarized material.
digest′, *v.t.,* to arrange methodically for study; to dissolve in the stomach.
digest′ed, *p.p.,* digest.
digest′er, *n.,* one who arranges in order; that which assists the digestion of food; a vessel in which substances in water are exposed to great heat so as to extract their essences.
digestibil′ity, *n.,* the quality of being digestible.

25

549. **Recorder** – N. *recorder*, registrar, record-keeper, archivist, remembrancer; notary, protonotary; amanuensis, stenographer, scribe; secretary, referencer, receptionist; clerk, record-clerk 808 n. *accountant*; filing cabinet, record room, muniment r., Record Office.
chronicler, saga-man, annalist, diarist, historian, historiographer, biographer, autobiographer 590 n. *narrator*; antiquary 125 n. *antiquarian*; reporter, columnist, gossip-writer 529 n. *newsmonger*; candid camera.
recording instrument, recorder, tape-r.; record, disc, long-player 414 n. *gramophone*; dictaphone; teleprinter, tape-machine, ticker-tape; cash register; turnstile; seismograph, speedometer 465 n. *gauge*.

26 As already mentioned, A4 and A5 are the two sizes of paper now in most common use. The following table gives the number of spaces across a page of A4 and A5 in both elite and pica pitch; also the number of lines to the page.

	A4	A5 (shorter dimension at top)	A5 (longer dimension at top)
Spaces across the page			
Elite (12 to the inch)	100	70	100
Pica (10 to the inch)	82	59	82

27   **2.** *Each other* is now treated as a compound word, the verb or preposition that governs *other* standing before *e.* instead of in its normal place: *they hate e. o., they sent presents to e. o.,* are usually preferred to *e. hates the other(s), they sent presents e. to the other(s)*. But the phrase is so far true to its origin that its possessive is *e. other's* (not *others'*), and that it cannot be used when the case of *other* would be subjective: *a lot of old cats ready to tear out e. other's* (not *others'*) *eyes*; *we e. know what the other wants* (not *what e. o. wants*). Some writers use *e. o.* only when no more than two things are referred to, *one another* being similarly appropriated to larger numbers; but this differentiation is neither of present utility nor based on historical usage. The old distributive of two as opposed to several was not *e.*, but *either*; and *either other*, which formerly existed beside *e. o.* and *one another*, would doubtless have survived if its special meaning had been required.

  3. *Between e.* For such expressions as 'three minutes b. e. scene' see BETWEEN 3.

28 Your boss has left the following message on the dictaphone. List the reference books you would need to consult to carry out his instructions.

Would you confirm my Singapore–Heathrow flight on 26 October with Singapore Airways? I think it leaves here at 9.15 pm. I also need the following information: the flight time between here and London, the time difference, the present exchange rate. Check the temperature there would you? It may be a nasty rumour that England is always cold and wet. I'll be spending two nights in London before I go to Birmingham. Would you find out how far it is between the two places.

Miscellany

Exercise 1   *Necessary conditions*

Most grammar books talk about 'real' conditional sentences. There is another type of conditional sentence which we can call a 'necessary' condition:

> **REAL CONDITIONS**
>
> (a) If it rains this afternoon, I shall come home by bus.
>
> This is called a 'real' condition because the event is in the future and we do not yet know if it will rain or not. The speaker is suggesting a choice:
> (b) If it rains this afternoon → I shall come home by bus.
> (c) If it doesn't rain this afternoon → I shall walk home.
>
> Note the tenses used:
>
>   If + present → future
>
> **NECESSARY CONDITIONS**
>
> (a) If you phone long distance after 1800 hours, it is cheaper.
> (b) If you drop a match in petrol, it burns.
> (c) If you go to Nigeria, you need a smallpox vaccination.
>
> These are 'necessary' conditions because they are true at all times – if one happens, the other must happen. Notice that the speaker has no choice in the matter. Again, note the tenses usually used:
>
>   If + present → present

Use the information given in the following paragraph and the table on page 88 to complete the necessary conditions printed underneath.

> The monetary unit of Trinidad and Tobago is the dollar, made up of 100 cents. Coins: 1, 5, 10, 25 and 50 cents. Notes: $1 (red), $5 (green), $10 (grey), $20 (mauve), $50 (rust) and $100 (blue).

1 If the note is blue, it is a $100 note.
2 If __, it is a $5 note.
3 __ $1 note.
4 __ grey.
5 __ rust.
6 If it is midday in Sierra Leone, it is __ in Sudan.
7 If it is midnight in Ghana, it is __ in Singapore.
8 If it is 1000 in Iceland, it is __ in Trinidad.
9 __ the United Kindom, it is 1900 hours in Thailand.
10 __ Kenya, it is 1130 in Tanzania.

Work in pairs to construct more sentences like these, using the world time table. Choose a time in one place and ask your partner what the time is somewhere else.

5

Exercise 2 *Pronouns (2)*

Certain pronouns – **it**, **this**, **that**, **these**, **those** – can be used to replace or refer back to other words.

Which word or words do each of the italicised words in the following passage refer back to or replace?

Financial reports present a picture of the operations of a business over a definite period of time – one year, six months or three months. [1]*They* provide a history of the firm's operations which can be used as a guide to establish [2]*its* future policies.

There are two basic financial reports – the balance sheet and the income statement. [3]*These two* are the keys of business planning. [4]*They* tell the management of a firm how much [5]*it* owns, how much [6]*it* owes and how much profit or loss resulted from [7]*its* activities. From a study of [8]*these two reports* [9]*they* receive a picture of past operations and the condition of the business at the present time.

[10]*The first of these* reports is an itemised statement of the assets, liabilities and capital of a business at a specified date. [11]*The second* is sometimes referred to as the profit and loss statement because [12]*it* presents a picture of the income received, the expenses incurred, and the net profit or loss resulting from operations for a certain period of time. A study of the income statement will tell the management of a business how the profit (or loss) occurred. [13]*This* information is essential in determining future policies for the business.
(Adapted from G A Reid, *Modern Office Procedures*, Pitman, Canada, 2nd edn, 1978.)

Replace the words italicised in the following passage with one of these:
it, its, this, that, these, then, they, the former, the latter.

Carbon paper is used to make copies of letters, invoices and despatches at the time [14]*the letters, invoices and despatches* are written. [15]*Carbon paper* was first used in 1806. It is not known whether the carbon paper [16]*which was first used in 1806* was widely used, but it is known that [17]*the carbon paper which was first used in 1806* was used by members of the police force. [18]*Members of the police force* used [19]*the carbon paper which was first used in 1806* for recording statements, passing messages and taking notes.

The carbon paper used [20]*in 1806* was very different from [21]*the carbon paper* used today. [22]*The carbon paper used in 1806* consisted of a porous sheet that had been soaked in a suspension of carbon black and then dried off. [23]*The porous sheet that had been soaked in a suspension of carbon black and then dried off* was then inserted between a top sheet and a writing sheet, and behind [24]*the writing sheet* was a writing plate. Pressure from a metal stylus transferred carbon to both the top sheet and the writing sheet. [25]*The top sheet* was retained as a copy and [26]*the writing sheet* used for the outgoing document.

Modern carbon paper was introduced to commercial work by an American, L H Rogers. He saw some improved carbon paper which had been made for a newspaper company. He recognised the superiority of [27]*the improved carbon paper* and started to manufacture [28]*the improved carbon paper* himself. In 1874, on seeing a demonstration of the first practical typewriter made by Sholes and Glidden, he persuaded the Remington Company to use [29]*the improved carbon paper* in their machine.
(Adapted from F G Holliday (ed), *The Manual of Stationery, Office Machines, and Equipment*, The British Stationery and Office Products Federation.)

Exercise 3 *Punctuation: commas*

In the two lists below find the words in list B which refer to the same things as the words in list A:

Example: 1 January = New Year's Day

A		B	
1	90 mm	a	4 July 198–
2	32 °F	b	parentheses
3	1330 hours	c	MI
4	guide keys	d	etcetera
5	brackets	e	inverted commas
6	period	f	six million
7	XL	g	$3\frac{1}{2}$ in
8	%	h	omission
9	ISO	i	full stop
10	(	j	home keys
11	4/7/8–	k	40
12	Michigan	l	1.30 pm
13	quotation marks	m	International Standards Organisation
14	6 000 000		
15	etc	n	0 °C
		o	per cent

In the following sentence, which two words or phrases refer to the same thing?

Nairobi, the capital of Kenya, is a tourist centre as well as the commercial capital of East Africa.

Nairobi = the capital of Kenya

Notice the punctuation.

16 Punctuate the following passage:

Trinidad and Tobago
Inland from Port of Spain is Arima the island's third most important town. Driving east from Port of Spain you can get to Sangre Grande a flourishing market town. Travelling from Sangre Grande you come to the spectacular Cocal miles of coconut palms stretching in endless groves along the shore through which you pass as though in some vast natural cathedral. There are breathtaking views of sand and sea to one side, and luxuriant tropical vegetation to the other. Finally you reach Mayaro Bay a perfect tropical paradise.

(Adapted from: Trinidad and Tobago Tourist Board Publication.)

17 Use the following chart to complete and punctuate
the passage:

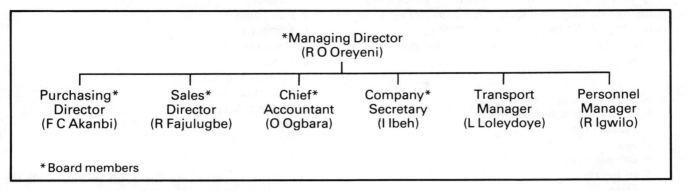

The diagram above an organisational chart shows
the management of a private limited company. This
company employs approximately 100 staff. The
owners of a limited company are the shareholders
joint owners of a company and they vote for those
members who make up the Board of Directors. In
this company they are the Purchasing Director __ __
Mr Fajulugbe __ __ and Mr Ogbara __.

The Managing Director __ has the job of co-or-
dinating the work done by the Board. __ the Company Secretary is responsible for organising the
work of the Directors. Mr Ibeh plays a vital role; he
communicates the decisions of the Board to the
Managers.

Examination preparation: *Form-filling*

1 These are the details to be entered on an examination form. Check that the form has been completed
correctly:

Christine Mumbwe; Zambia Institute of Technology,
Kitwe; Serial No P4 95103; 1116 Jambo Drive,
Kitwe; Centre Reference No CRN 4130; 14 July
198–.

5

ENTRY FORM for English for Office Skills only.   To be completed <u>before</u> the examination begins.

BOTH parts of this form must be completed in **CAPITAL LETTERS IN INK**.

This complete entry form must be **attached**—preferably stapled—on top of your worked papers. **Write your name and Centre Number on Test Paper.**

NAME. (Write clearly in CAPITAL LETTERS on the line below, your name in the form in which it should appear on a certificate if awarded.)

Christine Mumbwe

CENTRE REFERENCE NUMBER
P4 95113
DATE *14 / 8 / 8–*

SUBJECT **ENGLISH FOR OFFICE SKILLS**

EXAMINATION CENTRE *ZAMBIA INSTITUTE OF TECHNOLOGY Kitwe*

RESULT

SPECIMEN

SERIAL NUMBER (*As shown at top right-hand corner of question paper*) *CRN 4103*
These two parts must NOT be separated.

PITMAN EXAMINATIONS INSTITUTE, GODALMING, SURREY, ENGLAND

NAME *Christine Mumbwe*

CENTRE REFERENCE NUMBER
P4 95113
DATE *14 / 8 / 8–*

SUBJECT **ENGLISH FOR OFFICE SKILLS**

EXAMINATION CENTRE *1116 Jambo Drive Kitwe CRN 4103*

HOME ADDRESS *Zambia*

RESULT

SPECIMEN

After the examination papers have been marked, the bottom half of this entry form will be returned to you with the result entered on it.
<u>Do not destroy it.</u>   It may be required later.   The examiners do not enter into correspondence regarding the result of the examination.

865

2 The following form has already been completed. The instructions have been left out. Choose from the list given the most suitable instructions. Remember an instruction may be direct: *Write your full name* or a heading: *Full name*.

Note: Not all the instructions in the list given can be used.

a Must be completed in ink
b List in chronological order
c Please print
d Sex
e Do not write in numbered boxes
f In figures
g Date

h Delete as appropriate
i Block capitals
j Address
k Full name
l Signature
m Relationship
n From   to
o Write in capital letters
p For office use only
q Please tick box
r Age
s Date of birth
t Tel No

Now type or write out the form including all the necessary instructions.

HARRY MWANZA ....

Single/~~Married~~/~~Widow~~/~~Widower~~/~~Divorced~~

I am able/~~unable~~ to start work immediately

P.O. Box 3000 ....

MUFULIRA ....

....

Under 18		
Under 21	✓	
Over 21		

M	✓
F	

1a [ ]
1b [ ]
1c [ ]

Next of kin:		
Name		
JACKSON MWANZA	PO Box 3000 MUFULIRA	FATHER

Details of previous experience:

Employer's name and address	Nature of employment	
Z.O.K. PO Box 9 KABWE	CLERK	9/11/8 — 30/1/8 -
N.C.C.M. PO Box 001 KITWE	CLERK TYPIST	1/2/8 — 25/9/8 -

H. Mwanza ....   9th November, 198 -

Unit 6

Summary: Note summaries

Exercise 1
1 To show the meaning of levels of generality
2 To show how headings can be used to indicate levels of generality

1 The Venn diagram below illustrates the relationship between items of information. The bigger the circle, the more general the information.

The information in the Venn diagram can be rewritten as the set of notes on the right. Notice that the notes have two levels of generality:
a) Africa (the most general term)
b) The countries of Africa (less general)

Can you give
c) a more general term than Africa?
d) a less general term than a country?

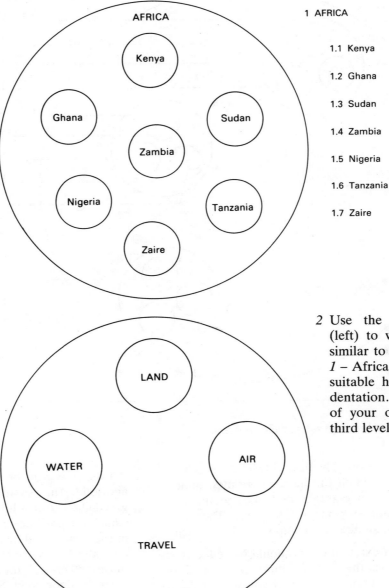

1 AFRICA

  1.1 Kenya

  1.2 Ghana

  1.3 Sudan

  1.4 Zambia

  1.5 Nigeria

  1.6 Tanzania

  1.7 Zaire

2 Use the Venn diagram (left) to write an outline similar to that in question *1* – Africa. Make use of suitable headings and indentation. Add examples of your own to make a third level of generality.

3 The Venn diagram below gives more information and more levels of generality than the ones on page 95. Study it and decide what is needed to fill in the blanks in the set of notes on the right with suitable information.

Notice how the headings on the right are indented and correspond to the circles. Each indented step corresponds to a *level of generality*:
— the title indicates the most general information – The World
— the main headings show the next level of generality – Continents
— the sub-headings show the next level of generality – Countries
— the sub-sub-headings show the lowest level of generality – ???

4 The following headings are all used on an employee evaluation form – a form that is filled in every year to show an employer how well an employee has worked during the previous twelve months. Arrange the headings in an appropriate order (main headings, sub-headings, etc) to construct a suitable form. (Do not number your headings – indent to show different levels of generality.)

Dress	Details of employee
Courteous	Co-operation
Name (in full)	Cleanliness
Accuracy	Job title
Initiative	Employee evaluation
Employee Evaluation Form	Personality
Cheerful	Self-confident
Department	Personal appearance
Punctuality and attendance	Work habits

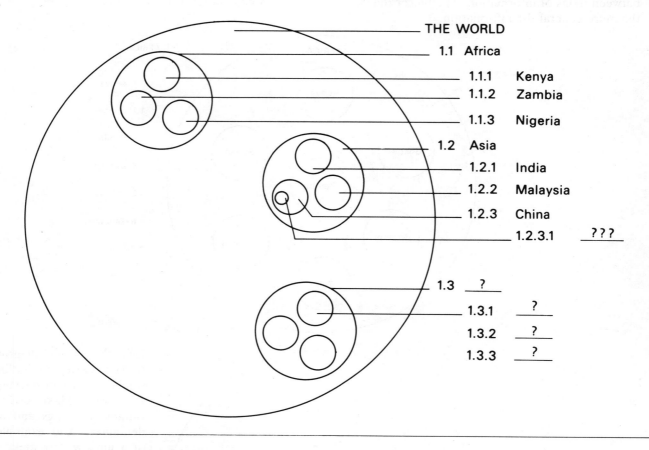

THE WORLD
1.1 Africa
1.1.1 Kenya
1.1.2 Zambia
1.1.3 Nigeria
1.2 Asia
1.2.1 India
1.2.2 Malaysia
1.2.3 China
1.2.3.1 ???
1.3 ?
1.3.1 ?
1.3.2 ?
1.3.3 ?

Exercise 2 *To use headings to produce an outline summary of a text*

Read the passage below. The title and all headings have been missed out. Match the headings printed underneath (*a–i*) to the paragraphs and arrange them to produce an outline summary of the text. The paragraphs have been numbered to help you refer to them.

1 The number of external doors should be reduced as far as possible as they are the most likely break-in point. Inspect all your doors as if you were a thief, paying particular attention to construction, locks and keys.

2 All doors should be at least five centimetres thick and solid. They should not have glass panels as even wired glass affords little protection against intruders. Check the position of the locks: there should be two in the positions shown in the illustration. A centred lock allows easy pressure at the top and bottom of the door – enough for a burglar to get a jemmy in and lever the door open. See that the frame is tough. We saw a cashier's door and frame pushed right out by a car jack braced against the corridor wall.

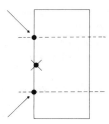

3 You need two mortice locks on every exterior door in the positions indicated above. There may not be such a thing as a 'thief-proof' lock, but there are many 'thief-resistant' locks on the market. These will put up a fight against a drill; their bolts will have rollers inside that will slide under the pressure of a hacksaw blade and the bolt will be 'dead' (ie it will not be sprung) so that it cannot be pushed back with a plastic card.

Open-shackle padlock   Close-shackle padlock

4 There must be millions of useless padlocks sold every year – as every bike-riding child and almost every adult can verify. The normal open-shackle padlock is a thief's dream – a tough steel lever can easily be inserted through the shackle and a sharp twist is enough to force it open.

A close-shackle padlock has most of its shackle shrouded, so that it cannot be levered open. When padlocked rooms are unlocked, the locks should either be locked on to the staple or removed altogether, otherwise the padlock may be lost, preventing locking, or it may be changed by a thief for one of his own for which he has a key.

5 Good locks are useless if the keys are left in them and get into the hands of the wrong person long enough to get a copy made (often while you wait). We do not believe, however, that really effective key security is possible. The realities of working with other people mean that we must trust each other, so that everyone who wants to get access to a key can get it. *Moral:* the only safe way is to have locks with registered keys for which blanks cannot be obtained from shops. It is a nuisance sending off to the maker whenever you need a copy, but it is the only way to be secure. Even registered keys are useless, however, if they are not used. Offices are particularly difficult to manage as the occupants do not all leave at the same time. Two bad habits may develop: the last person to leave may not have a key and so the premises are left open overnight or even over a week-end; over a length of time, everyone is given a key and there is a loss of security simply because there are so many keys in circulation. To overcome these problems,

ensure that the 'final exit' can be locked without a key, so that the number of keys in circulation can be limited.

6 Where windows are vulnerable, the most common solution advocated by the police and insurance companies is the installation of bars. Barring all windows is an expensive business but there seems to be no secure alternative, apart from the one suggested by a much-burgled businessman who said if he were starting again he would build with no windows at all! The cost of barring windows is difficult to estimate and there are other disadvantages apart from the cost: barred windows can be a risk to life in the case of fire as people cannot escape through them; they can be dragged off by a vehicle, especially if they are fitted to the outside of the building; they make window cleaning, painting and repairing difficult. If you wish to protect cash or small valuable items in a room, it may be worth considering a safe, which will give greater protection for lower cost.

7 The police regard lighting as an extremely effective deterrent, and so do we. Security lighting must, of course, be switched on through all the hours of darkness – about 4 000 hours a year. It is this cost of keeping the lights switched on which can make one system cheaper than another. The familiar tungsten filament light is incredibly wasteful and expensive but it is still widely used in security lighting. It is uneconomic because of its short life and because it produces so little light for the power consumed. There are several alternatives on the market:

6

Type	Tungsten	High pressure sodium	Mercury vapour	Low pressure sodium
Life	1 000 hrs	7 500 hrs	7 500 hrs	6 000 hrs
Watts	1 500	600	1 000	50
giving lumens	27 500	62 000	80 000	7 500

The last of these is the best buy: this is actually *low* pressure sodium, but, as can be seen from the table, it gives the greatest amount of light (measured in lumens) for the watts consumed and it is the cheapest in all respects.

(Adapted from a report in *Better Buys for Business*; additional material by Grahame Underwood, *The Architect's Journal*, May–November 1980.)

All the headings and the title are given in the list below. Decide which are main headings, which are sub-headings and which are sub-sub-headings. (Do not number your headings – indent to show different levels of generality.)

a Doors	*d* Windows	*g* Security lighting
b Keys	*e* Padlocks	*h* Door construction
c Locks	*f* Mortice locks	*i* Keeping out intruders

Exercise 3

1 To show that different people approach texts from different points of view

2 To write two sets of notes from different points of view

Different people approach a text from different points of view, depending on their interests, purpose, etc. A security officer in a company would approach the text in Exercise 2 with the purpose of finding ways of keeping thieves *out*. A thief would approach the same text with the purpose of finding ways *in*.

The writer says that one of the most effective ways of examining your security is to inspect it as if you were a thief. Make two sets of notes, one from the point of view of a company security officer (vulnerable points, good equipment, ways of discouraging thieves, etc) and the other from the point of view of a thief (vulnerable points, poor equipment that is easy to open, tools to use, etc). Use the text in Exercise 2 for your notes.

Exercise 4   *Writing a set of notes from personal observation*

Make a set of notes showing the ways in which the security of the room in which you are working or studying could be improved. Examine the doors, locks and windows and decide whether they would keep a thief out. Imagine that you want to keep small personal items (watch, jewellery, wallet, purse, etc) safe. The notes should be sufficiently clear and well displayed for someone in your college to understand.

PS: Using numbering systems to display notes, outlines and reports

Business documents such as reports and memos often employ a numbering system to make them easier to follow. These numbering systems can also be used to display notes and outlines.

The diagram below displays information at four levels of generality (see page 95).

The information in this diagram can be set out using two principal numbering systems:

OFFICE EQUIPMENT	OFFICE EQUIPMENT
I Office machines	1 Office machines
A Typewriter	1.1 Typewriter
1 Manual	1.1.1 Manual
2 Electric	1.1.2 Electric
B Photocopier	1.2 Photocopier
II Office furniture	2 Office furniture
A Desk	2.1 Desk
B Chair	2.2 Chair
1 Typist's	2.2.1 Typist's
2 Office	2.2.2 Office
C Cupboard	2.3 Cupboard
III Stationery	3 Stationery
A Envelopes	3.1 Envelopes
1 Banker	3.1.1 Banker
2 Pocket	3.1.2 Pocket
3 Window	3.1.3 Window
B Notepaper	3.2 Notepaper

Use the text below to make a set of notes on the languages of Africa. Set them out appropriately.

Languages of Africa

There are some three thousand languages and dialects in Africa, only a handful of which were written down until recently. There are generally said to be five main language families. The largest is the Niger–Congo family, spread throughout sub-Saharan Africa and including most of the languages of western Africa (for example Ga, Ewe and Ibo) and the Bantu languages of central, eastern and southern Africa (for example Zulu, Chichewa, Bemba and Swahili). Along the southern border of the Sahara and in the upper Nile Valley region are found the Nilo-Saharan languages. In northern and north-eastern Africa the Afro-Asiatic languages are spoken. These are divided into two main groups: the Hamitic (eg Hausa) and the Semitic (eg Amharic). The Bushmen and Hottentots of southern Africa speak 'click' or Khoisan languages, and Austronesian languages are spoken in Madagascar, whose peoples originally came from Indonesia. With this bewildering array of distinct languages, the use of a sixth group of non-African languages has become widespread. Arabic, French, English and Dutch (Afrikaans) are the principal examples of this non-African group.

(Adapted from *Peoples of Africa*, ed L Singer and R Wood, Marshall Cavendish, 1978.)

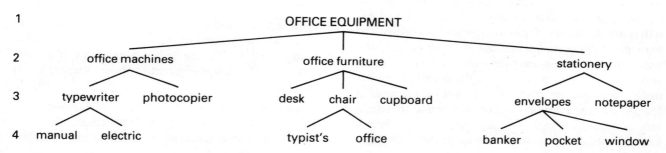

Comprehension: Constructing complete texts

Exercise 1 *To construct three complete texts*

Work in pairs. Below are three extracts from a newspaper: a news story, a general-interest story and an advertisement. The three headings are given across the top but the paragraphs have all been mixed up. Work together to sort them out to make three complete texts. (Each text should have four paragraphs.)

When you have constructed the three complete texts, compare your texts with those of another group. Do you agree about everything? If not, examine your texts and decide who is right.

MORE DUD NOTES FOUND

1 The Chinese, who believe that a 'lucky' number will add years to life and thousands to their bank accounts, will eagerly pay hundreds of dollars for the right licence plates. Plates bearing an 8, for example, are much sought after, since the Cantonese for eight ('bath') rhymes with the word meaning 'prosperity'.

2 Write today for a brochure to: The Registrar, Institute of Computer Studies, PO Box 93, Manila.

3 Three more counterfeit $20 notes were found in Newcastle yesterday, bringing to nearly 100 the total of such notes discovered in recent weeks.

4 At the end of your course you will take the Institute's own internationally-recognised examination and, if successful, you will be ready to launch yourself into your new career in electronic data processing.

A NEW CAREER IN COMPUTING

5 Full- and part-time courses are held in our well-equipped Centre and you will be taught the most common computer languages in use today on the most up-to-date equipment by our staff of highly-qualified specialists.

6 Last week five counterfeit notes were discovered by a bank clerk in Sydney. It is thought that all five were exchanged by one person.

7 Every five or six weeks the Hong Kong government holds an auction of merchandise that is so valuable that it must be kept under wraps until the day of the sale. Chinese paintings perhaps? Local gold or silver? No – just plain black and white HK$2 car licence plates.

8 A police spokesman warned bank clerks and shopkeepers throughout New South Wales to be on the lookout for the counterfeit notes. They can be recognised as each one carries the same serial number – ZU36104107.

WHAT'S BEST IN NUMBERS

9 Combinations of numbers can also produce the right spells. A 32 is 'saamyi', which sounds like the Cantonese word for business. Put an eight at the end and a happy entrepreneur would have 328 – 'prosperity in business' – on the bumper of his car.

10 Is the Hong Kong Government making money out of people's superstition? 'The sense of luck brought by a number is purely imaginary,' said Mr John Chan, a Transport Department official. All proceeds go to charity.

11 A similar series of counterfeit notes surfaced in Melbourne in 1975. No one was ever arrested and the plates from which the counterfeit notes were made were never discovered. Police say that a connection with the Melbourne counterfeitings cannot be ruled out.

12 The Institute of Computer Studies, established in 1966, offers first-class tuition in computer programming, information processing and systems analysis.

Exercise 2 *To construct a page of a newspaper*

This exercise is a more demanding version of Exercise 1. This time you have to construct page 7 of a newspaper, complete with several stories, advertisements and other features. Work in pairs. Altogether there are 29 items to be arranged to make the complete page.

1 Quick-thinking teachers ordered all the children to shelter under their desks until the wind died down. 'There was no panic and no one was injured,' said Headmaster, Mr P Butcher. 'This was due entirely to the dedication of the staff.'

2 TODAY'S WEATHER

3 Newington, Mon. A runaway bull was shot by police after running amok through the village of Newington today. Two bulls escaped from the village market – one was recaptured almost immediately, but the other ran off, eluding its would-be captors. Eventually it was cornered on a farm outside the village. Villagers were unable to tether the bull and finally had to call in the police to destroy the animal humanely.

4 NEWS IN BRIEF

5 You will end the month on a high note. After an uncertain start to June, you will find money matters easy to deal with. Play your hunches – they will bring rich rewards.

6 New legislation to control the building and operation of small airfields is being drafted by the Government. The new legislation is a response to the numbers of unlicensed airstrips which have mushroomed around the country in recent years, bringing with them an increase in smuggling and illegal movement in and out of the country.

7 It was 2.20 in the afternoon and pupils were all working quietly when the gale struck. Mrs S Carr, Class 4 teacher, said the storm came without warning. 'No thunder – one minute all was quiet, the next I thought a war had started. It sounded just like a bomb.'

8 PRISONERS FLEE

9 A well-established grocery company invites applications for the following posts:
   i) Delivery man (must have clean driving licence)
   ii) Mechanic (must possess C & G or equivalent)

10 Western Star, Wednesday, 30 May 198–

11 Western Shipping Ltd, PO Box 135, Colster. Tel 93-65850

12 The Minister revealed that Immigration Authorities had been pressing for tighter controls for several years as the unauthorised fields offered opportunities for fugitives from the law both to enter and leave the country.

13 THIEF JAILED

14 We offer scheduled container services to the Caribbean, USA and Canada. Crating and shipping to all ports in South America.

15 VACANCIES

16 page 7

17 Kabompo, Tues. Painter A R Osman, 24, was jailed today for stealing paint and building materials valued at $33 from his employer, KP Construction.

18 Dry and warm, with a high of 33° and a low tonight of 28°. Outlook: Continuing warm but with isolated showers building up to storms over the week-end.

19 LUCKY ESCAPE FOR CHILDREN

20 Queensbury, Tues. Three prisoners awaiting trial on charges of illegal possession of firearms escaped from Queensbury Police Station last night. The discovery of their escape was not made until morning. The search for the three continues.

21 WESTERN SHIPPING LTD

22 The new proposals were disclosed in Parliament yesterday by Transport and Aviation Minister, Mr A P Alif. Mr Alif informed the House that the Government viewed with 'deep concern' the number of illegal airfields that have been built in recent years in various parts of the country.

23 The cost of repairing the damage to the building has not yet been assessed. It is reckoned that the classroom block will be out of use for at least three months. In the meantime pupils are continuing their lessons in the school dining hall.

24 Please submit applications with references and a recent photograph to:
The Advertiser
Box No 0665
c/o Western Star
Head Street
Butterworth

25 Children at the Concord Primary School, Washington, had a lucky escape from tragedy yesterday when gale force winds whipped through the village before a violent storm. The lashing, 100-kilometre-an-hour, winds ripped the roof from their classroom block and carried it several hundred metres before dumping it on the school football field.

26 YOUR BIRTHDAY STARS

27 Fully-comprehensive insurance. If you have anything to ship, large or small, contact us now for a FREE estimate.

28 BULL SHOT

29 NEW AIRFIELD LAWS ON THE WAY

PS: British and American English

There are not as many differences between British and American English as is often thought. The list gives some of the most important ones, including those in commerce. Use this list and, if necessary, a dictionary to 'translate' the sentences below from American to British English.

1 I paid a check into my savings account.
2 I'm changing my automobile – I'm getting rid of my station wagon and buying a sedan and a trailer instead.
3 The automobile mounted the sidewalk and crashed through the window of the drugstore.
4 The kerosene heater fell over and the drapes caught fire.
5 They're paying for their new phonograph by instalment plan.
6 I arrived here at ten of two and now it's twenty after three.

The sentences below mean different things in British and American English. State what each underlined word means in both varieties of English.

Example: I need a new vest.
American = sleeveless garment worn by men under a jacket (a waistcoat in British English)
British   = a piece of underwear worn over the upper part of the body (an undershirt in American English)

7 Gas seems to be escaping from that tank.
8 Can you tell me where the subway is?
9 My trunk has been broken into.
10 My boot needs repairing.
11 The restaurant is on the first floor.
12 The project will cost nearly a billion dollars.
13 (On the telephone) 'Thank you, operator, I'm through now.'
14 We have tabled the motion for discussion at today's meeting.
15 We arrived here on 6.2.198– and we're leaving on 11.4.198–.

US	UK
apartment	*flat*
billion	*one thousand million (1 000 000 000)*
bonds	*stocks*
busy (phone)	*engaged*
check	*tick*
checking account	*current account*
corporation (Inc)	*limited company (Ltd) (PLC)*
drapes	*curtains*
elevator	*lift*
estate tax	*death duties*
fall	*autumn*
first floor	*ground floor*
gas/gasoline	*petrol*
hood (of car)	*bonnet*
instalment plan	*hire purchase*
kerosene	*paraffin*
over	*PTO*
overpass	*flyover*
period	*full stop*
property tax	*rates*
realtor/real estate agent	*estate agent*
retirement pension	*superannuation*
savings account	*deposit account*
schedule	*timetable*
second floor	*first floor*
sedan (car)	*saloon (car)*
shipment	*consignment*
sidewalk	*pavement*
stocks	*shares*
subway	*tube/underground (train/railway)*
trillion/one million million (1 000 000 000 000)	*billion*
trunk (of car)	*boot*

Collect your own examples of differences between British and American English.

Note: Most examining boards will accept either British or American English as long as they are used consistently – it is important that you do not jump from one system to the other.

6

```
NORTH-EASTERN ELECTRICAL INC

xxxxxxxxxxxxxxxxxxxxxxxxxxxxxxx

February 6, 198-

Electrical Importers
P O Box 2887
Nairobi
Kenya

Gentlemen:

xxxxxxxxxxxxxxxxxxxxxxxxxxxxxxxxxx
xxxxxxxxxxxxxxxxxxxxxxxxxxxxxxxxxx
xxxxxxxxxxxxxxxxxxxxxxxxxxxxxxxxxx
xxxxxxxxxxxxxxxxxxxxxxxxxxxxxxxxxx
xxxxxxxxxxxxxxxxxxxxxxxxxxxxxxxxxx

Very truly yours
```

AMERICAN STYLE

```
NORTH-EASTERN ELECTRICAL CO LTD

xxxxxxxxxxxxxxxxxxxxxxxxxxxxxxx

6 February 198-

Electrical Importers
P O Box 2887
Nairobi
Kenya

Dear Sirs

xxxxxxxxxxxxxxxxxxxxxxxxxxxxxxxxxx
xxxxxxxxxxxxxxxxxxxxxxxxxxxxxxxxxx
xxxxxxxxxxxxxxxxxxxxxxxxxxxxxxxxxx
xxxxxxxxxxxxxxxxxxxxxxxxxxxxxxxxxx
xxxxxxxxxxxxxxxxxxxxxxxxxxxxxxxxxx

Yours faithfully
```

BRITISH STYLE

American business letters follow slightly different conventions from British-style letters. The two examples show the differences in a formal business letter. Use the letters to complete the table below.

	AMERICAN STYLE	BRITISH STYLE
Date:	....	....
Formal greeting:	....	....
Less formal greeting:	Dear Mr Smith:	....
Formal close:	....	....
Less formal close:	Sincerely yours	....

Composition: Expanding notes

Exercise 1 *To use notes to write a memorandum*

Read the following dialogue from a telephone conversation:

You:	Good afternoon. Machine Hire. Can I help you?
Mr Mukasa:	I'd like to speak to Mr Mbela.
You:	I'm sorry but he's out at the moment. May I help? I'm Mr Mbela's secretary.
Mr Mukasa:	Well, it's really quite important. I'd like the matter to be dealt with urgently. We received a letter from you this morning threatening legal action if we didn't pay our bill. Now this bill was paid two weeks ago! It's really quite amazing. We've been doing business with you for well over four years and we've always paid promptly.
You:	Oh, I see. Well I'll certainly look into this for you at once and I'll see that Mr Mbela knows about it. May I have your name please?
Mr Mukasa:	It's Mukasa from TSI Limited.
You:	Ah, yes Mr Mukasa. You're down Independence Avenue, aren't you? On the Kariba Industrial Estate?
Mr Mukasa:	That's right. You know even if our bill had been outstanding, I would have thought you would have given me a ring – not this threatening letter business. We've been good customers long enough.
You:	Well, Mr Mukasa, I'm sure there has been some clerical error which we can sort out. Do you happen to have the invoice in front of you? If you can give me the number, I can trace your account quickly.
Mr Mukasa:	As a matter of fact I do. It's 449/4329/AB. Did you get that?
You:	449/4329/AB. I'll look into this straight away Mr Mukasa. If there are any further problems I'll ask Mr Mbela to phone you when he gets back.
Mr Mukasa:	I suggest you sort it out pretty quickly. I can go elsewhere for these machines you know.
You:	I'm sure there is a simple explanation.
Mr Mukasa:	I certainly hope so. Goodbye.
You:	Goodbye.

Write the notes you would have made during that call.

After the call, you checked the files and made the following notes:

```
Checked files - TSI's bill overdue 1 wk
- TSI paid 10 days late - clerk told to
send warning letters to customers over-
due by 1 mth - clerk sent TSI form
letter used only for second warnings -
this seems to be the only error like
this.
```

From the notes on the phone conversation and the above notes, write a memo for your boss about the problem. Use today's date and your own name.

Exercise 2 *To add missing information*

How do you decide what information you require in a document? Imagine you are the person receiving the document and ask yourself if, from the document, you know:
a) what the document is about – the background to the situation;
b) the purpose of the document;
c) what action if any needs to be taken.

1 Decide what is missing from the message below. Rewrite it using information in Exercise 1.

MEMORANDUM

To: Clerical Assistants   *From:* Supervisor

Date: 4 July 198–   *Subject:* Warning letters

Please check that the correct letters of reminder are sent to customers.

---

2 Your boss started to draft a letter of apology to Mr Mukasa. It is not complete. There is no background information and no apology. Rewrite the letter adding the appropriate information. Display it suitably.

Having checked our files, we discovered that indeed you were sent the letter in error. Such letters are usually reserved for customers whose payment has been outstanding for over four months.

Exercise 3 *To expand messages which are too brief*

The following messages do not give enough information for the receiver to understand them fully. Rewrite the messages adding appropriate information. The notes below the messages are a guide to the missing information.

1 My colleagues and I send you our congratulations.
2 My curriculum vitae is enclosed. If you require any further information, I can be contacted at the above address.
3 The stitching is, as you have pointed out, not up to our usual standard. This particular batch was unfortunately overlooked by the controller. Please accept our apologies.
4 We should be grateful if you would forward the rates for a similar advertisement to appear each month for the next six months.
5 Mr Quin will be visiting Nigeria in November and will make arrangements to meet to discuss future trading.

Notes:
a Half-page ad in last mth's issue of *Office Skills*
b complaint re trousers
c heard yesterday appointed Regional Manager
d Far East
e ad in today's *Gleaner*
f new African rep
g gd no of orders from ad
h lots of experience, lived in Africa 12 yrs
i audio typist
j thoroughly deserve promotion
k available for interview any time
l been in export business all working life
m can return faulty order or sell as seconds
n sending replacement order by air
o great asset
p wish every success in new post
q charge only $115 for the order if kept

Exercise 4 *To supply details required in examination questions*

The following examination questions ask you to supply your own details. Decide from the notes below each question which details would be appropriate and then answer the questions.

1 As secretary to a Social Club (give a name) write to a bus company indicating that you would like to hire a bus from them for a trip for your members. Give as many details as you can to enable the bus company to help you.

Notes:

Would like to hire bus – blue one if possible – no beer drinkers – 2 wks – any time between 25 April and 19 July – no children – 14 people – tour Kama Game Reserve – Wildlife Club

2 As a new arrival in a town, write to the Town Council asking to be given a house. Give details of your particular needs.

Notes:

Arrived two weeks ago – in local guest house – need spare room for relations – wife and two children – family can't come until get accommodation – want to keep chickens – this town has the best houses in the country – married too young – wife's mother thinks I'm lazy – both children under 5 – wife pregnant.

Exercise 5 *To answer an examination question requiring details to be added*

Using between 150 and 200 words, write a letter for your company, J S Wallace & Co Ltd, Wallace House, Eldon Road, Stock, Stockshire, 4SD FF5, to the Headmaster of Hetley Secondary School, Hetley Road, Stock, 4SD FF8, saying how pleased your company has been in the past years with youngsters from Hetley School who have been hard-working, loyal and efficient. Explain that two vacancies for office juniors have arisen and you are wondering if he can recommend any suitable pupils who will soon be leaving his school. Give details of the type of work envisaged.
(*LCCI* – English for Commerce, Intermediate.)

PS: Proof-reading (4)

We usually read for *meaning*. Read the letter below once and answer the following questions:

1 Who is the letter from?
2 What kind of machine is the Sana LX?
3 Why can't the machine be repaired immediately?
4 How long does a parcel take sent from overseas by surface mail?
5 What does Mr Kunda advise the customer to do?

Refer: 431/JW

DATE

Mr. Zulu
Chisuma Machines Ltd.
P O box 1979
Nairobi

Dear Mr Zulu

Sana LX

We have examined your machine the 'Sana LX', which we collected from you on 22 May 1980.

The fault has been traced but we are sorry to inform you that as your your machine is an old model, we do not have the required parts in stock. We could order the parts from overseas, but as you must appreciate, this would take at laest 3 months by surface mail. By air the cost would be excesive.

May we suggest that replacement would be more economical than repair? The cost of calculators has droped considerably since you bought your present model.

Enclosed are our latest catalogue and price-list. All items listed are in stock.

Please give us your instructions regarding the 'Sana LX'.

Yours sincerely,
NAME OF CO.

J. K. Jenwa
NAME
Manager

Enc

How many errors did you find in the body of the letter? There are 10 typing errors. Go back and find them all.

Remember to check *all* the information in the letter, not only that in the body of the letter. Is any information missing? There are 10 other errors apart from those in the body of the letter. Rewrite the letter correctly.

Oral/Aural: Oral instructions

Exercise 1 *To practise accurate listening*

Work in pairs. A: With your book closed, write down what B dictates. B: Dictate the following to A.

B: *1* 1, 2, 3, 4
    2 Monday, Tuesday, Wednesday
    3 2, 4, 6, 8
    4 January, February, March
    5 A, B, C, D

Change over.
A: *6* 1 000, 2 000, 3 000
    7 1979, 1980, 1981
    8 30, 20, 10
    9 X, Y, Z
    10 15, 14, 13

Change over.
B: *11* A, B, C, E
    12 300, 200, 150
    13 E, F, G, I
    14 First, second, first
    15 1977, 78, 78

Change over.
A: *16* Monday, Tuesday, Thursday
    17 18, 19, 20, 22
    18 3 000, 2 000, 1 200
    19 2, 4, 6, 8, 7
    20 AB, CD, EF, FG

Exercise 2 *To check understanding of typographical instructions*

Find which parts of the invoice match the descriptions given.

```
┌─────────────────────────────────────────┐
│              INVOICE                      │
│                                           │
│   FAST COPY                    Cheque sent/│
│   High St                      3.II.8-    │
│   Colster                                 │
│                                           │
│   Telephone: (9432) 64132                 │
│                                           │
│   Date:   2/2/8-                          │
│   Invoice No:   C 6781                     │
│                                           │
│   ┌─────────────────────────┐             │
│   │ Polly Writers           │             │
│   │ 10 Stock Street         │             │
│   │ Colster                 │             │
│   └─────────────────────────┘             │
│                                           │
│   Photocopying charges as at 2.2.8-       │
│                                           │
│     48 copies at 5¢ per copy....... 2.40  │
│    307 copies at 6¢ per copy.......18.42  │
│                                           │
│                         Total: 20.82      │
└─────────────────────────────────────────┘
```

1 normal abbreviation
2 underlined heading
3 in figures
4 normal handwriting
5 block capitals
6 dotted line
7 script
8 in capital letters
9 in numerals
10 in roman numerals
11 in arabic numerals
12 in brackets
13 broken line

Work in pairs and dictate the following instructions to each other.
A: Dictate the following to B.

Write:
14 *first*, *second* and *third* in normal abbreviations.
15 *diary* in capital letters and underlined.
16 *4 321* in arabic numerals.
17 *Total* in normal handwriting followed by a dotted line.
18 *Two*, *four* and *six* in roman numerals.

Change over.
B: Dictate the following to A.

Write:
19 the normal abbreviation for *telephone* and *number* in normal script.
20 *address* in block capitals followed by the words *capitals please* in normal handwriting.
21 *fifteen thousand, one hundred and three* in arabic numerals.
22 2nd December 1981 in figures and underlined.
23 roman numeral *seven* followed by the word *recommendations* in capital letters.

Exercise 3 *To check understanding of instructions giving the position of items on a page*

Work in pairs. A: Dictate the following to B. B: Use a piece of A5 paper and follow A's instructions with your book closed.

A: *1* Halfway along the page, about three centimetres from the bottom, draw a square approximately one cm by one cm. Put a tick just under the square.
    2 Draw another square the same size to the right of the one you have drawn and parallel to it. Leave about two cms between the squares. Put a tick in the middle of that square.
    3 Draw two squares above and parallel to the first two again leaving about two cms between the squares.
    4 In the right-hand square, put a dot in the centre. In the left-hand one put a dot in the top left-hand corner.

5 To the left of the upper left-hand square, draw another square of the same size. Put a dot in the bottom right-hand corner.

6 Draw another square of the same size to the right of the row of three. Put a dot just below this square.

7 Draw four squares above the top row. The squares should be the same size as and parallel to the squares you have already drawn.

8 Repeat the instruction above.

Change over. B: Give A your drawing and give A the following instructions. A: Follow B's instructions using the same piece of paper.

B: 9 Divide the left-hand top square into three equal columns.

10 Divide the square to the right of this into two halves with a vertical line.

11 Leave the square to the right of this blank.

12 Divide the right-hand square at the top into two halves by a broken vertical line.

13 In the square below the one with three columns, draw a diagonal line from the top left-hand corner to the bottom right-hand corner.

14 In the square above the one with a dot in the top left-hand corner, draw a diagonal line from the top right-hand corner to the bottom left-hand corner.

15 Shade in the last square on the right in this row with diagonal lines going in the same direction as the line in the square at the opposite end of this row.

16 Divide the blank square in this row into quarters by two diagonal lines.

Check that the drawings are correct.

There are many routes you could take from the bottom row of squares to the top row.

Example:

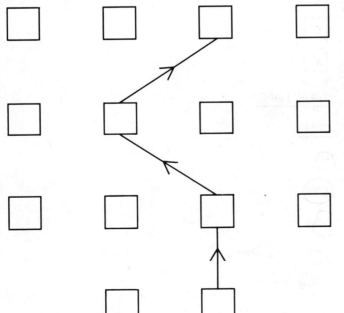

Copy the squares exactly so that each person has the same drawing. Plan four routes from the bottom to the top row.

Work in pairs and without letting your partner see your routes, and without pointing or gestures guide your partner through each route.

Example: Start at the square with the tick in the middle. Go to the square with the dot in the centre. Etc.

Can your partner follow your directions accurately?

Exercise 4 *To practise following directions to produce a document*

Work in pairs. A: Describe the following page out of a diary so that B can produce it accurately.
B: Follow A's instructions with your book closed.

A:

> JANUARY
>
> Reminders ....
>
> ....
>
> 11   Monday
>
> ....
>
> 12   Tuesday
>
> ....
>
> ....

Change over.
A: Follow B's instructions.

ORDER FORM			
Description	No	Price	

Exercise 5 *To practise examination questions which require the production of a document from oral instructions*

Work in pairs. A: Read the following instructions to B once, at a slow steady speed.

B: Listen to A's instructions. Do not start drawing until A has finished. Try and picture in your mind what the finished document will look like.

A: You are to draw up a chart showing details of salaries. At the top of the space, in the centre, write the title AVERAGE SALARIES in capital letters, and underline it.

Draw a line vertically beneath the title, dividing the page into halves.

Near the top of the left-hand column write the figure 1972. Write the capital letters A, B and C on the left of the same column, so that B is about two inches below A, and C two inches below B. Next to the letter A write the word Professional in your normal handwriting. Underneath Professional write £3 000 in figures.

In the same way write Clerical and £2 000 next to B, and Skilled and £1 900 next to C.

In the top of the right-hand column write the figure 1973.

Underneath 1973 write 'Figures not available' in your normal handwriting.
(*PEI* – English for Office Skills.)

Change over.

B: Your employer gives you the following instructions.

'I want you to draw up a new form which will be filled in by new employees. Give it a central heading PERSONAL INFORMATION SHEET in capital letters. Draw a narrow left-hand margin. Write Works No at the top of this – nothing else. Now we want the following items of information from the employee: name, date of birth, home address, department, last employer. Give each item a number, for example, 1. Name. Make sure the employee has enough room to write the information; provide dotted lines for this, and start each item with the number next to the margin. Draw a line across the page underneath the questions, and underneath that line put the heading FOR OFFICE USE ONLY in capitals.'
(*PEI* – English for Office Skills.)

PS: Examination instructions

Work out what the written examination instructions would be for the following:

Example:

The instruction would be: Put a tick in the box.

1	☐	[o]
2	☐	[x]
3	_____	YOUR NAME
4	ONUS	ONUS
5	h	(h)
6	the	(the)
7	hte	(hte)
8	its the president	It's the President.
9	5	five
10	22 June 1979	22.6.79

11	First, second, third	1st, 2nd, 3rd
12	ambiguous	more than one meaning
13	Ⓐ Ⓑ Ⓒ Ⓓ	Ⓐ Ⓑ ● Ⓓ
14	foreign	indigenous
15	I can swim better than any of you said the boy	'I can swim better than any of you,' claimed the boy.

The following are instructions taken from examination papers. Two sample answers are given for each. Decide which answers are shown correctly.

16 What is the article mainly about? TICK *ONE* ONLY.

a	CARS	TRAINS ✓	HOVERTRAINS

b	CARS	TRA̶I̶N̶S̶	HOVERTRAINS

17 *The second box is for a correction*, if you have to make one. Strike out what is incorrect.

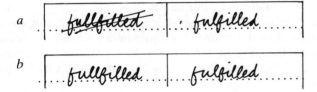

18 Rewrite the sentences given below in the space provided. Punctuate them correctly.

Im a stranger here can you direct me to the west-minster bank asked the american

a "I'M A STRANGER HERE. CAN YOU DIRECT ME TO THE WESTMINSTER BANK?" ASKED THE AMERICAN.

b 'I'm a stranger here. Can you direct me to the Westminster Bank?' asked the American.

19 Each of the sentences below contains *one* error of grammar or syntax. Ring the error. In the space provided, write the correction.

a Do you know who's pen this is?   **Whose**

b Do you know (who's) pen this is?   **whose**

20 Identify each error exactly by putting a ring round it.

Eg co(mp)etition

a WHEN TO SELL YOUR CA(r)
More than (20)00,000 use(○)cars change hands in Brit(ia)n .....

b WHEN TO SELL YOUR (CAr)
More than (2000,000) (use) cars change hands in (Britian) .....

21 In each sentence, write the correct word in the space provided to complete the sentence. Make your choice from the words following each sentence.

a Everyone should make a *fair* contribution to society. (fair, fare)
b Everyone should make a .... contribution to society. (fair, fare)

22 Which word on the right is nearest in meaning to the word on the left. Underscore only one word.

a option
  abstain
  vote
  dilemma ✓
  choice

b option
  abstain
  vote
  dilemma
  <u>choice</u>

Note: ALL YOUR ANSWERS MUST BE WRITTEN IN INK. ALL WORKINGS TO BE DONE IN INK. THE WHOLE EXAMINATION MUST BE WRITTEN IN INK. } = DO *NOT* USE PENCIL

6

Miscellany

Exercise 1 *Prepositions*

Use the following sentences to complete the rules on the right for each of the italicised prepositions. Write a new example for each preposition.

Example: **In** is used when talking about an area, and **at** is used when talking about a specific place.

I work in Hong Kong at the Polytechnic.

Sentences:

1 a Her dictating machine is similar *to* mine. In fact I think it is the same make.

  b This typewriter has a different typeface *from* the one I use at home.

2 a With some electric typewriters, you can replace one typing element (or golf ball) *with* another if you want a different typeface.

  b It is very useful for typing documents where a variety of styles is required if you can substitute one golf ball *for* another.

3 a There was a sales meeting *on* Wednesday.

  b The next meeting will be *in* May.

4 a He has been a lot happier *since* he started his new job.

  b He was working as an assistant accountant *for* three years.

5 a The work used to be shared *between* the typist and the secretary.

  b Now the typing work is shared *among* the six girls in the pool.

6 a My boss agreed *to* the extra expenditure required to buy a new machine.

  b My boss agreed *with* me that a new machine would be a good idea.

7 a I prefer using an electric machine *to* a manual one.

8 a Make sure the report is typed *by* 11 o'clock as the meeting is at 12.

9 a The ZIP code in American addresses is now composed *of* five or nine figures.

  b The ZIP code in American addresses comprises five or nine figures.

10 a The improvement of your speeds is dependent *on* regular practice.

  b Shorthand skills can never be independent *of* language skills.

Rules:

A You can agree a) .... an idea, but agree b) .... a person.

B Use a) .... when talking about two people, but b) .... when talking about more than two.

C Use a) .... after similar and b) .... after different.

D A is composed a) .... B and C, but A comprises B and C.

E a) .... means not later than.

F Use a) .... after dependent but b) .... after independent.

G You can replace A a) .... B, but substitute B b) .... A.

H After prefer use a) .... as in: I prefer A b) .... B.

I Use a) .... if it is followed by a period of time and b) .... if followed by a point in time.

J a) .... is used with days and dates which include the day, and b) .... is used with longer periods of time.

Decide which are the correct prepositions to complete the following:

I have wanted to have an electric typewriter [11] .... a long time. I suggested the idea to my boss some time [12] .... February, but although he agreed [13] .... me that it would be a good idea, he couldn't put in a request as the budget for equipment had already been allocated. I told him that I had preferred electrics [14] .... manuals [15] .... my last job where I had used one.

Although it looked as though I wouldn't be getting an electric typewriter, I thought I would do a little research on prices, just in case. I work [16] .... a reasonably large town and there are a number of office equipment shops. Compared [17] .... manuals, the electric models were a good deal more expensive. The main difference [18] .... the two types, apart from price, is that the electric machine is less tiring to use as the features normally operated by the typist, eg carriage return, are all automatic. This means that the typist can type [19] .... longer periods with much less fatigue.

When I found out the prices of electrics, I thought my boss would never replace my manual [20] .... an electric machine. So I was most surprised, when, [21] .... Monday morning he asked me to put in a requisition for an electric typewriter [22] .... the end of the week. The requisition had to consist [23] .... three quotations which of course I had already.

My boss had forgotten that the budget for equipment was not independent [24] .... the other departments and if their budgets had not been allocated we could order equipment through a different department.

Exercise 2   *Spelling: silent letters*

The following are methods that have been found useful for remembering spellings:

Method 1

Write out the word you want to remember missing out one letter at a time.

> *Example:* –anoeuvre
> m–noeuvre
> ma–oeuvre
> man–euvre
> mano–uvre
> manoe–vre
> manoeu–re
> manoeuv–e
> manoeuvr–

Method 2

Find smaller words within the word you want to remember.

> *Example:* In KNOWLEDGE there are KNOW, LEDGE, NOW, EDGE and OWL.

Method 3

As you write the word you want to remember, pronounce the word as it is spelt, not how it is said.

> *Example:* As you write SCISSORS, pronounce the C as a K – say SKISSORS.

Method 4

Make part of the word into a picture in your mind.

> *Example:*

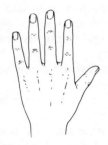

kerchief   for HANDKERCHIEF

Method 5

Think of words you know how to spell which are spelt the same way as a word you want to remember. Make up a sentence including the words and memorise the sentence.

> *Example:* For MARRIAGE: I age when I think of marriage in a carriage.

Use the list of words on page 175 to make up your own examples of each method.

Write out the following words putting in the silent letters:

1 colleages
2 sutlety
3 sychology
4 miniture
5 veicle
6 Febuary
7 gage
8 garantee
9 undoutedly
10 campain

Each of the following definitions makes a word which has a silent letter. Find the silent letters and make another word out of them. The first letter of each word is given.

> *Example:* a) a piece of land surrounded by water
> b) a fellow worker
> c) the day before Thursday
> The words are ISLAND, COLLEAGUE and WEDNESDAY.
> The silent letters spell SUD.

11 *a* the institution of a man and a woman legally linked on a permanent basis (M)
    b a division of a page into a vertical block (C)
    c to distrust (D)
    d a tool used for cutting (K)
12 *a* on a very small scale (M)
    b a weapon with a long thin cutting blade (S)
    c an agreement to lend money to buy a house (M)
    d the pattern produced by the length and loudness of notes in music (R)
13 *a* frequently (O)
    b something owed (D)
    c a standard measure (G)
14 *a* complete confusion (C)
    b buying and selling (B)
    c the season after summer (A)
    d to pay attention (L)
15 *a* harmonious co-operation (L)
    b to reply (A)
    c organised attempt to get support (C)

6

Exercise 3 *Dangling participles*

Here is an example of one of the most common errors in English.

   × Walking through the field, a snake bit me. ×

Who was walking – the snake or me? This should be rewritten:

   Walking through the field, I was bitten by a snake.

Rule: The participle (walk*ing*) must agree with the subject in the second part of the sentence (I): I was walking, I was bitten.

Rewrite each of the following according to the instructions underneath. In each case you should avoid a dangling participle.

1 We were driving through the game park when an elephant charged us.
   Begin: Driving . . .

2 He was an only child and his parents gave him everything he wanted.
   Begin: Being . . .

3 She worked for the company for five years and was then promoted to supervisor.
   Begin: Having . . .

4 The mechanic serviced the typewriter. It was then cleaned.
   Begin: Having . . .

5 As he crossed the road, a bus knocked him over.
   Begin: Crossing . . .

6 The driver lived through the crash but the delay in getting him to hospital killed him.
   Begin: Having . . .

7 Sheila lost Mary's book and so Mary asked her to pay for it.
   Begin: Having . . .

8 The bank gave him a job as a cashier as he had obtained a good pass in mathematics.
   Begin: Having . . .

9 My father wrote me a letter because I had asked him for some money.
   Begin: Having . . .

10 I was working late. The caretaker locked me in.
   Begin: Working . . .

11 Looking through the window, the bus was coming.
   Correct this sentence.

12 Sailing on the lake, the water looked beautiful.
   Correct this sentence.

13 Entering the building, a sad sight struck us.
   Correct this sentence.

14 Lying on the grass, a branch fell on her head.
   Correct this sentence.

15 Driving along the main road, a pedestrian stepped in front of my car.
   Correct this sentence.
   (*11, 12, 13 PEI* – English for Office Skills.)

Examination preparation: *Punctuation of direct and indirect speech*

Direct speech:

   ✓ She said, 'I shall be late as my car has broken down.'

   ✓ 'I shall be late,' she said, 'as my car has broken down.'

   ✓ 'I shall,' she said, 'be late as my car has broken down.'

   ✓ 'I shall be late as my car has broken down,' she said.

   ✓ 'I shall be late,' she said. 'My car has broken down.'

   × She said', I shall be late as my car has broken down'.

   × She said', I shall be late as my car has broken down'.

Indirect speech:

   × She said that, she would be late as her car had broken down.

   × She said that, 'she would be late as her car had broken down.'

   ✓ She said that she would be late as her car had broken down.

Decide whether each of the following contains a) direct speech, b) indirect speech, c) no speech at all. Punctuate them appropriately.

1 Mr Henry London has recently been appointed Governor of Colster Prison.

2 Could you tell me the right time please asked the boy.

3 After his sixteen-hour flight, John Britton said I've flown 17 000 kilometres and I'm exhausted.

4 I won't travel in John's car again until its brakes have been fixed declared Mary.

5 The policeman said he had discovered a gun and a camera in the suspect's room.

6 A gun and a camera were said to have been discovered in the suspect's room.

7 The timetable states that the train leaves at noon.

8 It is said that walking under a ladder is unlucky.

9 You'll find roads in Morocco are a motorist's delight. They're well-engineered, wide and excellent to drive on.

10 Go the the Sahara said the agency clerk and you won't regret it.
   (*2, 3, 4, 9, 10* adapted from *PEI* – English for Office Skills.)

Unit 7

Applications and interviews

The documents in Assignments 1 and 2 form the basis of assignments throughout the rest of the unit. These assignments should be done individually and then be discussed by the class as a whole before moving on to the others.

Situation 1

You work in the Personnel Department of Tropicana Food Canners, a company based in San Fernando, Trinidad. It is part of your job to deal with the administrative side of staff recruitment. These documents have just landed in your 'In' tray.

JOB DESCRIPTION	
JOB TITLE	Secretary
RESPONSIBLE TO	General Manager
LOCATION	Head Office
HOURS OF WORK	0830–1700 Monday–Friday
DUTIES	Taking and preparing correspondence Dealing with incoming mail Taking/receiving telephone calls Typing and layout of reports and special documents Maintaining filing system Making travel arrangements Keeping accounts Supervising and liaising with other staff Entertainment of guests/customers
QUALIFICATIONS	Advanced Secretarial Certificate: 100 wpm shorthand 40–50 wpm typewriting Knowledge of basic book-keeping methods English Language – O level or equivalent
BACKGROUND EXPERIENCE	Experience preferable, particularly in dealing with visitors and members of staff at all levels
HOLIDAY	3 weeks per annum

TROPICANA FOOD CANNERS
100 Coffee Street San Fernando Trinidad W I

Tel 652-2793   Telegraphic   Tropicanners
                   Address:

To: *Personnel Manager* Date: *27 Aug 198-*
From: *Office Manager*

PERSONNEL REQUISITION

Description of personnel required

Date required: *1 Oct 198-*

Number required: *1*

Job title: *Secretary*

Department: *to Gen. Manager*

Salary range: $ *1500* to *2000*

Permanent or Temporary: *P*

Full-time or part-time: *F-T*

Qualifications: *S/hand 100 WPM*
Typing 40-50 WPM
English Lang O Level
Maths O level
Book-keeping

Age range: *25-40*

Reasons for requirement

Replacement or addition: *R*

If replacement, who is being replaced?
Miss Lloyd

If addition, give reasons:

7

Assignment 1 *Drawing up a job advertisement*

Use the documents in your 'In' tray to draw up a suitable job advertisement to be placed in 'The West Indies Chronicle' next week. As the vacancy is for a secretary, it is important that all replies should be typewritten.

Situation 2

The following letters are replies to the advertisement you placed in 'The West Indies Chronicle'. As you work in the Personnel Department of Tropicana Food Canners, part of your job is to organise any interviews. It is company policy to restrict the number of candidates for interview to three.

---

101 High Street
San Fernando

7 September 198-

The Personnel Officer
Tropicana Food Canners
100 Coffee Street
San Fernando

Dear Sir

I should like to be considered for the post of secretary as advertised in 'The West Indies Chronicle'.

I am 19 years of age and have just completed a one year full-time secretarial course at the Excel College where I obtained a Pitman Higher Secretarial Group Certificate giving me:

> English for Office Skills - First Class
> Shorthand Typist 100 wpm
> Typewriting Advanced (50 wpm)
> Private Secretarial Duties - First Class
> Book-keeping Intermediate

I left school in 197- with English Language, Mathematics, Caribbean History and Caribbean Geography at General Proficiency level of the Caribbean Examination Council.

I shall be glad to provide any further information if you need it and I can attend for interview at any time.

Yours faithfully

A. Daly

Ann Daly

13 Wrighton Road
Port of Spain

15 September 198-

Dear Sir

I read your advertisement in the daily news paper & it looks like the
sort of job I have been looking for.

I am 18. I have attended Smiths Business College where I did typing
and shorthand and how to do office machinery. At the moment I am working for Charles Mitchell and Co which is an insurance firm. I do
typewriting and some bbok-keeping for them, which I am good at.

I really want to change my job and would like to come for an interview.

Yours faithfully

Valerie Chan

V Chan

12 Main Street
Scarborough
Tobago

5 September 198-

The Personnel Officer
Tropicana Food Canners
100 Coffee Street
San Fernando
Trinidad

Dear Sir

I should like to be considered for the post of secretary as advertised
in 'The West Indies Chronicle'.

I am 19 years of age. I attended St Peter's High School where I passed
English and Mathematics at General Proficiency level for the Caribbean
Examinations Council. I then went on to do a one year secretarial course
at Smith's Business College where I obtained a Pitman's Secretarial Group
Certificate with shorthand at 100 wpm and typewriting at 40 wpm. The
Certificate includes Book-keeping Intermediate.

I am at present working as a secretary in the Tourist Board Office where
I also do some reception work.

My family is moving to Trinidad which is why I am looking for another
post.

I shall be willing to attend for interview at any time.

Yours faithfully

M. Chapman

Mary Chapman (Miss)

7

21 Murray Street
Port of Spain

6 September 198-

The Personnel Officer
Tropicana Food Canners
100 Coffee Street
San Fernando

Dear Sir

I wish to apply for the post of secretary which was advertised in this week's 'West Indies Chronicle'.

I enclose my curriculum vitae.

I shall be willing to attend for interview at any time.

Yours faithfully

B. Cheddie

Betty Cheddie

CURRICULUM VITAE

NAME   Betty Ann Cheddie

ADDRESS   21 Murray Street
                    Port of Spain

AGE   26   DATE OF BIRTH   3 August 195-

EDUCATION   GCE O Level - English Language
                                     Mathematics
                                     Economics
                                     Geography   197-
                    RSA Stage III Typewriting
                    RSA Stage II Accounting
                    RSA 100 wpm Pitman Shorthand   197-

EXPERIENCE   Office Junior   197- to 197-
                    Imprint Caribbean Ltd
                    Port of Spain

                    Typist/Receptionist   197- to present
                    Hasham's Printing Products
                    150 Tragarete Road
                    Port of Spain

REFEREES   Mr Mitchell, The Manager, Hasham's Printing
                    Products, 150 Tragarete Road, Port of Spain

                    Mrs Chrichlow, Head of Commercial Studies,
                    Smith's Business College, Port of Spain

21 Frederick Street
Port of Spain

5 September 1980

The Personnel Officer
Tropicana Food Canners
100 Coffee Street
San Fernando

Dear Sir

I wish to apply for the post of secretary as advertised in 'The West
Indies Chronicle'.

When I left school I worked as a shorthand typist for eight years until
my marriage. My children are now grown up and I wish to return to work.
I am 44 years old.

I have a typing speed of 45 wpm and a shorthand speed of 100 wpm. I have
English, Mathematics and Commerce at 'O' level. I do not have any book-
keeping qualification although I could pick up the necessary knowledge
quickly.

I shall be willing to attend for interview at any time.

Yours faithfully

J. Peraud

Joan Peraud (Mrs)

---

21 Belmont Circular Rd
Port of Spain

The Personnel Manager
100 Caffe St.
San Fernando

Dear Sir

I read your advert in The W. Indies Chronic-
al. I would like to apply for the job. I am 16 years old
and have just finished a business studies course
at Mucuago Senior Secondary Comprehensive School. I
am studying English and Commerce at CXC. I have already past Pitman Elementary Typewriting.

I have just taken exams in typewriting at 45
wpm and Shorthand at 80 wpm But I am still
waiting for the results.

I am good at learning new things and my
teachers say I am a good worker. I know if I was
chosen for the job I would be very happy.

Yours faithfully.

G. Persad

Assignment 2 *Using letters of application to choose suitable candidates for interview*

Make a list of the qualifications, etc required for the advertised post from the documents in Situation 1. Use this list and the letters of application to choose three suitable candidates for interview. Write down the names of the candidates you have chosen.

Situation 3

The work involves a series of interviews. Work in groups of six. Each member of the group must play the role of someone taking part in the interviews. The six roles are:

Interviewers	Interviewees
A B Kennard, Personnel Manager	Candidate 1
W O Adams, Office Manager	Candidate 2
S T Stevens, General Manager	Candidate 3

Agree among yourselves who will play each role. If you do not have six in your group, you can go ahead with the interviews without the Office Manager or without Candidate 3.

The three shortlisted candidates have now arrived to be interviewed for the post of secretary to the General Manager of Tropicana Food Canners. The three interviewers should arrange themselves around a table and place a chair in a suitable position for the interviewees. The interviewees should wait outside the room and then be invited in one by one.

Assignment 3 *Practising interview techniques*

Interviewers: The Personnel Manager should act as chairman of the interviewing panel. The panel should interview each of the candidates in turn. Each interview should last 10–15 minutes. Study the briefing sheets on pages 118–20 and use them to help you ask and answer questions. After the three interviews, discuss the candidates and agree which one should be given the job.

Interviewees: You will each be interviewed by the panel, who will then decide who should be offered the job. Study the briefing sheet on page 120 and use it to help you answer and ask questions. You will each need to study again the letter of application that 'you' wrote when originally applying for the job.

Briefing sheet

Personnel Manager: A B Kennard

You are A B Kennard, the Personnel Manager of Tropicana Food Canners. You are responsible for the appointment and dismissal of all staff, for all wages and salaries and all other matters concerning employment conditions, benefits, welfare and training. You are the chairman of the interviewing panel.

Your part in the interview:

1 Welcome the candidate, ask him/her to sit down and introduce yourself and the other interviewers.
2 Ask the candidate to outline any previous work experience and say what he/she liked or disliked about previous jobs.
3 Ask the Office Manager if he/she has any questions to put to the candidate.
4 When the Office Manager has finished, ask if the General Manager has any questions to put to the candidate.
5 Ask the candidate if he/she has any questions. You will have to answer some of these questions. Use the information on the right to help you.
6 Thank the candidate and ask him/her to wait outside until all the interviews are finished.
7 Discuss the candidates with the other interviewers and agree on which candidate should be offered the job.

Information which can be given:

a *Office hours* are 8.30 am to 5 pm, Monday to Friday. *Lunch:* 12.30 to 2.
b *Holidays:* three weeks. Dates would have to be agreed with the General Manager.
c *Pay:* the salary range is given on the Personnel Requisition. Do not give an exact salary figure to any candidate. Say that salary is according to qualifications and experience. Extra salary is given for passing relevant examinations.

Briefing sheet

Office Manager: W O Adams

You are W O Adams, the Office Manager of Tropicana Food Canners. You have responsibility for Office Administration, including all secretarial and typing work.

Your part in the interview:

1 The Personnel Manager will introduce you to the candidate and will ask him/her to outline previous work experience.
2 The Personnel Manager will ask you if you have any questions to put to the candidate. Ask the candidate to list his/her secretarial qualifications.
3 Ask the candidate if he/she has any qualifications or experience in book-keeping. If so, get details from the candidate.
4 Tell the candidate that he/she would be responsible for keeping the records for the General Manager's entertainment budget. Ask him/her to outline the records that should be kept.
5 The Personnel Manager will ask the candidate if he/she has any questions. You will have to answer some of these questions. Use the information on the right to help you.

Information which can be given:

a The General Manager's secretary has a small office equipped with a telephone (all calls to the General Manager come through the secretary's extension), a two-year old electric typewriter, audio typewriting equipment and several filing cabinets.
b The company allows secretaries to use either shorthand or audio typing equipment – they have no preference.
c The company has a typing pool for all routine and copy typing. Copy typists do not carry out confidential work such as typing the General Manager's correspondence or reports.
d The company has a separate reprography department with several photocopiers and its own staff.

Briefing sheet

General Manager: S T Stevens

You are S T Stevens, General Manager of Tropicana Food Canners. You have overall responsibility for the day-to-day running of the company. The three candidates are being interviewed for the job of your secretary.

Your part in the interview:

1 The Personnel Manager will introduce you to the candidate and will ask him/her to outline previous work experience.
2 The Office Manager will then ask the candidate to answer some questions.
3 Tell the candidate that you would expect him/her to arrive at the office 30 minutes before you each morning. Ask what the candidate would do in these 30 minutes.
4 Entertaining customers is an important part of your secretary's job. Ask the candidate how he/she would entertain an important American customer for the evening. The customer is a strong supporter of the church.
5 The Personnel Manager will ask the candidate if he/she has any questions. You will have to answer some of these questions. Use the information on the right to help you.

Information which can be given:

a Most of the work involved in this job is routine secretarial work – see Job Description.
b The successful candidate will have to be able to work unsupervised – handle routine correspondence and telephone calls, etc.
c You normally entertain 10 or 12 customers a month. This usually means taking them to lunch. You normally expect to spend one or two evenings a month entertaining. You would expect your secretary to be willing to help you with this.
d You sometimes work late, perhaps once a week. You would expect your secretary to stay behind to help you if necessary. There is no extra pay for work in the evening.
e Your last secretary left because there was too much work in the evenings. Try to avoid telling candidates this.

Briefing sheet

You are one of the applicants for the post of secretary to the General Manager of Tropicana Food Canners. Study again the advertisement for the job and familiarise yourself with the relevant letter of application. You will need to make use of information from these documents during the interview.

Your part in the interview:

1 You will be called into the interview room one by one. The Personnel Manager will introduce the members of the interviewing panel. All three will ask you questions.

2 You will be asked if you have any questions. You should ask questions about at least five of the following points plus any other relevant questions you can think of.

Candidate 1	Candidate 2	Candidate 3
a Hours of work? Overtime?	Overtime – how often? – rates?	Hours of work? Overtime?
b Holiday – how long?	Holiday – can take any time?	Holiday – can take 3 weeks together?
c Salary?	Is extra paid if extra exams passed?	Can use shorthand instead audio?
d Duties?	What type of equipment available?	Own office? Electric typewriter?
e How much entertaining?	Evening work – how often?	Evening work?
f Reason last secretary left?	Reason last secretary left?	Reason last secretary left?

Situation 4

One candidate has now been selected for the post. Although the decision was given to all the candidates verbally, they must be informed officially in writing.

Assignment 4a *Drafting a letter offering the successful candidate the post*

Draft a letter to the successful candidate informing him/her that he/she has been successful. Offer your congratulations. Confirm the salary that has been agreed upon and the date on which the candidate should start work. The candidate should be given an outline of the duties that he/she will be required to perform. Ask the candidate to confirm that he/she intends to accept the post.

Assignment 4b *Drafting a letter to the unsuccessful candidates*

The successful candidate has now accepted the post. Draft a letter to be sent to the two unsuccessful candidates. Thank them for attending the interview and inform them that they were unsuccessful.

Miscellany

Exercise 1 *British and American spelling*

There are not many differences between British and American spelling. A few rules make some of these differences easier to remember. Use the following lists of words to complete each of the rules underneath.

BRITISH	AMERICAN
armour	armor
colour	color
flavour	flavor

1 There is a group of words in British English ending with the suffix __. In American English this suffix is spelt __. For example, the person who lives next door is the n_____ in British English but the n_____ in American English.

BRITISH	AMERICAN
calibre	caliber
fibre	fiber
theatre	theater

2 Words ending with the suffix __ in British English end with __ in American English. For example, another word for middle is c_____ in British English but c_____ in American English.

BRITISH	AMERICAN
catalogue	catalog
monologue	monolog

3 Words ending with **-gue** in __ English are spelt with a __ in __ English. For example, a discussion between two people is spelt d_____ in British English but d_____ in American.

BRITISH	AMERICAN
dial/dialled/dialling	dial/dialed/dialing
level/levelled/levelling	level/leveled/leveling
wool/woollen	wool/woolen

4 Root words ending in an __ double the __ before a suffix beginning with a __ in __ English but not in __ English. For example, a person who travels is a t_____ in British English but a t_____ in American English.

BRITISH	AMERICAN
defence	defense
pretence	pretense
offence	offense

5 Several words ending __ in British English end in __ in American English. For example, an official paper giving you permission to do something is spelt l_____ in British English but l_____ in American.

There are also differences with individual words. Make two lists, one headed BRITISH and the other headed AMERICAN. Decide which list the following words should go in and fill in the corresponding place in the other list. Use a dictionary.

	BRITISH	AMERICAN
Example: rumor	rumour	rumor
6 glamour		
7 sulfur		
8 storey		
9 appall		
10 fulfil		
11 skillful		
12 jewellery		

Fill in the blanks in the following passage with *either* British spellings *or* American spellings. Be consistent.

The development of central Africa has, in many ways, been linked with the development of transport in the area. At the end of the nineteenth century the railway was pushed northwards into the 13 _____ (center/centre) of Africa when the railway company was given a 14 _____ (licence/license) to extend its operations from Zimbabwe into 15 _____ (neighboring/neighbouring) Zambia.

The railway company's engineers 16 _____ (favored/favoured) crossing into Zambia north of the Victoria Falls, but many 17 _____ (travelers/travellers) wanted to see the spray and 18 _____ (vapor/vapour) from the Falls where the water crashed over the 19 _____ (gray/grey) rocks into the river below. Despite the 20 _____ (scepticism/skepticism) of the engineers, men 21 _____ (labored/laboured) 22 _____ (skilfully/skillfully) throughout 1905 to erect a bridge high above the Zambezi. Meanwhile track was laid north of the river so that the building 23 _____ (program/programme) should not be delayed.

With the completion of the railway, a farming belt grew up alongside the tracks in Zambia. Mechanised 24 _____ (ploughs/plows) were introduced and the first capital of the country was established in the new farming town of Kalomo. However, the site of the town was not a healthy one and in 1906 the local bank refused to cash 25 _____ (checks/cheques) unless the government took steps to control malaria. It was decided that it would be cheaper to move the capital and a new town was laid out at Livingstone with 26 _____ (metaled/metalled) roads and proper 27 _____ (curbs/kerbs) instead of muddy tracks. With tarmac roads motor cars with pneumatic 28 _____ (tires/tyres) could operate between the major towns.

After trains and cars came reliable 29 _____ (aluminium/aluminum) 30 _____ (aeroplanes/airplanes), which appeared after the second world war. These opened up the more remote areas once ground had been cleared and 31 _____ (leveled/levelled) for airstrips. The introduction of a flying doctor service meant that medical staff could quickly reach outlying villages and serious cases could be flown back to the towns where there were operating 32 _____ (theaters/theatres) in modern hospitals.

7

Exercise 2 *eg* and *ie*

> *eg* means 'for example'. It comes from the Latin 'exempli gratia' but can be remembered in English as **e**xample **g**iven.
>
> I shall be in Rome all next week. Why don't we arrange a meeting one day – eg Tuesday?
>
> Tuesday is an example of a day of the week. It is only one day of the week. This is shown in this diagram:

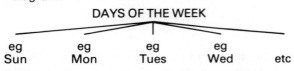

DAYS OF THE WEEK

eg	eg	eg	eg	
Sun	Mon	Tues	Wed	etc

Which words in the sentences below mean the same as *eg*?

1 Several cities in the world, for instance San Francisco, Hong Kong and Newcastle-upon-Tyne, have recently built rapid transit train services.

2 Many countries, such as Zambia and Australia, have changed to decimal currency since 1960.

3 The job offers various perks, for example free lunches and company medical insurance.

> *ie* means 'in other words'. It comes from the Latin 'id est' but can be remembered as **i**n **e**xplanation or **i**n **e**quivalent language.
>
> I shall be in Rome all next week – ie 22nd to 29th.
>
> '22nd to 29th' is another way of saying 'all next week' – they mean the same thing. This is shown in this diagram:
>
> | ALL NEXT WEEK | = | 22nd TO 29th |
> |---|---|---|

Which words in the sentences below mean the same as *ie*?

4 Rapid transit services, that is, high speed train services with frequent stops, have been built to ease the traffic problems in busy cities.

5 Since 1960 many countries have changed to decimal currency, that is to say a currency where 100 small units equal one larger unit.

6 Salary scale: $750–$984. Salaries are per Hegira month, in other words a month is reckoned as 29½ days.

Fill in each of the gaps in the passage below with either *eg* or *ie*.

> ### NINETEENTH-CENTURY TYPEWRITERS
>
> The typewriter was not invented by one man. There were numerous 'inventions', many of which never saw the light of day because, 7_____, the typist could not see what she had typed until the letter was finished. The Sholes-Glidden machine was possibly the first commercially-produced typewriter and appeared on the market in the 1870s. Sholes himself maintained: 'This (8_____ the typewriter) will enable them (9_____ women) more easily to earn a living.'
>
> Some government departments, 10_____ the Inland Revenue, were pioneer employers of women, who were considered capable of important tasks, 11_____ typing letters to the Treasury. In 1888 an official informed anyone who wanted to hear of the advantages of women, 12_____ their speed and accuracy. But one advantage was of overwhelming importance: 'they receive lower remuneration and are entitled to no superannuation' – 13_____ they were cheap. Women were called typewriters and the machines they used were known as type writers.
>
> The nineteenth-century office typewriter (14_____ the machine, not the user) was heavy to lift and unattractive to look at. Various improvements were made – 15_____ Edison developed an electric version in 1872 but electric machines were not commercially available until the 1920s. And the girl in front of the typewriter 100 years ago spent at least a quarter of an hour on daily maintenance, 16_____ oiling.

(Adapted from Alan Delgado, *The Enormous File*, John Murray, 1979.)

Exercise 3 *Writing a curriculum vitae*

A curriculum vitae is a summary of a person's qualifications, educational background, experience, etc. It is used when applying for a job and is sent with a covering letter.

Use the information in the following letter to type or write out a curriculum vitae. Use the headings given after the letter. These headings are not in a sensible order.

(*Note:* An example of the layout of a curriculum vitae can be found on page 116.)

```
                                                    61 Chacon Street
                                                    Port of Spain
                                                    Trinidad


         28 September 1980


         The Manager
         Trinidad Chamber of Commerce
         69 Frederick Street
         Port of Spain
         Trinidad


         Dear Sir

         I should like to be considered for the post of stenographer as
         advertised in today's 'West Indies Chronicle'.

         I am 25 years old.  I attended Saint Martin's Secondary School in
         San Fernando, Trinidad and obtained four GCE O Levels in English
         Language, Mathematics, Economics and Accounts.

         At present I am working as a secretary to the manager at Hessick
         and Jardine Manufacturing Company, Trincity Estate, Port of Spain.
         I have been with this company for one year.  Before taking this
         post I worked for eighteen months as a receptionist/typist for
         External Telecommunications Limited, P O Box 3, Port of Spain.  I
         left this post as I was not given any opportunity to use my short-
         hand and I wanted to maintain my speeds.

         Before starting work for External Telecommunications Limited, I
         went straight from school to Brown's Private Secretarial College,
         San Fernando where I completed a one year full-time secretarial
         course.  I passed RSA Stage III Typewriting, 100 wpm Pitman Short-
         hand and Stage II Commerce.

         References can be obtained from my shorthand teacher, Mrs King, at
         Brown's College and from the Manager at Hessick and Jardine.

         I shall be available to attend an interview at any time.  Should
         you need more information I shall be pleased to supply it if you
         contact me at the above address or telephone me at home after 1730
         hours on 62-39876.

         Yours faithfully

         E. M. Chan

         Elsie Mary Chan (Miss)
```

7

CURRICULUM VITAE   EDUCATION
EXPERIENCE   TELEPHONE NUMBER
MARITAL STATUS   ADDRESS
FULL NAME   REFEREES
DATE OF BIRTH   QUALIFICATIONS

Plan and type or write out your own curriculum vitae.

Examination preparation: *Indirect speech*

Match the following sentences with a description of each from the list given beneath:

Example: I can type at 50 wpm. Statement.

Interviewer: Good afternoon, Miss Daly. Please sit down. (Miss Pereira, I do not want any interruptions for the next 30 minutes.) Did you have any difficulty finding us?

Interviewee: Not at all, the map you sent was very clear.

Interviewer: Good! Now you have a Pitman Higher Secretarial Group Certificate, haven't you?

Interviewee: Yes. I received an award for having the best speeds of the year in my college.

Interviewer: Indeed, that's very good! Now you haven't any work experience. I warn you working in an office is quite different from college work. We can't afford to make mistakes here. Have you ever worked in an office?

Interviewee: Well, yes. Between leaving school and starting my course I worked as a clerk for Muir Marshall.

Interviewer: At least you have been inside an office. That helps. During your course did you use any office machines?

Interviewee: Oh yes, we had a model office and we were given practical assignments each week. We learnt to use a spirit duplicator, a stencil duplicator, different calculators, a switchboard, ...

a Statement	*e* Order	*i* Exclamation
b Warning	*f* Suggestion	*j* Promise
c Request	*g* Greeting	*k* Complaint
d Question	*h* Reply	

Change the sentences below into indirect speech. Replace *said* in each with a form of one of the words *a–k*. Imagine that the sentences are taken from telephone conversations and you have to pass the messages on to your boss immediately.

Example: He said, 'We are opening our new factory in September.'
He stated that they are opening their new factory in September.

1 'Our order is over two weeks late,' she said.
2 He said, 'Would you send us a pro-forma invoice for customs?'
3 'I should send your order straight away since supplies are limited,' he said.
4 'Do you still supply parts for the Triptex machine?' she said.
5 'The shipping documents were sent last week,' she said.
6 She said, 'Can you attend for interview on 10 October?'
7 'You could make a part payment of $200 now and pay the rest by September,' she said.
8 'I don't think I can manage that,' she said.
9 She said, 'We can't possibly pay by the end of next week!'
10 'I will tell you the results of the interview on Monday,' she said.
11 'Be careful!' he said.
12 'I will be moving to Head Office next month,' he said.
13 'I should order some more labels now,' she said.
14 He said, 'Would you please let us have the information by the end of next week?'
15 'Do you know how to run off a stencil?' he said.

Unit 8

A clerical error

Situation 1

You work in the Stores Section of East African Plastics Ltd of Nairobi. It is the beginning of October and you have to carry out your quarterly stock-taking of stationery in the storeroom. After stock-taking orders will have to be placed with your usual suppliers to bring your stocks up to their *maximum* level.

Assignment 1 *Completing a Purchase Requisition from Stock Cards and a Price-List*

Use the stationery stock cards and the Kenprint price-list to complete the purchase requisition on page 127. The purchase requisition is sent to the Purchasing Department, who will send the necessary orders off to your suppliers.

Note: All prices in these documents are expressed in East African shillings. There are 100 cents in a shilling.

KENPRINT/Price List   *Please consult catalogue for details*

Description	Catalogue No	Price	Description	Catalogue No	Price
Envelopes (price per 100)			**Rulers** (price per 10)		
C 7/6	42101	41·50	15 cm	22063	17·80
C 5/6	42102	47·10	30 cm	22046	36·20
C 6	42103	51·40			
C 5	42104	64·00	**Scissors**		
C 4	42105	100·00	10 cm	48611	48·60
			15 cm	48690	53·90
Files (price per 25)			17·5 cm	48692	62·10
Manilla	74112	279·00	25 cm	48691	80·80
Computer files	74213	364·00			
Single pocket	74111	472·00	**Sharpeners**		
Double pocket	74537	160·33	Single hole	20491	·63
Slide Binder	74356	49·00	De luxe	20921	350·00
			Battery	20241	449·00
Paper (price per ream)					
Duplicating	F12522	59·20	**Stamps**		
Typewriting – Bond	F12641	96·00	DATE – PAID	1127	110·50
Typewriting – Copy	F12982	80·00	DATE	1176	15·60
			DATE – RECEIVED	1101	129·50
Paper Clips (price per 100)					
Large	39327	25·30	**Staplers**		
Small	39326	17·80	Giant	7711X	600·00
			Long Arm	47136	120·00
Punches			Gazelle	47232	102·00
Adjustable	49250	479·00			
4-hole	49366	223·00	**Staples** (price per 1 000)		
Lightweight	49384	60·00	No 16 (6 mm)	46033	·40
			No 19 (8 mm)	46271	·44
Rubber bands (price per 0·5 kilos)			No 46 (10 mm)	46238	·54
25 × 1·2 mm	55700	20·00			
50 × 1·2 mm	55737	20·00			
100 × 3 mm	55974	20·00			
Assorted	55727	20·00			

8

STATIONERY STOCK CARD

Item ... Paper clips (small) ... Max. stock 1000 boxes (1000's) ... Supplier ... Kenprint ... Min. stock 250 boxes

Bal. in stock
250
245
235

STATIONERY STOCK CARD

Item ... Files, manilla ... Max. stock 500 ... Supplier ... Kenprint ... Min. stock 50

Bal. in stock
885
863
763
713

STATIONERY STOCK CARD

Item ... Staples (8mm) ... Max. stock 1000 boxes (1000's) ... Supplier ... Kenprint ... Min. stock 250 boxes

Bal. in stock
190
90
63
50

STATIONERY STOCK CARD

Item ... Envelopes C4 ... Max. stock 5000 ... Supplier ... Kenprint ... Min. stock 500

Bal. in stock
922
878
877
677
612

STATIONERY STOCK CARD

Item ... Paper Punch (small) ... Max. stock 60 ... Supplier ... KZ Supplies ... Min. stock 10

Bal. in stock
1220
1100
900
875
675
600

STATIONERY STOCK CARD

Item ... Pencil sharpener (small) ... Max. stock 250 ... Supplier ... Kenprint ... Min. stock 50

Bal. in stock
58
57
55

STATIONERY STOCK CARD

Item ... Scissors, 10 cm ... Max. stock 100 ... Supplier ... Kenprint ... Min. stock 20

Date	Receipts	Issues	Bal. in stock
14.7.8-	✓	2	14
28.7.8-	76	✓	90
11.8.8-	✓	6	84
22.9.8-	✓	39	45
27.9.8-	✓	3	42

Bal. in stock (additional column entries)
177
175
125
113
111

PURCHASE REQUISITION   No 5785493

Department .... *Stores* ....   Date .... *1 Oct 8–*

Supplier .... *Kenprint Ltd* ....

.... *PO Box 41382 Nairobi* ....

Quantity	Unit	Description	Total Price
2		Date stamps	
		Paper clips (small)	
	each	Files, manilla	
100	each	Files (one pocket)	
		Staples (8 mm)	
	each	Envelopes C4	
1300	each	Envelopes C5	
1700	each	Envelopes C6	
2100	each	Envelopes C5/6	
		Paper punches (small)	
		Pencil sharpeners (small)	
4		Pencil sharpeners (electric)	
		Scissors, 10 cm	
23		Scissors, 17½ cm	
60	each	Rulers, 30 cm	
TOTAL		Shs	

8

Situation 2

It is now 29 November 198–. The order referred to in Situation 1 has been placed with Kenprint and was delivered to East African Plastics on 26 November. Unfortunately, there seems to have been a mistake. You work in the Sales Department of Kenprint and it is one of your jobs to deal with customers' queries and complaints. You have just received a letter of complaint from East African Plastics, together with a photocopy of their original order to you.

Assignment 2   *Locating errors in documents*

It is your job to try to discover what has gone wrong and, if possible, why and who made the mistake in the first place. Study the letter of complaint, p 128, the photocopy of the order, p 129, and your price-list, p 125, and try to decide who was to blame.

Make any notes you feel are relevant as you go through. You will need them in a later assignment.

EAST AFRICAN PLASTICS LTD

Tel: 679421   Kimathi Street   Telex: EAP 212
           P O Box 6941 NAIROBI

28 November 198-

Kenprint Limited
Umfango Street
P O Box 41382
Nairobi

Dear Sirs

Order No 1460/BC

The above order was delivered on 26 November 198-.

We were dismayed to find that you delivered 440 000 C4 envelopes
(Catalogue Number 42105). We ordered only 4 400.

As you can imagine this error has created numerous problems including one of storage. We have had no alternative but to store
the excess outdoors.

Enclosed is a copy of our order form. We hope to receive a corrected invoice and your decisions regarding the envelopes soon.

Yours faithfully

John Ajok.

J Ajok
Purchasing Dept

Enc

Situation 3

It is 1 December. You are W Warui, the Sales Manager of Kenprint Limited. The letter of complaint above has been passed on to you for reply.

Assignment 3   *Agreeing on what went wrong*

In Assignment 2 you decided individually what went wrong in Situation 2. Now agree on this in groups.

Situation 4

You work in the Sales Department of Kenprint Limited. The Sales Manager asks you to have a meeting with your colleagues to think of all the possible solutions to the problem in Situation 2.

Assignment 4a   *Solving a problem through discussion*

Work in groups of four. Think of and discuss *all* the possible solutions to the problem. Make notes if necessary.

ORDER

From: East African Plastics Ltd
Kimathi Street
P O Box 6941
Nairobi

To: Kenprint Ltd
Umfango Street
P O Box 41382
Nairobi

Date: 10 October 198-

Please supply:

Quantity	Description	Cat No	Unit Price
2	Stamp - Date	1176	15.60
287	Paperclips small	39326	17.80
18	Files - manilla	74112	279.00
4	Files - single pocket	74111	472.00
388	Staples No 19 (8 mm)	46271	.44
4 400	Envelopes C4	42105	100.00
13	Envelopes C5	42104	64.00
17	Envelopes C6	42103	51.40
21	Envelopes C5/6	42102	47.10
5	Punch, lightweight	49384	60.00
139	Sharpener, single hole	20491	.63
4	Sharpener, battery	20241	449.00
58	Scissors, 10 cm	48611	48.60
23	Scissors, 17.5 cm	48692	62.10
6	Rulers, 30 cm	22046	36.20

Deliver to   As above

Signed: John Ajok.

8

Assignment 4b *Reporting a problem and deciding on action*

Divide into pairs. Each pair: find another not working with you in Assignment 4a. Each pair should give an oral report on all the solutions they decided upon in Assignment 4a. Then as a group, decide on
1 The action to be taken.
2 What the action involves, eg writing a letter, a memo, etc.
3 What must be said in each document.

Situation 5

You are W Warui. It is 2 December.

Assignment 5a *Writing a tactful letter*

Draft then type or write the letter of reply and its envelope to East African Plastics Limited, based on the decision made in Assignment 4b.

Assignment 5b *Writing a memo as follow-up to a decision*

Write or type a memo to the Despatch Department telling them of the decision made in Assignment 4b and of any action required of them.

Situation 6

It is 15 December 198– and all the necessary action has been taken. Now that the problem is solved, the Managing Director of Kenprint, Mr G H Nyong'o, has called for a summary of the confusion that arose over the East African Plastics' account and the action that was taken to sort it out. You are W Warui, Sales Manager of Kenprint and have been involved with this situation throughout.

Assignment 6 *Summarising a series of documents*

Produce the required summary of the situation. Refer to all relevant documents, meetings and actions taken. Arrange your summary chronologically, explaining what happened on each date, what documents were sent, what actions were taken and who was involved. Display your summary in the form of a memo. The first entry has been done as an example:

12 October 198–: East African Plastics' order number 1460/BC dated 10 October was received by Kenprint (photocopy enclosed). This order was processed and sent to the warehouse for despatch.

Miscellany

Exercise 1 *Index and table of contents*
Using an index to a book

There are several methods of looking for information which does not seem to be included in an index:

i) Items of several words may be indexed under the second, third or fourth word. Look for other words in the item you want.
If you cannot find UPPER CASE LETTERS, try LETTERS, UPPER CASE. If you cannot find DUPLICATING MACHINES, try --

ii) Items may be indexed under another word meaning the same thing. Look for another entry with the same meaning.
If you cannot find POST, try MAIL.
If you cannot find STENCIL DUPLICATING, try --

iii) Items may be indexed in more detail than you realise. Look for an entry which is an example of the item you want.
If you cannot find DUPLICATING MACHINES, try INK DUPLICATING.
If you cannot find TELEGRAPHIC COM-MUNICATION SERVICES, try --

iv) Items may be indexed in less detail than you realise. Look for an entry which includes the item you want.
If you cannot find CROSSED CHEQUE, try CHEQUE.
If you cannot find DICTATING MACHINES, try --

Here are 15 items not included in the index on the right. Use the methods suggested above to find the headings under which you would find the relevant information.

1 types of business correspondence
2 calculating machines
3 filing systems
4 notes, consignment
5 bar graphs
6 inter-office memoranda
7 xeroxing
8 indexing systems
9 receiving telephone calls
10 orders, purchase
11 stencil addressing machines
12 analysis of sales
13 customer invoices
14 registered post
15 salutations in business letters

Index

Absent folder card, 46–7
Adding and calculating machines, 26, 78, 101–2
Addressing machines, 99–100
Alphabetical filing, 41–2, 43, 44, 45, 55, 56
Area sales analysis, 84–6

Business letters, 33–7, 56

Cheques, 92
Consignment notes, 60–61
Credit control, 31
Cross reference, 47
Customer files, 18–19
Customer list, 6–17
Customer orders, 20–22, 26, 27–30
Customer record cards, 5, 22, 26, 42, 43, 44

Dictating machines, 102–3

Flow chart, 32
Follow-up filing, 45–6

Geographical filing, 42–3
Giro credit slip, 93
Goods received notes, 75–7, 93
Graphs, 86–8

Ink duplicating, 70, 73, 75, 96–7
Invoicing, 57–9, 61, 78, 89

Lateral filing, 48
Ledger cards, 89–90, 92

Mail, 38–40
Memorandums, 54–5

Numerical filing, 44–5

Photocopying, 98–9
Price-list, 4
Project, 94–5
Purchase orders, 73–4, 77
Purchase requisitions, 70–73

Ready reckoner, 24–5

Sales analysis, 78–81, 83–5, 87–8
Sales order forms, 22–4, 31, 32, 35
Sales summary, 82–3, 85, 86
Spirit duplicating, 1–3, 5, 57
Statements, 91–2
Stock availability, 31
Stock record cards, 63–4, 70, 73, 75
Stock schedule, 64–9, 70
Strip indexing, 49
Subject filing, 43–4
Suspended filing, 48

Telephone, 50–53
Total quality comparison, 83–5

Visible card indexing, 49

8

Using a table of contents

Here is an incomplete table of contents. Below are the missing chapter headings, but they have been mixed up.

TABLE OF CONTENTS	
Chap	Page
1 The Training Office	1
2	20
3	33
4	38
5	41
6	50
7	54
8	57
9	60
10	63
11	73
12	78
13	89
14	96
Index	104

a Internal Communications
b Filing and Indexing Systems
c Stock Control
d Customer Orders
e Despatching
f Office Machinery
g Purchase and Receipt of Goods
h Business Letters
i Accounts and Statements
j The Mail
k Analysis of Sales
l The Telephone
m Invoicing

Use the index on page 131 to decide the order of the chapter headings.
(Adapted from K Gosling, *The Clerical Training Office*, Pitman, second edn, 1975.)

Exercise 2 *Dictionary use – appropriate meanings*

Many English words have more than one meaning. When we look a word up in a dictionary there are often several meanings from which we must choose the correct one to fit the context. Passages 1 and 2 contain several fairly easy words, all of which have several meanings. Match each word underlined in the passages to the correct meaning from the dictionary entries below.

carbon n. **1** a chemical element. **2** an electrode used in arc welding. **3** short for carbon paper or carbon copy.
certain adj. **1** sure, convinced. **2** some; not specified but existing.
clear adj. **1** transparent. **2** distinct, plain.
copy n. **1** reproduction; one thing made to look like another. **2** written material ready for typing or printing. **3** any single example of a book, newspaper, etc.
copy v. **1** to make a copy of something. **2** to do exactly the same as someone else.
degree n. **1** extent; level. **2** academic qualification. **3** 360th part of the circumference of a circle. **4** marking on a scale, eg degree of temperature.
fast adj. **1** quick. **2** ahead of the correct time. **3** firm; fixed firmly.
fast adv. quickly, swiftly.
file n. **1** a collection of papers arranged for reference. **2** a row of soldiers or other people. **3** a steel tool for cutting or smoothing.
file v. **1** to place in a file. **2** to cut with a file.
manual adj. done with or operated by the hands.
manual n. a handbook containing information or instructions.
then adv. **1** at that time. **2** next. **3** therefore, so, in consequence.
type n. **1** a sort, a pattern. **2** letters for printing.
type v. **1** to use a typewriter. **2** to state that something belongs to a particular type.

1 Making [1]carbon copies

It is usual to [2]copy all correspondence for the [3]files. Carbon paper is still used for making [4]copies in many offices. All carbon copies should be [5]clear, free from smudges and easy to read.
It is important to know how many copies are required before you start to [6]type. Most companies have a policy calling for a [7]certain number of copies for each [8]type of job. If you are not [9]certain how many copies are needed, look it up in the company [10]manual.
(Adapted from G A Reid, *Modern Office Procedures*, Pitman, Canada, 2nd edn, 1978.)

2 Ribbons for typewriters

These are mostly made of inked fabrics which may be cotton, silk or nylon. The [11]degree of inking varies from light to medium and heavy. For some typewriters – both electric and [12]manual – a plastic [13]carbon-coated ribbon (which should be used only once) is also available.
Ribbons may be single or two coloured, with black and black and red record being the most popular. Record ribbons are inked with [14]fast dye which makes a permanent impression. A ribbon switch enables the typist to select the part of the ribbon (top or bottom) she wishes to use. Many prefer to keep the top of the ribbon in constant use: the typing will [15]then be as [16]fast as possible because the ribbon does not have to rise to its highest extent when each key is struck.
(Adapted from E Mackay, *The Typewriting Dictionary*, Pitman, 1977.)

Exercise 3 *Punctuation: semicolon (2)*

A semicolon can be used instead of a full stop between two sentences where the second sentence is:
a) a contrast
b) an alternative
c) a conclusion

What is a contrast? Find contrasting pairs of words in the following list:

Example: add and subtract

1	black	11	cold
2	quiet	12	short
3	buy	13	export
4	long	14	cheap
5	refuse	15	private
6	expensive	16	busy
7	public	17	accept
8	difficult	18	hot
9	sell	19	easy
10	white	20	import

What is an alternative? Find alternatives in the following:

Example: by sea or by air

21	by phone	31	audio
22	coffee	32	telex
23	shorthand	33	quire
24	Fahrenheit	34	manual
25	fully blocked	35	eraser
26	ream	36	centigrade
27	capitals	37	indented
28	cable	38	lower case
29	correction paper	39	by letter
30	electric	40	tea

Find five contrasts or alternatives in column B to the statements in column A:

A
41 The temperature in the office has dropped to 11 °C
42 We must sell this stock
43 The typists were asked to use the new invoice forms
44 The girls wanted to earn extra money
45 Our wages have gone up 12 per cent

B
a before the beginning of April
b yet they still use the old ones
c to spend on clothes
d when Mr Todd gets back
e otherwise we won't be able to order more
f nevertheless they weren't prepared to do over-time
g still that doesn't mean we can afford a new car
h however the heating has been turned on
i which is really good
j as winter has arrived early this year

List the words in *a–j* that can introduce a contrast and those that introduce an alternative.

Rule 3: A semicolon is used to separate two clauses when the second clause is a contrast or an alternative to the first.

(Rules 1 and 2 are on page 19.)

Decide on suitable endings for the following and punctuate correctly.

Example: A good dictionary is usually expensive however..........
A good dictionary is usually expensive; however *it is worth having one's own copy.*

46 I haven't visited my family for three months however..........
47 I shall have to pass the examination this time otherwise..........
48 I hope I get the job I applied for still..........
49 Photocopying is fast..........
50 It is said that touch typists never look at the keys..........

Rule 4: A semicolon is used to separate two clauses when the second is a conclusion drawn from the first.

Pick out the sentence that has a conclusion in the second clause. The sentences are unpunctuated:

51 He went to bed early because he had an examination the following day.
52 He went to bed early therefore he was ready for the examination the following day.
53 He went to bed early otherwise he wouldn't have got up in time for his examination the following day.
54 He went to bed early still he was late for his examination the following day.
55 He went to bed early otherwise he wouldn't have got to his examination the following day.

Match each of the clauses (56–65) with another from the list. Rewrite them with the correct punctuation. There are five sentences in all.

Example: a) so it is wise not to plan any business meetings on that date
b) in Nigeria, October 1st is Republic Day and is a national holiday throughout the Federal Republic

In Nigeria, October 1st is Republic Day and is a national holiday throughout the Federal Republic; so it is wise not to plan any business meetings on that date.

56 in the main tourist centres of the Caribbean it is difficult to find a hotel room at the height of the season

8

57 therefore callers will not have to go through the switchboard operators
58 Kenya has many beautiful beaches and interesting game parks
59 so it is better and cheaper to walk to the Star Ferry
60 hence there is no need for the visitor to take a heavy suit
61 Jamaica has International Subscriber Dialling (ISD)
62 therefore it is advisable to book early
63 thus it is worthwhile to take time off from business to visit such places
64 taking a taxi between Kowloon and Hong Kong Island can be expensive because of the toll for the tunnel connecting the two
65 in the Caribbean the climate is sub-tropical and most businessmen dress informally

Examination preparation: *Problems with pronouns (3)*

A Double objects: *I/me*

Which of the following sentences are correct?

1 *a* He accused Sally and I of doing it.
  b He accused Sally and me of doing it.
2 *a* Sally and I were accused of doing it.
  b Sally and me were accused of doing it.

Simple rule: Think of the sentences without 'Sally': it should then be obvious that *1b* and *2a* are correct.

Use this rule to complete each of the following sentences with *I* or *me*:

3 The bad weather prevented my husband and __ from coming.
4 Please give him and __ our letters.
5 She gave my sister and __ some bad news.
6 Tom and __ were promoted.
7 Fast cars are not for people like you and __.
8 I think you and __ should discuss this matter again soon.
9 My husband and __ were prevented from coming by the bad weather.
10 My sister and __ received some bad news.

B Pronoun and *-ing* form

Which of the following sentences are correct?
11 *a* They couldn't understand even after me explaining it.
   b They couldn't understand even after my explaining it.
12 *a* He was satisfied with my apologising.
   b He was satisfied with me apologising.

Explanation: What couldn't they understand – 'me' or the 'explaining'?
What satisfied him – 'me' or the 'apologising'?
'explaining' and 'apologising' are both nouns. This is clear if we rewrite the sentences:

11 *c* They couldn't understand even after *my explanation*.
12 *c* He was satisfied with *my apology*.

Simple rule: In sentences like these, always use the possessive form (*my*, *your*, *his*, *her*, *our*, *their*) before *-ing*.

Use this rule to decide which of the sentences below are incorrect. Rewrite them correctly.

13 I object to you borrowing my books without asking.
14 He was surprised at my asking such a question.
15 They will not agree to your having a month off.
16 She was pleased at them offering her such a good pay rise.
17 I recollect you telling me about that meeting.
18 He has agreed to me leaving early on Friday afternoon.
19 I remember him discussing it with us.
20 She was upset at their lying about the matter.
21 Had you forgotten him not speaking at the meeting?
22 You talking about it is no good – you must do something about it!

Unit 9

Safety in the office

Situation 1

You are a secretary in the Accounts Department of a fairly large firm. You share an office with the Accountant and three clerks. On 15 December 198–, one of the wages clerks, Sebastian Grey, emptied an ashtray into his wastepaper bin which was beside his desk. He then left the office to go for lunch. Everyone else had already left for lunch. He had been gone for about ten minutes when he realised he had left his library book on his desk. He had brought it in that morning so he could change it at lunch time. He went back to the office to get it and found that the paper in his bin was on fire. He picked the bin up to take it to the tap outside and in doing so he burnt his hands and dropped the bin. You came in from lunch and put the fire out with water from the kettle. You found some bandages in the first-aid box and dressed his burns. The burns were not serious and Sebastian was back at work after three days.

Assignment 1a   *Drawing up and completing an accident report form*

The Office Manager has asked you to submit an accident report. You find that the company does not have a standard report form but the Office Manager has some notes on what should be included on the form. Draw up the form from the notes and add any headings you think are relevant. Then complete the form using the details of Sebastian's accident.

Notes for Personal Accident Report Form:
1 Details of injured person – name, job, dept, etc.
2 Details of accident – where, when, treatment given, etc.
3 Description of how accident occurred – leave about 10 lines for this
4 Space for name and signature of person writing the report – also date
5 Witnesses
6 Details of injuries

Assignment 1b   *Writing a notice of a meeting*

As a result of Sebastian's accident, the Office Manager asks you to arrange a meeting with the other workers in your office to discuss ways to improve safety in your office. Write a notice asking those concerned to attend a meeting giving a brief description of what the meeting will be about.

Situation 2

Below is a picture of the office where you work.

(From B Paisley and J Parker, *People at Work*, Pitman, 1980.)

9

Assignment 2a *Listing hazards in the office*

Work in pairs or groups. Discuss and list all the possible hazards shown in the picture.

Assignment 2b *Writing a notice giving rules for safety*

Working in pairs, and using your list from 2a, draw up a notice to be given to all employees on the 'Do's and Don't's' for safety in the office.

Example: Do not put broken glass in wastepaper bins.

Situation 3

Your company does not have a general policy on safety. The Office Manager asks you to give him a report on the number of accidents over the previous year and to make recommendations to improve safety.

Assignment 3 *Writing a memo report*

Use the two passages below to write a memorandum for the Office Manager. Use the information in Passage 1 to present a table of minor accidents in 198–. Use Passage 2 to make your recommendations.

Passage 1

Minor accidents during 198–

In your department, Accounts, there have been five minor accidents during the year. This is not counting Sebastian's, which was the most recent. Two of the accidents were at the beginning of the year, two in May and two in the fourth quarter.

The Sales Department and Personnel each reported two accidents in the first quarter. Personnel didn't report any other accidents during the year, but Sales reported five other minor accidents: two in the second and fourth quarters and one in the third quarter. In fact more accidents occurred in Sales than in any other department.

Purchases had the best record having only one accident in August.

The Production Department had the worst record for accidents in previous years, but in 198– they had only three: one in the first quarter and two in the third.

Administration also improved on previous years with a total of four accidents: two in the second quarter, one in the third and the last was only recently, at the beginning of December.

Passage 2

Health and safety at work

How important are health and safety at work? Is an accident one of those things which happens only to other people? What does the secretary or office worker need to know? It is important for an employee to know the duties of an employer. The employer should ensure safe entrances and exits for the place of work. The working environment should be safe. This means there should be adequate fire precautions; the offices should be kept clean and free from pollution by dust, noise or vibration, etc. Welfare facilities such as first-aid arrangements, wash-rooms and sanitary conveniences are also associated with the working environment.

Any machinery or equipment should be safe. In the office this would refer to equipment such as typewriters, photocopiers, duplicators, etc. There should be warning notices where necessary, the issue of special instructions, and proper arrangements for the storage of flammable materials. Such substances may prove a danger to the office worker through inhalation of a gas or vapour, by accidental swallowing if liquids are inadequately labelled or stored in unmarked bottles, or by fire through careless storage or use. Cleaning solvents and substances such as spirit duplicator fluid may prove dangerous if improperly used.

The employer should provide information about possible hazards in the office or any precautions necessary in connection with their work. This information might also include a copy of the company's safety rules, the procedure to follow in the event of a fire or an accident and the procedures to be followed by which employees can ask questions relating to their health and safety.

Provision must also be made for the appointment of safety representatives from among the employees. Safety representatives should investigate potential hazards in the workplace, investigate reports of unsafe working conditions and inspections of the workplace.

The employee should take reasonable care for his own safety. Someone who lit a cigarette while filling a container with flammable liquid would not be taking reasonable care. An actual accident concerned two girls in an office who were killed within seconds when a can of flammable liquid was knocked over and the vapour ignited.

It has been estimated that over 80 per cent of accidents can be directly attributed to 'human error', and this is why there should be also a heavy emphasis on safety awareness and safety training.

(Adapted from an article by Joyce Stananought, 'Health and Safety at Work', *Memo/2000*, January 1980.)

Situation 4

One of your recommendations to the Office Manager was to provide clear instructions for employees on what to do if there is a fire in the office. He has asked you to make two lists of instructions: one of what to do in case of fire and the other of procedures which must be followed at all times. He has given you his notes to make the lists.

Assignment 4   *Writing clear instructions*

Use the following notes to write clear, numbered instructions in a suitable order for the two lists described above. Give headings.

Keep corridors free. Attack the fire if at all possible. Don't block fire exits with chairs, cupboards, etc. Don't take risks if you think the fire is too big for you to put out yourself. Make sure that fire doors are kept shut at all times. Make sure workers know where the fire exits, fire bells, extinguishers and first-aid cupboards are. There should be no smoking in the duplicating room. If the person who finds the fire can't tackle the fire alone,

the fire bell should be rung. If possible all doors and windows should be closed. Somebody should ring the fire brigade. Don't use the lift. Check that everyone is out of the room. Leave the building by the nearest route and don't come back for any reason until authorised to do so. Make sure the fire exit doors are unlocked during working hours and clear of obstruction.

Situation 5

Three weeks after Sebastian's accident your Office Manager has decided to buy some ready-made signs to increase safety on your floor of the building. He gives you a catalogue of signs and a floor plan of the offices.

Assignment 5   *Making a requisition form*

Use the floor plan and the catalogue (pp 138–9) to decide which signs and how many you would need to order. List the items you choose on a requisition form, which you should design yourself.

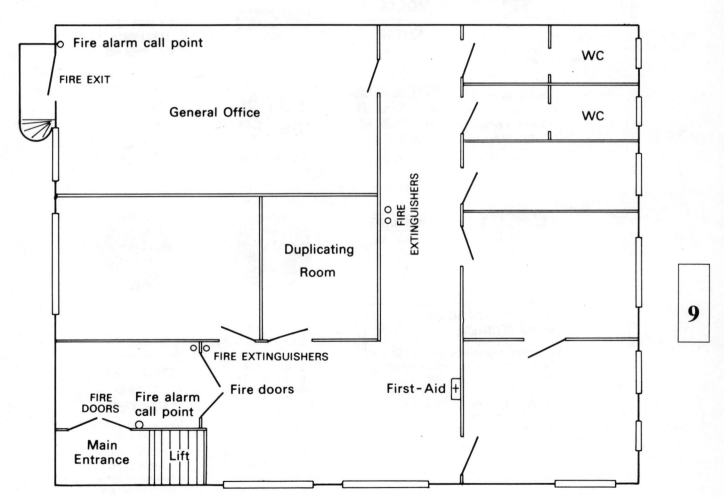

9

FIRE EXIT
5093 G

FIRE EXIT ▶
5095 G

◀ FIRE EXIT
5094 G

EMERGENCY STOP
4247 N

These Goggles are for use with this Grinder only
NOT TO BE TAKEN AWAY
1364 N

IMPORTANT
REPORT ALL ACCIDENTS IMMEDIATELY
1402 NA
3402 N

MASKS MUST BE WORN WHEN WORKING HERE
1361 UH

smoking permitted
1687 Q
3687 Q

FIRE ALARM
4056 G

STRETCHER
1409 D

toxic gas
1652 Q
3652 Q

DANGER 415 VOLTS
4317 N

1001 PK

FIRE EXTINGUISHER
5055 G

FIRE DOOR KEEP CLOSED
1137 H
3137 H

THIS DOOR TO BE KEPT LOCKED SHUT WHEN NOT IN USE
1145 N
3145 N

SMOKING OR NAKED LIGHTS POSITIVELY FORBIDDEN BEYOND THIS POINT
5021 R

PETROLEUM MIXTURE HIGHLY FLAMMABLE NO SMOKING OR NAKED LIGHTS
1010 AR

OUT OF ORDER
1242 NA

MIND THE STEP
1285 D

FIRST AID BOX
1404 D
3404 D

FIRST AID POST
1405 G
3405 G

1346 PK

1347 PK

KEY TO SIGN SIZES & MATERIALS

Enamelled Aluminium—1000 Series
Self Adhesive Vinyl—3000 Series

P - 400×400mm	U - 200×100mm
K - 200×200mm	A - 400×300mm
H - 400×200mm	D - 300×100mm
N - 200×150mm	G - 450×150mm
R - 600×450mm	Q - 300×250mm

Luminous Self Adhesive Vinyl
— 4000 Series

Reflective Aluminium
— 5000 Series

DANGER
LIFT MACHINERY
UNAUTHORISED ACCESS PROHIBITED
DOOR TO BE KEPT LOCKED SHUT
1283 N

DANGER DEEP WATER
1284 R

EMPLOYEES ARE POSITIVELY FORBIDDEN TO RIDE IN THIS LIFT
1273 U
3273 U

EMPLOYEES ARE POSITIVELY FORBIDDEN TO RIDE ON THIS HOIST
1274 UH
3274 U

PRICE-LIST for SIGNS INCORPORATED

Sign	Price	Sign	Price		Price
5093 G	3·05	1409 D	1·20		
5094 G	3·05	1404 D	1·20		
5095 G	3·05	1405 G	1·25		
5055 G	3·05	1364 N	1·15		
5021 R	3·40	1402 N	1·15	A	1·55
		1361 U	1·10	H	1·35
4056 G	2·55	1687 Q	1·40		
4247 N	2·30	1001 P	1·60	K	1·30
4317 N	2·30	1137 H	1·35		
		1652 Q	1·40		
3402 N	1·15	1145 N	1·15		
3404 D	1·25	1010 A	1·55	R	1·75
3405 G	1·35	1241 N	1·15	A	1·55
3687 Q	1·55	1285 D	1·20		
3137 H	1·40	1346 P	1·60	K	1·30
3652 Q	1·55	1347 P	1·60	K	1·30
3145 N	1·15	1283 N	1·15		
3274 U	·95	1284 R	1·75		
3273 U	·95	1273 U	1·10		
		1274 U	1·10	H	1·35

Miscellany

Exercise 1 *Consistent use of pronouns*

One can be used to mean people in general. This use is formal.
You has the same meaning but is used more informally.

If you use *one* or *you*, make sure you keep to the same pronoun. Decide which are the correct pronouns to complete the following:

1 One does not like to have __ position challenged.
2 When travelling by bus, __ cannot be sure that you will arrive on time.
3 I hope you identify __ when answering the telephone.
4 We hope you received our catalogue and look forward to __ order.
5 If one wants a job done, it is better to do it __.

Make sure all the pronouns you use are correct. Choose the correct pronouns to complete the following:

6 The supervisor thanked each girl personally for __ co-operation.
7 Each of the clerks in the office had completed __ work before 1600 hours.
8 Every student had to collect __ report at the end of each term.
9 The company had to increase __ production or would be forced to close.
10 They had only __ to blame for the problems.
11 It was suggested that everyone should complete __ own questionnaire.
12 All the secretaries were asked to collect the mail __ as the mail room was being modernised.

In the following passage, the writer has not paid attention to using pronouns correctly. Find the mistakes and correct them. (Decide whether to use *one* or *you*.) Check that verbs agree.

One cannot be expected to remember a large number of details. Research has shown that your memory cannot cope with many more than eight items at once. The answer for the secretary is to write down what needs to be remembered. Your diary is one of the most important reference books. The secretary must make sure that not only your diary but also that of their employer is kept up to date. Double-booking is an avoidable problem but frequently happens; often you cannot be blamed. To avoid this you should make sure her boss tells her what he is doing daily. It should be a habit for you to check both diaries immediately she arrives at work. If her employer does not check his diary then they should be reminded of their appointments.

Appointments that are tentative can be written in pencil until it is confirmed. Then one must remember to enter it into her employer's diary.

The efficient secretary will check the entries in their diary and cancel it after one has satisfied oneself that the appointment was kept or the necessary action taken. If a matter is left outstanding, she will note them down.

9

Exercise 2   *Proof-reading: word division*

Rules for word division

DO NOT DIVIDE	DIVIDE

DO NOT DIVIDE

a unless absolutely necessary – undivided words are easier to read;

b one-syllable words;

c figures or sums of money;

d abbreviated words;

e proper names;

f the final word on a page;

g leaving two letters at the beginning or end of a line;

h between any two letters which make one sound.

DIVIDE

i between syllables;

j before a suffix;

k between hyphenated words;

l between the same two consonants unless they are at the end of a root word;

m between two different consonants if they are sounded differently.

Give examples of each of the rules where possible.

The passage below is badly typed because too many words have been divided at the ends of lines. Decide which words should not be divided and which words are incorrectly divided. Type or write the passage dividing words at line-ends according to the rules.

Committee procedures and documents

Meetings are such an essential component in the business world that all typists and secretaries should be familiar with the documents used and the proceedures adopted.

Before the meeting the secretary must ensure that a Notice is sent to all those entitled to attend, giving the day, date, time, and place of the meeting. The minimum length of time which must elapse after the notice is sent out and before the meeting is held is stated in the organisation's rules or constitution. For an annual general meeting it is usually twenty-one clear days and seven to fourteen clear days for an ordinary meeting.

An Agenda is a list of items of business to be discussed at a meeting. It is compiled by the secretary in conjunction with the chairman, and is usually combined with the notice of the meeting so that those people attending the meeting have some time to think about the matters to be discussed. Occasionally, it may not be available until the meeting, hence the importance of the notice.

It is the secretary's responsibility to ensure that suitable accommodation is available for the meeting, and to have to hand all the papers and documents which may be required for it. During the meeting the chairman will take the items in the order in which they appear on the agenda. He is responsible for the conduct of the meeting and his decisions must be accepted by all the members present. He sometimes has the casting vote, ie a vote used to make a decision when the votes 'for' and 'against' a motion are equally divided.

After the meeting, the secretary types a draft of the minutes for the chairman's approval before subsequent duplication and distribution to the members.

Minutes, which are an accurate, concise and clear record of the business transacted at a meeting and the decisions arrived at, are approved at the next meeting and signed by the chairman as constituting a true record of the proceedings. They are written in the third person and in the past tense. Their safe keeping is of paramount importance since they provide a permanent record which is available for reference purposes.

(Adapted from an article by Ken Fisher, 'Typing in Block', *Memo/ 2000*, August 1980.)

Exercise 3 _Report writing_

Only short informal reports are dealt with here.

A report is usually divided into three main sections:

1 _Introduction_ – a) This states the reasons for the report (who asked whom to do it).
b) What the report is about.

2 _Findings_ – a) The information asked for. (This may be broken down into suitable headings.)

3 _Conclusion_ – a) Conclusions.
b) Recommendations if asked for.

Remember: a) To give a title
b) To sign it
c) To date it

Reports are impersonal.

Example: ✓ It was found that . . .
✗ I found that . . .

Change the following into impersonal statements:

1 The Sales Manager asked me to report on the work of our Sales Representatives.
2 I really like Robert Lee and he seems to get on well with other people.
3 I noticed that the cord from the electric fire was stretched between the desks.
4 We should like the typists' desks to be 'L shaped'.
5 I attended a public meeting in the Town Hall on 5 October.
6 The Office Manager asked me to investigate the reason for delays in locating files.
7 I found that there would be full-scale distribution throughout the country.
8 You must make sure that each cheque is backed by a cheque guarantee card.
9 I think it would be better to have requisition forms for files and then we would know who had a file.
10 You asked for a report on the furniture and equipment I considered essential.

The following report is mixed up. Sort it out and display the information, putting in a title and headings. Sign it and date it.

11 The new office provides work space for four clerks, two typists and one supervisor. Equipment: 5 chairs, 2 typists' chairs, 1 office table, 7 waste paper bins, 1 two-door cupboard; Furniture: 1 plain paper copier, 1 guillotine, 3 four-drawer filing cabinets, 4 two-drawer desks, 2 'L shaped' desks, 1 three-drawer desk, 1 set of parcel scales, 2 long carriage electric typewriters. On 16 January 198– a memorandum from the General Manager requested a report on the essential furniture and equipment required for the new office which is near completion. As requested the list does not include stationery and minor items. The items listed will be required to make the office a self-contained unit.

Use these examination questions to answer the questions given below:

12 Your school/college has been offered a donation by a charitable trust to improve its library facilities. The trust's own suggestions are that it provides more magazines, periodicals and fiction works for the library or that it donates a photocopier for students' use, which would be placed in the library. As Secretary to the Students' Association you have been asked by the trust to discuss the suggestions with the students. After the discussion you are requested to write a report which outlines _briefly_ the existing library facilities, and which conveys both students' opinions of the trust's suggestions and their own ideas for using the donation in the library. Your report should be informal but should be arranged under suitable headings.
(_RSA_ – Clerical and Secretarial, Stage II, Communication in the Office.)

The best title for the report would be:
_a_ Trust's Donation
_b_ Improvement of Library Facilities
_c_ Students' Association Meeting

13 You are working as a secretary or clerk and you have had a junior assisting you for a year. The Personnel Manager is considering the future of this junior and requests you to write a report on him/her. The employee concerned has not been satisfactory in a number of ways, but you get on well with him/her as a person and you do not wish to cause too much harm to his/her promotion prospects, while at the same time remaining loyal to your employer's interests. Write an appropriate report.
(_RSA_ – Clerical and Secretarial, Stage II, Communication in the Office.)

The most appropriate introduction would be:
_a_ Introduction
In response to a request from the Personnel Manager, a report on the progress of A R Tam's work from July 1980 to July 1981 is given below. The report will form the basis of recommendations for Mr Tam's future role in the company.
_b_ In order to consider the future of Mr Tam, the Personnel Manager would like me to report on him.
_c_ Dear Sir
With reference to your query about Mr Tam, I present below a report on his progress over the last year.

9

14 You have been sent by your firm on a course lasting up to three days. Write a report, describing briefly the content of the course and indicating how your newly-acquired knowledge will be of use to your employer. You may choose any appropriate topic or one of the following suggestions may be used: (a) a course at head office concerning the aims and the structure of the organisation; (b) how to operate a particular advanced piece of equipment; (c) modern secretarial methods; (d) computer applications; (e) business education.

(*RSA* – Clerical and Secretarial, Stage II, Communication in the Office.)

The most appropriate set of headings would be:

a Introduction
　Findings
　Conclusion
b Terms of reference
　Procedure
　Findings
　Conclusions
　Recommendations
c Introduction
　Description of the course
　Application of the course
　Conclusion

15 As Area Manager, write a report to the Sales Manager on the work of your three area sales representatives. One man has achieved an excellent rise in sales though the reason for this increase is not of his making; the second has shown an unexpected increase in sales while the third reflects a worsening situation. Give the likely reasons.

(Adapted from: *PEI* – English for Business Communications, Intermediate.)

The best description of the salesmen's work would be:

a One man has achieved an excellent rise in sales, the second has shown an unexpected increase and the third reflects a worsening situation.
b *Total Sales of Area Representatives*
　R Brown　– $168 500
　J Collins　– $57 000
　K Carlos　– $33 500
c

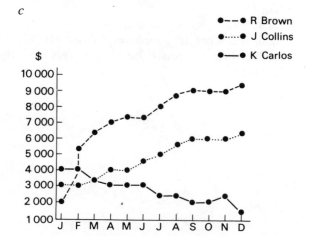

Examination preparation: *Trap words*

Choose the correct word to complete each sentence.

1 Because Miss Lee is __ herself, she expects everyone else to arrive on time. (punctual/punctilious)
2 Even though she lives __ a long way from work, she always manages to arrive before 9 o'clock. (quiet/quite)
3 Miss Lee's first task in the morning is to __ the mail. (sought/sort)
4 She opens all the letters __ those marked 'Confidential'. (accept/except)
5 She then makes a __ reply to each of the letters she can answer without advice from her boss. (draft/draught)
6 Usually letters of complaint which require a __ reply are left for her boss to deal with. (tactful/tactical)
7 With letters of complaint, it is difficult to know the best __ of action, particularly if the complaint is justified. (cause/course)
8 With some letters, Miss Lee does not have __ to the required information to be able to give an answer. (excess/access)
9 __ Miss Lee used to leave all the letters until her boss could deal with them, but now she can answer most letters without consulting her boss. (Formerly/Formally)
10 Her boss leaves letters and instructions on the dictaphone. The only problem is that he tends to __ and she is not always sure what he has said. (utter/mutter)
11 Match each of the words in brackets in the above to one of the following definitions:
　a tried to find
　b a flow of air in an enclosed space
　c in the past
　d having little or no sound or movement
　e an amount which is greater than necessary
　f the right or opportunity to obtain something
　g anything producing an effect
　h following accepted procedures
　i direction to take
　j to say something audibly
　k fairly
　l very careful about small details
　m to separate into groups
　n prompt or arriving at the correct time
　o to speak indistinctly or in a low voice
　p avoiding giving offence
　q using plans to do something
　r something written which may be revised later
　s to take something which is offered
　t apart from

Which of the words in brackets fit the blanks in the following?

12 a) .... describes something well over a thousand years old and b) .... usually means something newer, about one hundred years. We can talk about c) .... Egypt at the time of the pharaohs but not d) .... Egypt. (ancient/antique)

13 a) .... means spoken words and b).......... means using too many unnecessary words. (verbose/verbal)

14 a) .... means to move something to a higher position and b) .... means somebody or something moves up. We can say that the river c) .... every year. (rise/raise)

15 a) .... describes something that is worth so much that its cost cannot be calculated and b) .... describes something that has no value. We can say that skis are c) .... in the Sahara. (valueless/invaluable)

16 If something is a) .... there is not enough to meet the demand but if something is b) .... it is thinly scattered. A population can be c) .... (sparse/scarce)

17 a) .... means the state of having no strength left and b) .... means very thorough. You can say a search was c) .... if you looked in every possible place. (exhaustive/exhausted)

18 a) .... means unreal, existing only in the mind, but b) .... means the ability to think of things not in your experience. If you are frightened of something which is not frightening then your fears are c) .... (imaginative/imaginary)

19 a) .... describes living with others and b) .... describes enjoying being with other people. Someone can live alone and still be c) .... (sociable/social)

20 An a) .... is a cover of paper used to put letters in but to b) .... means to cover something completely. A large coat can c) .... someone. (envelope/envelop)

21 A a) .... is a bed with another bed below or above, but a b) .... is a bed on a ship or a train. (bunk/berth)

9

Unit 10

Waste in the office

Background reading

Read the following passage and then answer the questions underneath. The passage will provide useful information and ideas for the situations and assignments in the rest of this unit.

When the Post Office introduced its considerably increased scale of charges, a new priority suddenly emerged in offices throughout the land: somehow, without damage, to cut down the cost of using the telephone lines. Every system has slack in it somewhere, and the first steps towards tightening look easy enough. Ban all personal calls, and give instructions that all normal business calls be brief, made out of peak hours, and not initiated until the caller has assembled all the facts relevant to the prospective interchange.

The real first step towards the goal of greater economy and/or cost-effectiveness is to master the implications of the tariff. It can be six times dearer to make the same call in the morning as after six in the evening. Although it was direct dialling rates which went up most steeply, there's still a very heavy penalty for using the operator. So a generally applicable rule is – avoid involving the operator if you possibly can.

It's not likely that business will follow the tariff to its logical conclusion and turn afternoon into morning, night into day and weekend into week so that the Post Office is forced to reverse the whole thing. What may be worth while is to get departmental heads to analyse the time pattern of telephone calls made in their zone of responsibility, and so evolve some genuine guidelines for staff. Some types of call can be readily 'batched' for transmission after one o'clock.

'Don't hang on, get them to call back.' Since everyone's staff is being instructed to minimise telephone usage, anyone who knows you need him more than he needs you is going to keep virtuously silent. In telephone-intensive jobs like selling, progress chasing and credit control, this kind of economy will be strictly limited. One simple saving is available to firms with sales or other staff in the field who need to 'ring in' to the office. A fairly high charge is now made to ask the operator to transfer the charges – so the canny thing to do is to make a quick, cheap call to ask the firm to ring you in your call box.

If this cost-conscious vigilance is going to be adopted and sustained it is important to give staff as much support as possible. A new device called Telecost will tell you how much you're spending as well as how long you're taking. Operating normally as a digital clock, it is 'programmed' by a set of small cards each bearing a different charge rate. When the caller looks up a dialling code, he selects the card for the charge rate shown, and presses a button when he makes his connection. The accumulating cost of the call will then be displayed until he presses the button again on replacing the receiver.

If your problem is not so much getting information from one person to another as getting particular people to come and answer their telephone, then you could well save on your telephone bills by installing a pocket paging system. In a department where incoming calls are important, and response is virtually unnecessary, it could be worth eliminating an extension and installing an answering telephone.

At current rates a message sent by telephone can cost as much as three times as the same message sent by telex. So the telex service is well worth serious consideration wherever hard copy confirmation is required – it may well in a comprehensive communications system be much more economic than an explanatory telephone call followed by a confirmatory letter.

(Adapted from a passage in *LCCI*'s Secretarial Studies Certificate Examination, Communications. The passage is adapted from an article that originally appeared in 'Business Systems and Equipment'.)

1 'Somehow, without damage, to cut down the cost of using the telephone lines.' Without damage to what?

2 '. . . the first steps towards tightening look easy enough' (paragraph 1). In your own words, give one 'first step' mentioned by the writer.

3 '. . . there's still a very heavy penalty for using the operator' (paragraph 2). Give an example from later in the passage of a penalty for using the operator.

4 '. . . the implications of the tariff' (paragraph 2). What are the implications of these parts of the tariff?

   a It can be six times dearer to make the same call in the morning as after six in the evening (paragraph 2)

   b A fairly high charge is now made to ask the operator to transfer the charges (paragraph 4)

5 You want to speak to Mr Long but he is on another line. The operator asks you if you would like to wait. What, according to the writer, should you do?

6 Explain in your own words what the Post Office would be forced to do if business followed 'the tariff to its logical conclusion and turn(ed) afternoon into morning, night into day and weekend into week' (paragraph 3).

7 The writer suggests drawing up 'genuine guidelines for staff' (paragraph 3) and mentions one such guideline. Explain in your own words what this guideline is.

8 'Don't hang on, get them to call back' (paragraph 4). The writer mentions several types of work where this would not be possible. Give two types of work mentioned by the writer.

10

9 You make a 12-minute call to a number which has a charge rate of 3·50 cents for two minutes. What two readings will be displayed on the Telecost at the end of your call?

10 At the end of every day your principal customers ring you to tell you how many packets of potato crisps and what flavours they have sold in the day's trading. This enables you to decide how many packets and of what flavour to produce the following day and the different quantities to deliver to these customers at the end of each week. You give no information to these customers when they ring. What, according to the writer, should you consider doing as an economy measure?

Situation 1

Following the receipt of a particularly large telephone bill (see page 148) and a recently-announced increase in telephone charges, it has been decided to hold a staff meeting at Associated Industries Limited. The meeting is to decide on ways of reducing the company's telephone bills in the future.

Assignment 1 *Discussing and noting down ways of economising on the use of the telephone*

There are five people at the meeting:

A B Simon – Secretary to the General Manager
T B Martin – General Manager
B H Moss – Telephonist
S B Roberts – Transport Manager
R A Wells – Office Manager

Work in groups of five and each choose a role (if there are fewer than five people in your group, leave out the role of Transport Manager).

The Office Manager should chair the meeting. Discuss the problem using the information on your briefing sheets (pages 146–7) and any ideas of your own. You should reach agreement on a list of proposals for economising. Note down the points as you will need this information for the next assignment. This role play involves a number of delicate problems because it is known that some people are misusing the company telephone in some way. These problems should all be discussed fully.

Briefing sheet

Secretary to the General Manager:
A B Simon

Your part in the meeting:

1 The Office Manager, who will chair the meeting, will outline the problem briefly.
2 Everyone will be asked to discuss the problem and make suggestions. These suggestions should be discussed one by one and agreement reached on each one. You should make contributions using the information below. You may also use your own ideas.
3 Make a list of the points agreed during the meeting for the next assignment.

Information:

a You think a lot could be gained by getting people to use the phone more responsibly. A lot of people spend more time (and so money) on the phone than they realise – can't they be timed in some way?
b You know that your boss, the General Manager, wastes a lot of time on the phone – insisting on dealing with routine calls you could easily handle, chatting with business colleagues, not thinking of shortening calls, etc.
c You think the company should invest in a telex – telex messages are cheaper than telephone calls and provide a written record.
d You receive some personal calls at work, but you never make outgoing calls. Incoming calls are all right because they do not cost the company money, do they?

Briefing sheet

General Manager: T B Martin

Your part in the meeting:

1 The Office Manager, who will chair the meeting, will outline the problem briefly.
2 Everyone will be asked to discuss the problem and make suggestions. These suggestions should be discussed one by one and agreement reached on each one. You should make contributions using the information below. You may also use your own ideas.
3 Make a list of the points agreed during the meeting for the next assignment.

Information:

a You are appalled at the way in which the telephone bill has risen recently. You are determined that everything possible should be done to cut these bills.
b You have heard of some American companies where there is a 'quiet hour' every day – no internal calls can be made, say, between 9 and 10, and incoming calls are taken by an answering machine. You think this would prevent a lot of interruptions and get people into the habit of writing memos instead of making more expensive internal calls.
c You like the idea of checking on each department to find out which are the real wasters. How can this be done?
d You know that many people make and receive personal calls at work. This must be stopped. How?

Briefing sheet

Telephonist: B H Moss

Your part in the meeting:

1 The Office Manager, who will chair the meeting, will outline the problem briefly.
2 Everyone will be asked to discuss the problem and make suggestions. These suggestions should be discussed one by one and agreement reached on each one. You should make contributions using the information below. You may also use your own ideas.
3 Make a list of the points agreed during the meeting for the next assignment.

Information:

a You know more about the company telephone system than anyone else – you operate it!
b Your job is made more difficult because of the way that people use the telephone system:
— they use you as a telephone directory instead of looking numbers up for themselves.
— customers and other businesses do not know extension numbers when they call; this wastes your time.
— some people are nearly always engaged; you know that many spend a lot of time making and receiving personal calls when you are trying to get them.
— you know that the Transport Manager in particular makes and receives a lot of personal calls.
— everyone comes in at 0900 and immediately starts phoning and so jamming your switchboard – many of these calls could be made later in the day when calls are cheaper.

Briefing sheet

Office Manager: R A Wells

Your part in the meeting:

1 You are to chair this meeting: control the discussion at all times and ensure that agreement is reached on all points.
2 Briefly introduce the problem: the company's telephone bill has roughly doubled in the last year (see the bills on page 148) and a further rise in phone charges has just been announced.
3 Ask for suggestions from those at the meeting and make sure each suggestion is fully discussed and some agreement is reached. You should contribute to this discussion yourself using the information below and ideas of your own.
4 Make sure everyone makes notes on the decisions reached.

Information:

a You think there should be a total ban on personal calls. How can this be achieved without upsetting people?
b The telephonist has complained to you that the job is becoming increasingly difficult – can ways be found of reducing pressure on the switchboard? At present all calls, incoming and outgoing, must go through the switchboard.
c You are fairly sure that the General Manager's secretary makes personal calls at work.
d Some employees spend a lot of time chatting on the internal phone, particularly to the telephonist.
e Telephone calls are cheaper before 0900 hours. Could everyone start work at 0830 and so make their calls at a cheaper rate?

Briefing sheet

Transport Manager: S B Roberts

Your part in the meeting:

1 The Office Manager, who will chair the meeting, will outline the problem briefly.
2 Everyone will be asked to discuss the problem and make suggestions. These suggestions should be discussed one by one and agreement reached on each one. You should make contributions using the information on the right. You may also use your own ideas.
3 Make a list of the points agreed during the meeting for the next assignment.

Information:

a You receive quite a lot of personal calls from your friends and family; this doesn't matter because it costs the company nothing and anyway, many of your friends do not have telephones.
b You *do* make quite a lot of personal calls from your office, but you do this when no one else is there and so no one knows about it.
c You think the telephonist is very inefficient: you often need to get hold of customers and contractors first thing in the morning and the telephonist seems to take ages to get your numbers for you.
d You think the telephonist must spend a lot of time chatting to friends on the phone – no one can check up on a telephonist!

10

Situation 2

The results of the meeting in the previous section have to be circulated to all staff to inform them of the measures to be taken to reduce the company's telephone bills in the future.

Assignment 2   *Summarising in report form decisions reached at a meeting*

Under the heading, 'Economy in the use of the telephone', draw up a list of all the measures agreed on at the meeting to reduce the company's telephone bill. Set your list out in the form of a memorandum addressed to all employees whose work involves the use of the telephone. Use a date in August and the name and position you took in the meeting in the previous section.

(Based on a question in *LCCI* – Secretarial Studies Certificate Examination, Communications.)

Situation 3

As part of the exercise to economise on telephone expenditure, it has been decided to ask the Post Office/telephone company to check that your recent bill is correct.

Assignment 3a   *Writing a letter querying a telephone bill*

Write to the telephone company about your latest bill, explaining that it is very much higher than had been expected. Ask them to look into the situation and check that a mistake has not been made.

The bills will provide you with relevant information: the bill on the right is the latest one, and the bill on the left is the one for the same period last year. Use the name and position you assumed in Assignment 2 and a similar date.

Assignment 3b   *Writing a letter of reply*

Write a letter of reply from an Accounts Clerk at the telephone company to the letter written in Assignment 3a. Put the information below in a suitable order and include it in your letter, appropriately worded. Use your own name and a likely date.

— ask the customer to settle the bill as soon as possible
— explain that the units shown on the telephone bill are recorded on a meter; there is one meter for every telephone number
— the meters are very simple and reliable
— introduce your letter by referring to the customer's letter
— the meter connected to the customer's telephone line has been checked and no fault found
— customers often underestimate their telephone bills
— you cannot accept the customer's estimate instead of the reading shown on the meter
— the telephone company has introduced a service offering suggestions to firms regarding unauthorised use of company telephones by employees; this service is available on a different extension (give an extension number)

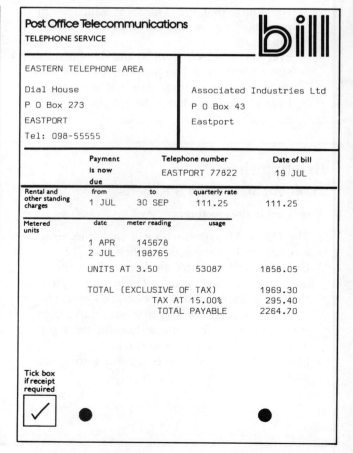

Miscellany

Exercise 1 *Making suggestions*

Suggestions are more tactful and more polite than commands: the listener may ask for a suggestion but does not have to take the advice given. There are many ways of expressing suggestions. Which of the statements below are *commands* and which are *suggestions*?

1 I suggest we go home as soon as possible.
2 Go home immediately!
3 How about going home now?
4 You ought to go home soon.
5 What about going home soon?
6 It may be worth going home soon.
7 You must go home now.
8 You are to go home immediately.
9 We'd better go home now.
10 Why don't we go home now?

Use the table to make suggestions in answer to the queries. The first one has been done for you as an example.

11 *a* All the o's on the stencil are blocked. What should I do?
   b I suggest you *clean the typeface on your typewriter*.

12 *a* The correction fluid hasn't covered the mistake completely. Any suggestions?
   b Why don't you . . .
13 *a* The copies are patchy. What shall I do?
   b You'd better . . .
14 *a* My typewriter is old and it's difficult to get good copies from stencils typed on it – the letter o's, a's, etc are often blocked. Can I do anything about it?
   b You could try . . .
15 *a* The correction fluid is too thick and the ink won't come through. What can I do?
   b It may be worth . . .
16 *a* The ink isn't dry on one sheet before the next one comes through the machine – I get ink from one sheet all over the next one. Got any ideas?
   b What about . . .
17 *a* Some of the characters, especially the o's and c's, have their centres cut out. What can I do?
   b You could try . . .
18 *a* The margins are unequal – there's a wide one on the left and hardly anything on the right.
   b If . . . then . . .
19 *a* I forgot to correct an error – one word has been typed twice. Can I do anything about it?
   b You could . . .
20 *a* The words I've retyped look much blacker than the rest of the stencil. What can I do about it?
   b You'd better . . .

STENCIL DUPLICATING – Problem-solving tips

Problem	Probable cause	Solution
Blocked characters	dirty typewriter typeface	Clean the typewriter typeface
	excessively worn typeface	Run the duplicator more slowly to obtain more heavily-inked copies
Visible corrections	error not completely covered with correction fluid	Strip the stencil back and apply more fluid to cover the error
	excess correction fluid	Place a piece of scrap paper behind the correction and run a finger across the area several times
	excess keystroke pressure applied when correcting error	Cover with correction fluid and retype using normal pressure
Uncorrected errors	poor proof-reading	Strip stencil back and apply correction fluid
Cut-out letters	keys struck too hard or machine impression lever set too high	Use a gentler stroke when typing; lower the impression setting
Smudged copies	newly-run sheets dropped into the receiving tray before the ink has dried on previous sheets	Use an ink that is quicker drying or slow down the speed of the duplicating machine
Light spots	inadequate inking	Release additional ink on the ink pad
Unequal margins	paper stacked off-centre or stencil typed off-centre	Move the paper in the feed tray to the left or right

(By permission. From Webster's Secretarial Handbook © 1976 by G. & C. Merriam Co., Publishers of the Merriam-Webster Dictionaries.)

10

Exercise 2 *Motions and resolutions*

Resolutions at formal meetings pass through the following stages:

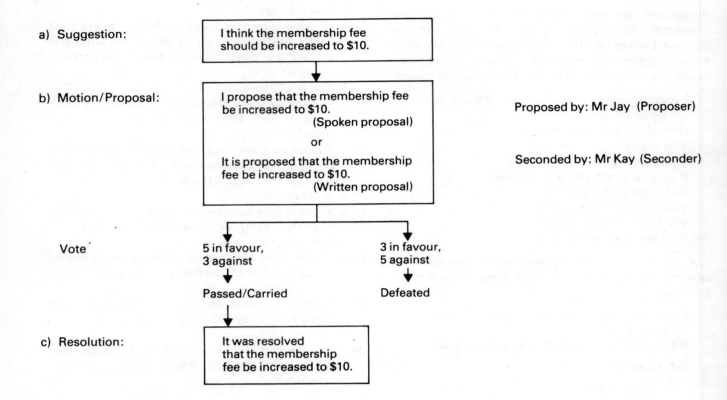

a) Suggestion: | I think the membership fee should be increased to $10.

b) Motion/Proposal: | I propose that the membership fee be increased to $10. (Spoken proposal) or It is proposed that the membership fee be increased to $10. (Written proposal)

Proposed by: Mr Jay (Proposer)

Seconded by: Mr Kay (Seconder)

Vote | 5 in favour, 3 against | 3 in favour, 5 against

Passed/Carried | Defeated

c) Resolution: | It was resolved that the membership fee be increased to $10.

As can be seen from the diagram, there are three stages through which decisions pass. The second and third stages (*motion* and *resolution*) have rather formal ways of being worded:

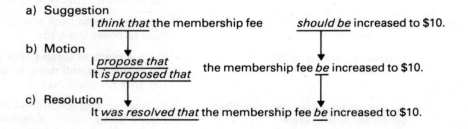

a) Suggestion
I *think that* the membership fee   *should be* increased to $10.

b) Motion
I *propose that*
It *is proposed that*   the membership fee *be* increased to $10.

c) Resolution
It *was resolved that* the membership fee *be* increased to $10.

Convert the following *suggestions* into a) motions and b) resolutions. Make sure that they are appropriately worded.
1 I suggest that the minutes should be taken as read.
2 I suggest that the Society should buy a safe.
3 I suggest that Mr Dee should be asked to resign as treasurer.
4 I think that Mrs Gee should be invited to become the new treasurer.
5 How about holding a Christmas Party on 22 December?

Exercise 3 *Minutes*

There is a range of different ways to record minutes of meetings. We may distinguish three types to illustrate this range, although in practice different elements of the three may be combined to produce what is required:

Verbatim transcript	Narrative minutes	Resolution minutes
Mr Wood: I think we should wait until next year before buying new machinery.	Mr Wood suggested that investment in new machinery should be postponed until the following year. Mrs Green disagreed. Mrs Green proposed the motion (subsequently carried) that . . .	4 PURCHASE OF NEW MACHINERY It was resolved that new machinery be purchased as soon as possible.
Mrs Green: Nonsense! That's a crazy idea! If we don't buy now . . .		

Verbatim transcripts are uncommon, except in records of court proceedings and Parliamentary debates (Hansard). The most common records of business meetings are *narrative minutes* and *resolution minutes*.

Decide which of the following statements apply to *narrative minutes* and which to *resolution minutes*.

1 They provide a record of the discussion at the meeting.
2 They give the names of members who stated particular views, proposed certain motions, etc.
3 They are brief.
4 They include no irrelevant material.
5 They record only motions that are carried.
6 They record only the decisions reached at the meeting and none of the discussion.
7 Disagreements at the meeting are not recorded.
8 You cannot see who said what.
9 The secretary cannot distort the record of the meeting as only the agreed wording of the resolutions is recorded.
10 Some members prefer them because they can see their own names written down in the minutes.

Use the dialogue below to write two sets of minutes: a) *narrative minutes* and b) *resolution minutes*. Make use of the following headings when writing both sets of minutes:

*Minutes of meeting of . . . at . . . on . . .
*Present
*Apologies for absence
*Minutes of last meeting
*Matters arising
 (Heading for each item on the agenda/resolution)
*Any other business
*Date of next meeting
(*These headings should be used whenever you are writing minutes.)

The dialogue is taken from the meeting of the Arts Society, which met at 7.30 on Monday, 1 March 198– in the Society's headquarters.

Mrs Dean (Chairman): Good evening, everyone. It's 7.30 and everybody seems to be here so let's get on with the meeting. I've received apologies for absence from Mr Armstrong – he's on holiday this week. Can we have the minutes of the last meeting please, Mr Lewis?

Mr Lewis (Secretary): Yes . . .

Miss Evans: I propose that the minutes be taken as read and signed as a true record.

Mrs Dean: Will someone second Miss Evans' motion? Mr Williams? Thank you. Those for? Motion passed unanimously. Now, any matters arising? Nothing? Good, let's move on to the next item on the agenda: the co-opting of a new member. Any nominations?

Miss Lee: I'd like to suggest Miss Read . . .

Mr Hawksworth: Oh no, not that woman. We asked her to help out last year and she hummed and hawed and finally said she couldn't.

Miss Lee: That was because she was handling a new project at the time and was under a lot of pressure. I've spoken to her and she says she has more time now and would like to join the Committee.

Mrs Dean: Miss Read has been nominated by Miss Lee. Is her nomination seconded?

Mr Fox (Treasurer): I'll second that.

Mrs Dean: Any other nominations? No. Then let's vote on Miss Read. Those for? Five. Against? Two. Motion carried. Miss Read is co-opted. Next item: a speaker for the Society's dinner in August. Any ideas?

Mr Hawksworth: How about the Mayor?

Mrs Sampson: What about a government minister?

Miss Lee: That's a bit risky: they get called away to meetings at the last minute.

Mr Lewis: I've heard that the new Chief Planning Officer at the City Council is very interesting and amusing.

Mrs Dean: We've had several suggestions. Can I have a motion? Do we have a seconder for Mr Hawksworth's proposal to invite the Mayor? Miss Evans? Thank you. Those in favour of the Mayor? Two? Those against? Five. Motion defeated. Do I have anyone to second Mrs Sampson's suggestion of a minister? No? Then we'll go on to Mr Lewis's idea of the Chief Planning Officer. Seconder? Miss Lee. Can we vote, please? Those for? Five. Those against? Two. Motion passed, five to two. Can we move on to Any Other Business? Nothing? Right, when shall we meet again? The first of the month as usual? All agreed. Right – that's the first of April, 7.30 in the Society headquarters again. Thank you. Good night, everyone.

10

Examination preparation: *Vocabulary questions*

There are several kinds of examination vocabulary questions requiring answers 'in your own words'. This can mean slightly different things in different types of question.

Replacing single words

The main problem is ensuring that you have the correct meaning of the word that is to be replaced.

Example:
When the Post Office introduced its new *scale* of charges . . .
    Does *scale* mean:
a a device for weighing things
b one of the stiff pieces forming the outer skin of a fish
c a film of solid chemicals covering a surface
d a set of numbers for measuring
e a set of prices for charging
f a proportion (especially in map making)
g a set of musical notes
h to climb up something

Choose the appropriate meaning: *e.* The sentence can then be rewritten in your own words:
When the Post Office introduced its new *set of prices for charging* . . .

Rewrite the following sentences, replacing the italicised word with a word or phrase of your own. (All the sentences are taken from the passage on page 145.)

1 When the Post Office introduced its considerably increased scale of charges, a new *priority* emerged in offices throughout the land. (paragraph 1)
2 . . . business calls . . . (should) not (be) *initiated* until the caller has assembled all the facts . . . (paragraph 1)
3 . . . the *canny* thing to do is to make a quick, cheap call to ask the firm to ring you in your call box. (paragraph 4)
4 If this cost-conscious *vigilance* is going to be adopted . . . (paragraph 5)
5 The telex . . . may well in a *comprehensive* communications system be more economic than an explanatory telephone call followed by confirmatory letter. (paragraph 7)

Explaining phrases (1)

Example:
Ban all *personal calls* . . .
The whole passage is about telephone *calls*, so it is *personal* which must be replaced with your own words. We might write:
Ban all calls *which concern private rather than company business* . . .

Which *one word* in the following phrases from the passage requires explanation? Explain each phrase in your own words.

6 Every system has slack in it somewhere. (paragraph 1)
7 peak hours (paragraph 1)
8 zone of responsibility (paragraph 3)
9 'batched' for transmission (paragraph 3)
10 telephone-intensive jobs (paragraph 4)
11 digital clock (paragraph 5)
12 pocket paging system (paragraph 6)
13 incoming calls (paragraph 6)
14 current rates (paragraph 7)
15 confirmatory letter (paragraph 7)

Explaining phrases (2)

Other phrases, however, have meanings which are greater than the sum of their parts.

Example:
cost-effectiveness (paragraph 2)
cost = price paid
effectiveness = the quality of producing results
cost-effectiveness = the quality of producing adequate results in relation to the price paid

The problem, then, is not only to be able to define the parts, but to see how the parts are related to each other. Explain each of these phrases from the passage in your own words.

16 prospective interchange (paragraph 1)
17 direct dialling (paragraph 2)
18 credit control (paragraph 4)
19 charge rate (paragraph 5)
20 hard copy confirmation (paragraph 7)

Unit 11

The Film Society meeting

Situation 1

At the last meeting of your college's Film Society, you were co-opted as Secretary. Your name is H Chan. You took the minutes at that meeting. Having drafted the minutes in narrative form, you asked the Chairman to check them for you. He read through them and told you that you had written them correctly as all previous minutes had been presented in narrative form; however the committee had been considering changing to resolution minutes. He explained that a lot of time was wasted in meetings arguing over who had or hadn't said something and whether what someone said was minuted. You and the Chairman discuss this and decide that as you had just taken over as Secretary it would be a good time to change to resolution minutes.

Assignment 1a   *Writing resolution minutes*

Below is part of the narrative minutes you drafted initially. Change them into resolution minutes.

Meeting of the Community College Film Society held on Monday 4 June 198- in the Students' Common Room at 1730 hours

Present: S Best, Chairman
            H Chan, Secretary
            H Bernard, Treasurer
            C Ortiz
            J Boodram

1   Apologies for absence

    Apologies were received from M Farnum, Vice-Chairman, and N Birch.

2   Minutes of last meeting

    The minutes of the last meeting, which had previously been circulated, were taken as read and signed by the Chairman as a correct record of the meeting.

3   Matters arising

    The Chairman asked if the Commerce Department had supplied the catalogue as discussed in Item 6. C Ortiz said that he had passed the catalogue on to the Secretary.

4   Secretary

    The Chairman reported that W Rudolfo had resigned as Secretary to the Club because she was nearing the end of her course and her time was taken up with studying for her final examinations. The Chairman read out her letter of resignation. She wished the Film Society success in the future and thanked the Committee for their co-operation. The Chairman proposed that a letter of thanks and best wishes should be sent to Miss Rudolfo. This was seconded by C Ortiz.

11

5 Appointment of new Secretary

J Boodram proposed that H Chan take over as Secretary as she was in the Commerce Department in the second term of her secretarial course. She had access to a typewriter and could practise her shorthand and typing in doing the minutes. This was seconded by H Bernard. H Chan agreed to undertake the job and to take the minutes for that meeting.

6 Attendance at the last film show

The film, The Rich the Poor and the Ugly, was shown on 25 May 198-. The Chairman reported that the attendance was very low for this film although it was thought to be a popular one. He asked the Treasurer how much the hiring charges were for this film. The Treasurer reported that the film was expensive to hire, £50. The Film Society had planned to share the expense with the University who had agreed to show the film on a different night. Unfortunately they had not been able to do this as the projector had been already booked by the Diving Club. The film had to be returned the following day otherwise the Society would have been charged for sending the film back late. This meant that the Film Society had to bear the full cost of hiring.

J Boodram stated that the posters advertising the film went up only one day before the showing. She proposed that the posters should be distributed at least one week in advance. This was seconded by C Ortiz.

The Secretary pointed out that one of the reasons for the low attendance might have been that there had been a disco at the Technical College on the same night. The Secretary proposed that future dates for showing of films should not coincide with any other events that members might wish to attend. This was seconded by H Bernard.

Assignment 1b *Writing a letter of thanks*

As Secretary to the Film Society, write a letter of thanks to W Rudolfo for giving her time to the job of Secretary to the Society. Wish her luck in her examinations. Invent any details you require.

Situation 2

You and the Chairman of the Film Society discuss the next meeting. You have the following conversation:

Chairman: Right. We'd better get the notice out for the next Committee meeting. This will be the last before the holidays unless we decide to have another after the examinations. I hope not. Anyway what did we decide under Date of Next Meeting?

Secretary: Let me see. Yes. We decided on Monday 16 June at the same time and in the same place as the last meeting. It's really good that we can use the Common Room. Still it's not used very much anyway – well not at that time of day.

Chairman: Has anyone sent you items for the agenda? The Commerce Department have asked us if we can show educational films in the evening. They don't have the time during class hours. We'll have to discuss it. There could be problems.

Secretary: Oh, yes. I was given the catalogue at the last meeting. I was talking to my shorthand teacher about it. The Department would leave it to us to choose which films we would like to have and we would order them through the Film Society.

The other item we ought to put on the agenda is the question of membership fees. If you remember we didn't have time to discuss this at the last meeting.

Chairman: Yes, we'll have to sort that one out. I think that's about all apart from the usual items. Anything else can be brought up under Any Other Business. You can send the Notice of the meeting and the Agenda at the same time. Did everyone get a copy of the minutes?

Secretary: They should have. I sent them over a week ago. I'll get the Notice and Agenda done in my lunch break tomorrow. Do you want to check them before I get copies made?

Chairman: No. I'm sure I can leave it to you.

Assignment 2 *Writing an agenda and a notice for a meeting*

Write the Notice and the Agenda for the next meeting of the Film Society. How many copies will you need to make of each?

Situation 3

At the next meeting there are two main items on the agenda on which decisions have to be made: the proposal that films should be shown for the Commerce Department and the membership fees.

Assignment 3 *Holding a meeting*

Work in groups of five and imagine you are members of the Film Society Committee having their next meeting. Decide who is:

a) Chairman   S Best
b) Treasurer   H Bernard
c) Secretary   H Chan
d) Committee Member   C Ortiz
e) Committee Member   J Boodram

If the class does not divide exactly into groups of five, those left should join one of the other groups to make six on the committee. The sixth person will be S Murray, another Committee Member.

Prepare your role using the following briefing sheets:

Briefing sheet   *Chairman:* S Best

You must control the meeting.

1 Open the meeting.
2 Ask if there are any apologies for absence.
3 Ask if everyone received a copy of the minutes for the last meeting.
4 Ask if you can sign the minutes as a correct record of the meeting.
5 Ask if there are any matters arising from the meeting. If anyone does not like the new style of minutes explain that it was your decision because they are shorter and clearer and save unnecessary arguments as well as being easier for the Secretary.
6 Ask the Committee for their views on hiring and showing films for the Commerce Department. Reach agreement on what should be done. If necessary take a vote to arrive at a resolution.
7 Ask the Committee for their views on membership fees. Decide whether there will be a change of policy on membership and whether the fees will be increased. At the moment members pay $5 each per annum giving free entry to any films shown.
8 Ask if there is any other business.
9 Agree on the time and date of the next meeting.
10 Thank the Committee and close the meeting.

Briefing sheet   *Treasurer:* H Bernard

Matters arising
1 You don't like the new style of minutes. You would like to go back to narrative minutes. You think narrative minutes are better because:
   a) people see their names in the minutes and this encourages them to take part in the meeting;
   b) if anyone disagrees with a decision this can be shown.

Films for the Commerce Department
2 You don't think the Film Society should hire and show films for the Commerce Department. At the moment the Society still owes $27 for the last film. To break even on educational films there would have to be an entrance fee and this would have to be fairly high to cover the costs. Also, not all Commerce Department students would come, especially if they have to pay quite a lot to get in.

Membership
3 You think the Society should no longer have a membership fee. This involves the extra cost of having membership cards printed. You think that there should be a new policy of charging an entrance fee of 60 cents for anyone who wants to come and see a film.

Next meeting
4 You can come to the Society's meetings only on Mondays as this is your free night. You are free on Fridays but this is when the Society shows its films.

Briefing sheet   *Secretary:* H Chan

Apologies for absence
1 Report that you have received apologies from N Birch and H Farnum.

Matters arising
2 Report to the Committee that you have sent a letter of thanks to the former Secretary, W Rudolfo.
3 If anyone objects to the new style of minutes, explain that resolution minutes are easier to take than narrative minutes. Point out that your shorthand speed is not good enough yet to take narrative minutes.

Films for the Commerce Department
4 You think it would be a good idea to show films for the Commerce Department. Suggest that the problem of paying for the hire of the films could be solved by asking the Commerce Department to pay 50 per cent of the costs. Tell the Committee that you have looked at the catalogue of educational films and the most expensive is $45 to hire. There are 86 people in the Commerce Department and if the Society charged an entrance fee the cost of the film could be covered.

Membership
5 You think that films should be open to members and non-members. Everyone should pay to see the film but non-members should pay more. You suggest the Society should charge 25 cents entrance to non-members and 15 for members.

11

Briefing sheet

Committee member: C Ortiz

Films for the Commerce Department
1 You think it is a good idea to show educational films. You suggest that the films could be shown on the same night as the Society's films. The educational film could be shown before the main film and posters could show when each film started so that members could come for the main film if they didn't want to see the educational film.

Membership
2 You think the Society should keep the membership fee at $5. Although there is going to be an increase in grants, everything else is going up, particularly the price of books. If the membership fee is raised then you would lose members and be no better off financially. Your idea is to open membership to the Technical College and the University to increase the number of members. At the moment membership is restricted to students at the Community College.

Next meeting
3 The Society's meetings have always been held on Mondays. This is no longer convenient for you as next term you are starting an evening class which is held on Mondays. Your class finishes at 2200 hours. Ask if the day of the meeting could be changed.

Briefing sheet

Committee member: J Boodram

Apologies for absence
1 You bring to the Committee's attention that N Birch has not attended the last four meetings. You do not think someone should be a committee member unless they are prepared to attend meetings. You propose that a letter should be sent to Mr Birch asking if he would still like to serve on the Committee.

Films for the Commerce Department
2 You agree with the Treasurer that the problem of showing films for the Commerce Department is one of finance. You think it can be solved. You don't think an entrance fee should be charged for an educational film. You suggest that the Commerce Department should be asked to pay the hiring charges and the Film Society could do all the administration, ie the ordering, the showing, the advertising, etc.

Membership
3 You think that the membership policy should remain as it is, but that the fee should be increased to $6 as from next term. You know that student grants are being increased at the beginning of the term.
4 You have made enquiries in the Commerce Department and they are prepared to run off membership cards as part of their office practice assignments. This means the Society could get the cards free.

Note: This sheet will not be used if there are five in your group.

Briefing sheet

Matters arising
1 You think resolution minutes are a good idea as it is much easier to see what has been decided.

Films for the Commerce Department
2 You don't think the Film Society should show educational films. You say that the Commerce Department should make time on the timetable for films as this would ensure that all students saw them. If the Society did this for the Commerce Department then other departments would expect the same service. In the end the Society would have to employ a secretary to do all the administration.

Committee member: S Murray

Membership
3 You think that the membership fee is already too expensive. Your opinion is that the Society should concentrate on really popular films to attract more members.
4 You think the films are not advertised adequately. You suggest that posters should be displayed well in advance of the showing of a film. You also propose that more posters should be put up around the college. At present only two posters are put up. The Principal's permission would have to be obtained to put up more posters.

Situation 4

The Commerce Department has agreed to cover the hiring cost of six films as long as the total does not exceed $240. They ask you, as Secretary of the Film Society, to choose the films from the catalogue you were given. They have supplied a list of the subjects covered in the Department. The subjects are arranged according to the number of hours each has on the timetable; the subject with the most number of hours is first:

Typewriting
Shorthand
Commercial English
Office Practice
Secretarial Procedures
Commerce
Book-keeping
Liberal Studies

Assignment 4a *Designing and completing an order form*

Draw up a short list of six films of definite interest to the Commerce Department. Make sure the hiring fees do not exceed $240 in total. Design an appropriate order form for Aria Films Limited and complete the form using the films you have chosen. Aria Films Limited also supply posters at $1·00 for ten.

Assignment 4b *Writing a letter of enquiry*

Write a letter to accompany your order enquiring about the films in the catalogue which *could* be of interest to the Commerce Department. Ask for further information about the subject matter and the level of audience the films are designed for.

Educational Films
Aria Films Ltd
PO Box 493
Bridgetown
Barbados

Catalogue No	Title of Film	Purchase Price	Rental Price 2 days	Rental Price 7 days
D 419	The Balance Sheet	345·00	45·00	55·00
E 768	Dictation – What the Boss Needs to Know	280·00	40·00	50·00
E 682	Statistics	110·00	20·00	25·00
F 925	Public Speaking	230·00	35·00	45·00
F 823	Handling Customers	230·00	40·00	50·00
S 213	Selling Techniques	280·00	40·00	50·00
T 310	Meetings – The Chairman	345·00	45·00	55·00
T 710	The Secretary and her Boss	280·00	40·00	50·00
T 639	How to Interview	345·00	45·00	55·00
T 320	Safety in the Office	280·00	40·00	50·00
T 390	Word Processors	325·00	45·00	55·00
T 365	Telephonist at Work	340·00	45·00	55·00
E 367	Reception Duties	110·00	20·00	25·00
C 879	From Producer to Consumer	280·00	40·00	50·00
C 237	International Trade	230·00	35·00	45·00

11

Miscellany

Exercise 1 *Word division*

Among the rules for word division are:

A. Divide before a suffix;
B. Divide between two consonants which are the same unless they are the end of a root word;
C. Avoid leaving two letters either at the beginning or the end of a line.

Note: All the rules are set out on page 140.

Make three columns to illustrate the above rules.

Example:

A	B	C
regret-ted	disap-pointed	essential

All the following words have double consonants. Decide which column each word should be put in. Some words can be put in more than one column. Put a hyphen where you would divide each word.

1 referred		*16* grammar
2 possesses		*17* appearance
3 accommodate		*18* immigrate
4 beautifully		*19* woollen
5 especially		*20* paralleled
6 slippery		*21* accessible
7 programming		*22* immediately
8 colleague		*23* planning
9 irrelevant		*24* intelligence
10 arrangement		*25* appropriate
11 omitted		*26* installation
12 necessary		*27* unnecessary
13 spelling		*28* occasionally
14 embarrassment		*29* successfully
15 addresses		*30* erroneous

Exercise 2 *Appropriateness*

Written communication in business can be formal or informal. Write the following list with the most formal at the top. (Some will be at the same level.)

1 Quotation
2 Minutes
3 Request for advice/information from a colleague
4 Letter of apology
5 Report
6 Letter of resignation
7 Letter confirming an order
8 Memo
9 Telephone message
10 Sales letter
11 Letter to well-known customer one is friendly with
12 Circular letter
13 Notice for staff notice board
14 Letter accepting a post

Write the following list beginning with the most appropriate for its purpose:

15 *a* Please do not smoke.
   b Visitors to these premises are asked to refrain from smoking.
   c No smoking.

Rewrite each of the following to be more suitable for its purpose:

16 If you see a fire, try and put it out yourself and if you cannot, ring this fire bell.
17 We are in receipt of your letter of the 15 inst for which we are most grateful.
18 We have taken cognisance of the fact that the remuneration is in excess of your normal fee.
19 If you want to make an external call rather than an internal call, then it is necessary to dial 9 and then dial the number you want, first checking you have got a dialling tone after dialling 9 otherwise you will not get through.
20 It is with extreme regret that I have to communicate that I am not in a position to accept the post you have so kindly offered.

Slang and informal expressions are inappropriate in business. Rewrite the following to make it more businesslike:

21

```
Dear Sir

We got your letter all right.It doesn't look like you remember
the letter we sent.

We've had a bit of a discussion about your idea and we don't think
it's really on to have a go at marketing the SLIV in Malawi.  The
kids there are not into computer games.

You may have better luck in the Far East but my guess is that
those markets are already sewn up.

We're real sorry we can't be a bit more positive.

Keep in touch.

Yours faithfully
```

Complaints must be appropriate. Be polite. There is nothing to gain in making people angry when you want action.
Which is the best way to complain?

22 You are waiting for an important order which has not arrived.
   a This delay is causing us financial loss.
   b I don't know why you cannot keep your promise.
   c Cancel our order.

23 A customer has not settled his account. This is the first reminder.
   a You had better pay up or we shall not be able to deal with you in future.
   b We cannot imagine why you have not paid yet; perhaps it is an oversight on your part. We humbly request payment as soon as you find it convenient.
   c May we remind you that your payment is overdue by two months.

24 You are asked to pay a bill you have already paid.
   a I advise you to sack your accounts clerk because I paid this bill some time ago. Somebody must either be very inefficient or a thief.
   b The amount you request was paid on 12 November.
   c I am surprised at this mistake; the bill has been paid!

25 Some of your employees spend too long on the phone.
   a As you know the phone is an expensive means of communication. I should be grateful if you would ask yourself these questions before you phone:
      1 Do I need to phone or would a letter do instead?
      2 Do I know exactly what I want to say?
      3 Can the call wait until it can be made within the cheap period?
   Thank you for your co-operation.
   b You all spend too long on the telephone. You are paid to work, not chat. If anyone is reported chatting on the phone, there will be serious consequences.
   c Do not use the phone more than is necessary.

26 You have ordered goods from a catalogue. When the goods arrive, they do not match the description in the catalogue.
   a Your goods are no good.
   b Your catalogue is written wrongly.
   c Unfortunately, the description in the catalogue led us to expect goods of a different quality.

27 Write the following letter of complaint:
From the Accounts Department Manager of Townsend & Bratby, 34 Midland Road, Rugby, to Coles Laminates, Highfields Road, Bedford, advising them that their account is now very much overdue and a payment is imperative. This is the second reminder on this matter.
(*PEI* – English for Business Communications, Intermediate.)

11

Exercise 3 *Prediction and proof-reading*

Divide the following under two headings: *Proof-reading* and *Normal reading:*

a Read each word.
b Miss words out.
c Notice the spelling.
d Find information.
e Notice the grammar.
f Notice the typing or print.
g Match the information to what we already know.
h Notice the punctuation.

When reading normally we do not read every word because we can *predict* what comes next.
What comes next in the following?

1 What's the __?
2 Would you close the door, __?
3 Would you like a cup of __?
4 Do not park __.
5 Smoking is bad for your __.
__ The teleprinter keyboard is a simplified typewriter __.
7 Look it up in the Post Office __.
8 Draw a rectangle the size of a post __.
9 Answer all __.
10 If you are told to write in ink, it means you should not use a __.

Read the questions below and use the passage on *Postal Codes* to answer them. Do this as quickly as possible.

11 Should a postal code be at the end or the beginning of an address?
12 Should a code be punctuated?
13 How many spaces should there be between the two parts of a code?
14 What should be typed beneath the code on envelopes?
15 Should the code be typed on the same line as the town?

Typing Postal Codes
1 Always place code at the end of the address as the last.
2 Always type the in the code in capitals.
3 Never type punctuation anywhere in the code.
4 Never underline the code
5 Type the code in line by itself when possible. Always leave one space between the parts of the code.
7 Never type anything below the code on envelope.

There are 10 items missing from the above text, but you should have been able to answer the questions without them.

Put these items in the text:

a an	*d* item	*h* two
b .	*e* marks	*i* 6
c ever	*f* on	*j* the
	g letters	

The following texts have been poorly copied. Use your prediction skills to complete them:

A

Rules for the Receptionist
1. Learn the name of the caller, the name of his (her company, and the purpose of the call.
2. Be pleasant and courteous, but firm. Make you callers feel welcome. Maintain an air (business-like efficiency.
3. Classify all callers:
   a) callers your employer will be glad to see
   b) callers your employer does not wish to se(
   c) callers whose needs can be better taken ca: of in another department
   d) callers you can look after yourself.
4. Always say "Good morning" or "How do y(do." Never say "Hello."
5. Go forward to meet a caller. Never shout acro the room.
6. Your personal appearance is important. Be su your grooming is above reproach.

B

ïps for a Successful Secretary
:eep on a card file the names, addresses, and usiness titles of persons or firms to which you ddress letters frequently.
nclude telephone numbers in your card file if ou have occasion to phone certain companies ·equently.
f you are responsible for a mailing list keep it on ndex cards. Changes can be made more easily nd quickly on these cards than on a typed list.
Jever use more than one card for each entry in a 1ailing list. All lists should be kept in alphabetic ·rder and revised frequently.
Ilways maintain a pleasant business-like attitude vhen dealing with the public. A slightly formal ttitude is an advantage when dealing with trangers.
·ry to give callers the impression that you are villing to assist them if possible.
Jever reply to rudeness with rudeness, or to nger with anger. The cool-headed, calm person ;ets things done and maintains good will.

C

Transcription Tips

1. Organize your materials before you begin ar arrange them for ease and efficiency.
2. Use your dictionary to check spelling and wor division.
3. Use a good reference book to check your gram mar.
4. Verify:
   a) names and addresses
   b) dates and figures
   c) any doubtful items.
5. Whenever possible, avoid dividing words.
6. Never leave a single line of a paragraph at th bottom of the page. Always type at least two line – three are preferable.
7. Proofread all work before you remove it from th typewriter.
8. Concentrate on your work. Be determined t produce the best quality work at all times.

D

Efficient Typing Skils

1. Do the important letters first. Check your work for important or rush items. Put these items on top and do them as soon as possible.
2. Check your supplies before starting work. Do you have sufficient letterhead paper, carbon paper, copy paper, and envelopes? Do you have an eraser?
3. Arrange all material conveniently in a logical and orderly manner or maximum efficiency.
4. Scan each letter for poblems – spelling of proper names and difficult words, grammatical constructions, facts to be checked and verified.
5. Solve your placemet problems for letters and tabulation before you begin.
6. Know the number o carbon copies to be typed before you type anyhing.
7. Proofread everythin!

Examination preparation: *Parts of speech*

In the puzzle below, the answers are correct but the clues are not in the correct part of speech.

Match each answer with a clue and rewrite the clue.

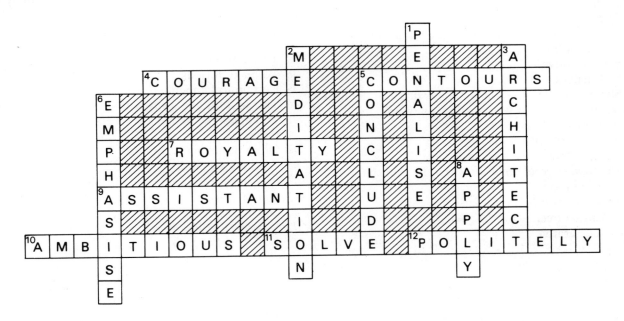

Example: 4 across is COURAGE. The clue should be *bravery* not *brave*.

a Think deeply
b Answer to a problem
c Summing-up, last part
d Line on a map, showing ground of the same height
e Punishment for breaking a rule
f Science of building

g Supporter of monarchy
h Courteous
i Brave
j Request for employment
k To help
l A stress or importance attached to something
m A strong desire for success

11

Choose the correct word from the choices given to replace the italicised words. If the word is a verb, make sure you add the correct ending if necessary.

13 Freda liked to do all kinds of work, so she *offered* to collect the money for coffee and tea each month.
   a volunteered
   b voluntarily
   c voluntary

14 To break the *lack of variety* in her job, she often did the filing for the other secretaries.
   a monotony
   b monotonous
   c monotonously

15 If her boss was in an important meeting, she would ask callers *in a courteous manner* to call back or leave a message.
   a polite
   b politeness
   c politely

16 She could deal with insistent callers with *the least amount* of fuss.
   a minimise
   b minimum
   c minimal

17 She wanted to *put in a request* for a transfer to the General Office where there was a varied workload.
   a application
   b applicant
   c apply

18 The General Office had a typing pool where the supervisor had to *share out* the work as it came in.
   a distribution
   b distributive
   c distribute

19 She hoped the situation would *get better* in the near future as her boss was starting a new job.
   a improve
   b improvement
   c improving

20 She *went beyond the truth* when she said she would die of boredom.
   a exaggeration
   b exaggerated
   c exaggerative

21 She really didn't want to *give up* working for her boss however much she complained.
   a abandonment
   b abandon
   c abandoned

22 She had been able to keep up her shorthand speeds particularly as her boss often *took charge at* meetings.
   a chairman
   b chairmanship
   c chaired

Some of the definitions below are followed by the wrong part of speech. Correct those that are wrong.

23 Perfect for the purpose — Ideally
24 Meet to try to reach an agreement — Negotiate
25 Not open to the public — Privately
26 Punishment for breaking a rule — Penalise *Penalty*
27 To obtain — Acquire
28 Newspaper writer — Journalism *t*
29 Can be clearly seen — Visibility *Visible*
30 Person who translates languages — Interpreter
31 Someone who sells goods — Retail *er*
32 From the east — Orient *al*
33 Able to handle situations without giving offence — Tact *ful*
34 Free from germs — Sterile
35 Able to be carried — Portable
36 Having no limits — Infinitely *Infinite*

Find one word which means the same as each of the following. The first letter is given.

37 To question a prisoner thoroughly — I *nterrogate*
38 To make furious — E *nrage*
39 Certain to happen — I *nevitable*
40 The act of doing away with — A *bandon*
41 To appoint someone as representative — D *elegate*
42 Often occurring, common — F *requent*
43 Working together — C *ollaborate*
44 Preconceived opinion, unfair bias — P *rejudiced*
45 Out of work — U *nemployed*
46 Outside surface — E *xterior*

(*PEI* – English for Office Skills.)

162

Unit 12

Flexitime

Background reading

Flexible working hours (or flexitime) is a system which allows employees to start and finish work when they choose, provided that:
a) they start and finish within times laid down by the company;
b) they are at work during a 'core time' (eg 10.30 am to 4 pm) when everyone is expected to be present;
c) they work an agreed total of hours every week.

The following article introduces the topic of flexitime. It has been divided into two parts: Part I gives an introduction and a conclusion, and mentions five problems which can be encountered when introducing flexitime systems; Part II gives solutions to the five problems. Match the solutions to the problems to construct the complete text.

KEEPING FLEXIBLE HOURS UNDER CONTROL

Part I

Introduction
Soon, management insisting on fixed hours will be considered old fashioned. Flexible working is here to stay and in this article I want to talk both to those who have not yet gone over to flexible hours (but no doubt will soon do so) and those who have done so but are finding some problems in keeping the situation under control.

In my opinion flexible hours should improve the lot of the staff and the running of the office. According to a market research survey of personnel managers, over 70 per cent have studied flexible hours in detail yet are waiting for staff to take the initiative. From my experience there are clear reasons why management is still reluctant to acknowledge flexible hours as the fundamental change in our working lives which I believe it to be.

1 Essential control
First – and way above the rest – is the fear of being unable to control people's movements. Certainly if flexible working is introduced with some slapdash pencil and paper method of keeping a check on everyone's hours worked then management is asking for trouble and, with unreliable characters in every society, they will get it. The first necessary ingredient of every flexible hours scheme is to keep an accurate, foolproof check on the number of hours people have worked over the month – and see that the other negotiated rules are respected.

This is as much for employee's benefit as anything else. There is nothing worse in an office than mutual suspicion between staff that others are cheating the system and getting away with it. The result is a lowering of enthusiasm for the job and a polluted atmosphere from which your best workers will soon wish to depart for pastures new.

2 Cost
Right after this worry of uncontrolled staff movement comes the problem of the cost of operating the scheme.

3 Supervision
The next problem to be overcome – and it is one which can genuinely persist if not realised for what it is – is the supervision of people on flexible working.

4 Communications
Leading on from this, however, is the matter of internal communications. Outside the core periods, people cannot be sure of contacting a colleague. I restricted my remark to 'internal' communications since, usually, outside callers can find an alternative person to help them provided supervisors sensibly insist that staff arrange adequate telephone cover at all necessary times.

5 Will the work be done?
Incidentally, I touched just now on another problem that is often raised – that of staff going home when there is still a heap of work to be done.

Conclusion
I cannot guarantee that a properly run flexible hours scheme will improve your office efficiency by leaps and bounds. Nor can I guarantee that if your present flexible hours scheme is a shambles, introducing a proper control system will cure it overnight. But if, like 99 per cent of industry and commerce, your management and staff get along pretty well together – the odd domestic tiff perhaps but nothing more – then flexible working hours offer an improved standard of life for the working day and a happier, more adaptable workforce as a result.

12

a I found that after a brief initial spell of difficulty, communications actually improve. Telephone calls or visits around the office tend to be restricted to the core periods, leaving the flexible periods free for more concentrated individual work. The day's planning, in fact, changes a little but the result is more orderly communications patterns.

b Right from the first day of the trial scheme, a control system should be used. This does not mean going back on to the clock. In fact clock cards are not the best method since they record actual times of arrivals and departures – contrary to the spirit of flexible hours. Electronic systems allow people to check in and out quickly with an ordinary key or identity card which they keep with them for security. Only the number of hours and minutes *worked* is recorded, not their actual times of arrival, although if they arrive after the start of core time, the fact is shown on the check-in unit.

c I find management tend to over-estimate the problem.

Manual control of a flexible hours scheme can cost eighteen minutes per person per four week period to administer. The comparable time for an electronic system is just over one minute.

In all, flexible working costs little to operate compared with the benefits it is possible to reap for both staff and management.

d I find that persuading staff to stay on willingly to finish a job is much easier for management when the staff know that every minute they spend can be taken off later. Staff who can see a peak coming, will plan ahead to stay late, working with a minimum lunch break to overcome it, knowing that, now, they are masters of their own time and effort. In short, staff respond with a more responsible attitude to their work.

Conversely, staff find a great benefit from being able to go home early if work permits without going 'cap in hand' to the boss to ask permission. As a reinstatement of human dignity that has more going for it than many managers may realise.

e Most organisations agree that the effect on supervision is similar to that at, say, lunch times or during supervisors' holidays. If the supervisor is good at the job, then work will have been set, people will know their targets and general duties and will work with those objectives in view.

In virtually all cases I have studied, staff do not react to flexible hours by arriving and leaving at all manner of odd times. They, in fact, keep more or less to their old fixed times – arriving and leaving a little earlier if anything – and keep the flexibility for emergencies such as peak workload or the wife's birthday (or a girl friend's birthday). Supervision just is not taxed enough to make the problem a serious one.

(Adapted from an article by Maurice Reynolds 'Keeping flexible hours under control', *Memo/2000*, July 1980.)

Situation 1

The company that you work for, Deans Toys Limited, hopes to introduce a system of flexible working hours. It has been decided to find out what company employees think of such a system – whether they are in favour and how they think such a system should operate. The questionnaire opposite has been drawn up to test their opinions.

Assignment 1a *Administering a questionnaire*

Administer the questionnaire to as large a group of 'employees' as possible, asking them to imagine that they work at Deans Toys Limited. They should imagine that Deans Toys' factory is situated where the college is and they are living where they live at present when working at this 'factory'. Either give the questionnaire to every member of the class or work in groups and ask students from other classes to complete it.

Assignment 1b *Collating the results of a questionnaire*

Work as a class to collate the results of all the questionnaires on the chalkboard. Go through the questionnaire question by question to find out the most popular answers to each one.

Assignment 1c *Summarising the results of a questionnaire*

Write a memo report to the Personnel Manager summarising the results of the questionnaire. Use the normal headings on a memo form.

STAFF QUESTIONNAIRE

The company hopes to introduce a system of flexible working hours in the near future. Please answer the following questions relating to a flexitime system.

1　Are you in favour of a flexitime system?　　　　yes ☐　no ☐

2　What is the earliest time that you could possibly start work?　　..............................

3　What time would you normally *expect* to start work if a flexitime system were introduced?　　..............................

4　Would it be impossible for you to start work earlier than 0900 hrs?　　yes ☐　no ☐

5　What is the latest time that you could possibly finish work?　　..............................

6　What time would you normally *expect* to finish work if a flexitime system were introduced?　　..............................

7　Would it be impossible for you to finish work later than 1700 hrs?　　yes ☐　no ☐

8　Would you be prepared to work overtime if necessary?　　yes ☐　no ☐

9　A 'core time' of six hours a day is proposed. During this time all staff would be expected to be at work. Which times would suit you best?

Starting at: ....

Finishing at: ....

10　When do you normally take your lunch hour?　　From .... to ....

11　Which of the following ideas do you like best (tick one)?
　　a)　One hour when all employees would take lunch.　☐
　　b)　A two-hour period during which all staff would take one hour for lunch.　☐
　　c)　Freedom to take your hour for lunch at any time.　☐

12　Any other suggestions? (Please write on reverse.)

Situation 2

Deans Toys Limited has reached the decision, in principle, to go ahead with the introduction of a flexitime system. A meeting is to be held to work out the details of the system to ensure that its introduction is as smooth as possible.

Work in groups of three. Each member of the group should take one of the following roles:

P J Vernon, Personnel Manager
C B Collett, General Manager
G J Churchward, Union Representative

Agree among yourselves who will play each role. If there are one or two members of the class left over, they should join other groups and express their own views as representatives of the staff.

Assignment 2 *Negotiating and reaching decisions within a meeting*

Hold the meeting within your groups and reach agreement on the details of the system. The Personnel Manager will chair the meeting and list the points which need to be agreed. All decisions should take account of the results of the survey carried out among the employees. Study the Briefing Sheet for your role (pages 166–7) and use it to help you participate fully in the discussion. Make notes on all the decisions reached at the meeting.

12

Briefing sheet

Personnel Manager: P J Vernon

The introduction of the new flexitime system will be your responsibility and you are anxious to have the agreement of the management and unions before it is started.

Your part in the meeting:

1 You are in the chair at this meeting. Welcome and introduce the two other members to the meeting and explain what has to be done.
2 Try to reach agreement on the following points:
   — Should the system be introduced?
   — If so, when?
   — What should the hours of the 'core time' be?
   — What should the hours of flexible working be?
   — What arrangements should be made for lunch?
   — Should this be introduced for a trial period?
   (Use the information on the right to present your own arguments.)
3 Ask the other members if they have any problems or doubts about the system. Discuss these.

Information:

a Ensure that you make full use of the article on page 163 and the results of the survey.
b All employees will be expected to work a total of 40 hours each week, as at present. Extra hours will be paid as overtime.
c You think a 'core time' of six hours from 1000 to 1600 would be best, but agreement from the other members is the most important thing.
d You favour a two-hour lunch period, with all employees taking one hour off.
e You have looked at the Flexiplan electronic control system – it is cheap, simple to install and operate, and reliable. All employees have their own plastic keys which they insert into the control every time they arrive at or leave work. The system records only the *total* number of hours worked per week, not the actual times of arrival and departure.
f You favour the introduction of the system as a permanent one – the cost and upheaval do not justify a trial period.

Briefing sheet

General Manager: C B Collett

You have overall responsibility for the production and day-to-day running of the factory. Although all personnel matters are the responsibility of the Personnel Manager, you have taken a keen interest in this scheme as you are anxious to see that production is maintained.

Your part in the meeting:

1 The Personnel Manager (who will chair this meeting) will welcome you and introduce the topics for discussion.
2 The Personnel Manager will lead a point-by-point discussion on the following topics:
   — Should the system be introduced?
   — If so, when?
   — What should the hours of the 'core time' be?
   — What should the hours of flexible working be?
   — What arrangements should be made for lunch?
   — Should this be introduced for a trial period?
   (Use the information on the right to present your own arguments.)
3 Bring up any problems or doubts about the system that you have and ensure that they are dealt with satisfactorily.

Information:

a You are basically opposed to the introduction of the system and want supervision to be as tight as possible.
b You are afraid that this is a way of reducing the 40-hour week. Check.
c You would like all employees to clock in and clock out, with the times of arrival and departure stamped on their time cards.
d You would like the 'core time' to include as much of the working day as possible.
e You would like everyone to have to start work at 0900 as at present.
f You suggest that everyone selects the eight hours they want to work and then work those same eight hours every day.
g You suggest a trial period of three months to see if production falls.
h What will happen if supervisors work different hours from other workers?
i What if there is a rush job? Will employees work late to finish it?

Briefing sheet   *Union Representative:* G J Churchward

It is your job to ensure that employees' interests are looked after when decisions are taken by the company.

Your part in the meeting:

1 The Personnel Manager (who will chair this meeting) will welcome you and introduce the topics for discussion.

2 The Personnel Manager will lead a point-by-point discussion on the following topics:
— Should the system be introduced?
— If so, when?
— What should the hours of the 'core time' be?
— What should the hours of flexible working be?
— What arrangements should be made for lunch?
— Should this be introduced for a trial period?
(Use the information on the right to present your own arguments.)

3 Bring up any problems or doubts about the system that you have and ensure that they are dealt with satisfactorily.

Information:

a You are generally in favour of the flexitime system but are worried that the management will use it as an excuse to reduce employees' other benefits.

b Will the longer working day be a way of extending the 40-hour week?

c What about overtime payments if people work longer than 40 hours?

d You refuse to accept clocking in and clocking out. Your union managed to have it abolished five years ago.

e You suggest a short 'core time' – perhaps 1000 to 1400.

f You think employees should have complete freedom of choice outside the core time – they should be able to work whenever it suits them and to change their hours from day to day.

g You suggest a trial period of six months and then another survey.

h Look at the results of the survey and ensure that employees' wishes are carried out as far as possible.

Situation 3

After consultations between management and employees it has been agreed that Deans Toys Limited will introduce a system of flexible working hours. An information leaflet, setting out the full details of the operation of the scheme, will be sent to every employee.

Assignment 3a   *Writing an information leaflet*

Using the notes you took in Assignment 2 on the details of the introduction and operation of the scheme, write a short leaflet which can be sent to each employee explaining the flexitime system.

Assignment 3b   *Writing a circular letter*

The information leaflet has now been duplicated and a copy of this is to be sent to all employees together with their plastic keys (for use in the time clock) and a covering letter reminding them of the essential features of the scheme and the date upon which it will come into operation. Compose the covering letter which the Personnel Manager will send to Mr John Gooch, a clerk in the Export Department. Your letter should include a 'tear-off' portion on which the employee can acknowledge receipt of the information leaflet and his plastic key.

12

Miscellany

Exercise 1 *Pronouns (4) – Substitution*

There are many ways of writing sentences more economically and avoiding repetition. Rewrite the sentences below using the word(s) in brackets after each. *Note:* Join all sentences marked with +.

Example: John walked into the room. + John switched on the light. (he)
John walked into the room and *he* switched on the light.

1 A man came round the corner driving a fast car just as Valerie was stepping into the road. The car hit Valerie but the driver didn't stop – the driver just drove on. (he, her, it)

2 John was late for work. + Carol was late for work. (both)

3 John and Carol were late for work. John and Carol's boss told John and Carol that John and Carol were late too often but John and Carol said that it wasn't John and Carol's fault. (they, them, their)

4 Where are the envelopes? I need another envelope. (one)

5 Which envelopes do you want? There are some brown envelopes and a white envelope. (one, ones)

6 Do you want an electric typewriter? No, I would prefer a manual typewriter. (one)

7 Mark and Claire applied for the same job. Mark is being interviewed on Thursday. + Claire is being interviewed on Thursday. (each)

8 Mark, Claire and Jenny applied for the same job. Mark is being interviewed on Thursday. + Claire is being interviewed on Thursday. + Jenny is being interviewed on Thursday. (all)

9 Mark did not get the job. + Claire did not get the job. (neither, nor)

10 Mark did not get the job. Claire did not get the job. (neither)

11 Mark, Claire and Jenny applied for the same job. Mark did not get the job. + Claire did not get the job. + Jenny did not get the job. (none, it)

12 John left early to go to an evening class. Carol left early to go to an evening class. (the same)

13 John left at 4 o'clock. I told him at 4 o'clock that I would be late in tomorrow. (then)

14 Look in the cupboard outside. You'll find the envelopes in the cupboard outside. (there)

15 John works for TPI. Carol works for TPI. (so does)

16 John works for TPI. Carol works for TPI. (do too)

17 John went to an evening class on Wednesday. John went to an evening class on Monday. (he, one, too)

18 Should I retype the whole letter?
Yes, please retype all of the letter. (it)

19 John was late for work. Carol was late for work. (too)

20 Carol sold her typewriter.
Why did Carol sell her typewriter? (she, do, that)

21 Do you think it will rain this afternoon?
I hope it won't rain this afternoon. (not)

22 How do you know that Joan is leaving?
I heard Joan say that Joan is leaving. (her, so)

23 I went to see my mother. + My mother lives in Zaria. (who)

24 Registered post and recorded delivery are both methods of sending valuable items through the post. Registered post entitles the sender to compensation if the item is lost. Recorded delivery provides proof that the item has actually been delivered. (the former, the latter)

25 Oil-based ink is more suitable than water-based ink. (–)

It can be irritating and time-wasting to discover that a file or folder that you need has been removed from its place in the filing cabinet and you have to search all over the office to find it. One way of avoiding this problem is to use 'absent cards'. These are left in the cabinet when a file or folder is removed. The card shows who borrowed the file and when. Anyone else needing the file can quickly trace it.

Use the absent cards to complete each of the sentences below. Fill in the blanks with the correct information and *rewrite the sentences using words of substitution to avoid any repetition.*

26 Mr Bose borrowed file number 154 on 15 February and returned file number 154 on __.

27 Mr Luckham has borrowed file number 167 recently. Miss __ has borrowed file 167 recently.

28 Miss Abrams borrowed file __ on 1 March and Miss Abrams returned file __ on 1 March.

29 I borrowed file __ this morning. Now I need another file.
   Certainly, Mrs Rose. Which file do you need?

30 Mr Loy took file __ on 7 March and returned the files he took on __.

31 Miss Seaton borrowed file number __ on 26 February. Mr Stanford borrowed file __ on 26 February.

32 Miss Seaton borrowed file number __ on 26 February. Miss Sankar borrowed file 134 on __.

33 Mrs Lee wanted file 135 on 5 March. She couldn't find file 135 because Mr __ had file 135.

34 On 27 February Mr Sankar looked in the cabinet for file 134 but file 134 was not in the cabinet. Mr Sankar looked again on __ and found that file 134 was in the cabinet and so Mr Sankar was able to borrow file 134.

35 Mrs Lee borrowed file __ on 28 February and returned file __ on 28 February.

36 Mrs Lee borrowed file __ on 28 February. Miss Low borrowed file __ on 28 February.

37 On 1 March Mrs Fung wanted file 179 and so Mrs Fung went to see __. __ had file 179.

38 Mr Persaud has got file __ at the moment. It says Mr Persaud has got file __ on the absent card.

39 Mr Loy borrowed two files on 4 March and Mr Park borrowed __ files.

40 Mr Park borrowed __ files on 4 March. Mr Park has not returned the files yet.

ABSENT

Date Taken	Folder No or Name	Taken By	Date Returned
4 MAR	121	D. LOY	7 MAR

ABSENT

Date Taken	Folder No or Name	Taken By	Date Returned
4 MAR	167	P. LUCKHAM	6 MAR

ABSENT

Date Taken	Folder No or Name	Taken By	Date Returned
1 MAR	182	S. ABRAMS	1 MAR
7 MAR	111	H. ROSE	

ABSENT

Date Taken	Folder No or Name	Taken By	Date Returned
15 FEB	154	D. BOSE	18 FEB
1 MAR	167	P. MUNROE	2 MAR
7 MAR	143	D. LOY	

ABSENT

Date Taken	Folder No or Name	Taken By	Date Returned
28 FEB	179	R. LEE	28 FEB

ABSENT

Date Taken	Folder No or Name	Taken By	Date Returned
26 FEB	134	D. SEATON	26 FEB
4 MAR	101	T. PARK	

ABSENT

Date Taken	Folder No or Name	Taken By	Date Returned
4 MAR	197	T. PARK	

ABSENT

Date Taken	Folder No or Name	Taken By	Date Returned
28 FEB	179	E. LOW	2 MAR
3 MAR	184	S. PERSAUD	

ABSENT

Date Taken	Folder No or Name	Taken By	Date Returned
26 FEB	134	R. STANFORD	28 FEB
1 MAR	134	A. SANKAR	3 MAR
4 MAR	135	D. LOY	7 MAR

ABSENT

Date Taken	Folder No or Name	Taken By	Date Returned
4 MAR	119	T. PARK	

12

Exercise 2 *Preparing telephone calls*

Use the following transcript of a telephone call to make a list of do's and don't's to help you make more effective telephone calls. You should find one point in each exchange. The exchanges have been numbered and the first one has been done as an example.

1 Caller: Hello. Is that 45918? Brown and Bridges?
  Voice: Well, yes it is 45918 but this isn't Brown and Bridges.

→ | **check the number before you dial** |

2 Caller: Try again. 4-9-5-1-8. (He dials again.)
  Telephonist: Good morning. Brown and Bridges.
  Caller: Oh . . . good . . .good . . .
3 Telephonist: Can I help you?
  Caller: Yes, I'd like to speak to Mrs Kay, please.
  Telephonist: I'm afraid we don't have a Mrs Kay working here.
  Caller: Oh, no . . . well maybe it should be Mrs Jay.
4 Telephonist: Just a minute – I'll check her extension number. . . . Right, I'm putting you through now.
5 Mrs Jay: Good morning. Sales Department, Mrs Jay speaking.
  Caller: Hello, Penny.
  Mrs Jay: Who's calling please?
6 Caller: It's Jack here.
  Mrs Jay: Jack? I'm sorry, I . . .
  Caller: You remember – Jack Gee.
7 Mrs Jay: Ah, yes, of course. What can I do for you, Mr Gee?
  Caller: Well, we'd like to know how you're getting on with our . . .
  Mrs Jay: I'm sorry, Mr Gee, but who is it you work for?
  Caller: Coleman and Parker. You remember.
8 Mrs Jay: Of course. Now, what were you saying?
  Caller: Well, we were wondering how you were getting on with them?
  Mrs Jay: 'With them'? What exactly are you referring to, Mr Gee?
9 Caller: You know, our order.
  Mrs Jay: Which order did you have in mind? We do a lot of business with you. Can you give me a reference?
10 Caller: Oh, yes. Hang on, I'll get the file. . . . Here it is: P3-4971657342XT.
11 Mrs Jay: Slow down. What was that again? P3-497 . . .?
  Caller: P3 - 497 - 165 - 734 - 2XT.
12 Mrs Jay: Got it. Just a minute, please, while I check on that. . . . Right, sorry to keep you waiting. The order's being made up this morning and will be ready for despatch later this afternoon. If you need it urgently, we can arrange to deliver it today, but it wouldn't be until after six o'clock.

  Caller: Oh, I don't know about that. I'm not sure if it's urgent. Hang around and I'll check with Mr Dee. . . .
13   . . . Right, I've asked him and he says we'd like it today and we'll arrange for someone to be at the warehouse until eight.
  Mrs Jay: Good. I'll see that that's arranged. Now, I have a note here saying that we have some goods to pick up from your warehouse. There are two crates . . .
  Caller: . . . Hold on. Let me get a pencil and paper. Right, go ahead.
14 Mrs Jay: Right. Two crates of light bulbs, four cartons of angle brackets and 15 packages of heavy-duty fuses.
  Caller: I've got that. [See message form underneath.]

TELEPHONE MESSAGE

To: Mr Dee
From: Mrs Jay, Brown and Bridges

Brown and Bridges' driver will collect the following this evening when he makes our delivery: 2 crates light bulbs
  4 ctns angle brackets
  50 packages h-d fuses

Message taken by: J Gee
Date: 24 May 198-   Time: 11.05

---

15 Caller: How are the kids?
  Mrs Jay: Oh, they're fine.
16 Caller: Good. Well, that's all I think. Oh, no, hang on a second, there is something else. I've got a note here somewhere. . . . Now, where is it?
17   . . . Yes, we need your new price-list. You did send one before but I think I lent it to someone down the corridor and she gave it to Jenny in the Accounts Department and she left it on her desk and it had gone next morning so maybe the cleaner threw it away by mistake or perhaps . . .
18 Mrs Jay: Don't worry, I'll send another one across with the driver. Now, let me just confirm . . .
  Caller: It's all right, I've got everything and I'll pass the message on to Mr Dee. Thanks. Goodbye.
  Mrs Jay: Goodbye. Please call again if you have any queries.

Exercise 3 *Composing forms and questionnaires*

If you were composing a form or questionnaire, how would you ask the following questions?

Example: What is your full name?
  → Name (in full)................................

1 Where do you live?
2 When were you born?
3 If I want to phone you, what should I dial?
4 Are you a man or a woman?
5 What kind of work do you do?
6 Put today's date in this space:
7 Sign your name here:
8 Where were you born?
9 When did you buy this item?
10 State here the total amount of money you are enclosing.

In recent years a lot of research has been carried out into the wording and layout of forms and question-naires. On the right is a list of suggested rules for writing questions. On the left is a list of questions and statements which break these rules. Match each example to the rule it breaks and then rewrite each example following the rule.

11 Monthly emoluments: ....

12 Title (please tick)
    Mr   ☐
    Mrs   ☐
    Miss   ☐

13 Do not complete this section if your car is not more than three years old.

14 Are you a bona fide visitor to this country?

15 Address: ....

16 Give your surname and all first/forenames in full, stating whether Mr/Mrs/Miss or other title.

16 ADDRESS
    STREET ....
    TOWN ....
    COUNTY/REGION ....
    COUNTRY ....

18 Sex: Male/Female (delete which is not applicable)

19 If examinations have been taken in the past three years, details should be given in the space below.

20 Are you under 65 and over 18?

a Do not ask questions with two parts: it is better to ask two separate questions.

b Avoid negative questions (double negatives are even more difficult to understand).

c Avoid passive verbs – active verbs are easier to understand.

d Use familiar words.

e Do not use foreign words or phrases.

f Ask questions needing a positive reply.

g Arrange boxes for answers immediately after questions – do not justify down the right hand side of the column.

h Do not use capitals throughout a question – lower-case letters are easier to follow.

i Make questions short.

j Leave sufficient space for people to write their answers.

12

Rewrite the following questionnaire, improving the
questions according to the rules suggested.

EMPLOYEE PROGRESS REPORT

PERSONAL DETAILS Employee's full name (give surname first)....

MR/MRS/MISS (delete which is not applicable)

What is the title of the job that the employee does?

Give the name of the department in which the employee works

....

Date on which the employee was first given a job with this

company ....

When was the employee given her/his present job?

Salary (per annum) ....

RATING

What is the employee's quality of work like? ....

What about personality and ability to cooperate with other

workers? GOOD/SATISFACTORY/POOR

Personal appearance   POOR/SATISFACTORY/GOOD

Attendance and punctuality EXCELLENT/FAIR

OVERALL
EVALUATION

How does the employee's overall performance compare with others

doing similar work?

unsatisfactory

average

above average

outstanding

EVALUATOR

What's your name? ....

Post?

Department ..... Sign here .....   Date .....

Examination preparation: *The examiner's point of view*

A is an examination question
B is a model answer.
C is a student's answer.
Decide where the candidate has lost marks.

Example:

A Rewrite the following sentence, correcting grammatical errors but otherwise changing the words as little as possible.
I am unable to find proof that either of the accounts have been settled. (2 marks)

B I am unable to find proof that either of the accounts has been settled.

C *I am unable find proof that either of the account has been settled.* ......①..

The candidate got one mark for identifying the error but lost one mark for copying the sentence incorrectly.

Now do the same with the following deciding exactly where each candidate lost marks:

1

A Punctuate the following where and if necessary, supplying any capital letters needed:
youre in trouble today samuel said the teacher (7 marks)

B 'You're in trouble today, Samuel,' said the teacher.

C *"You're in trouble today samuel," said the teacher.* ......③..

2

A There are 10 errors in the typescript below. Identify each error by putting a ring round it.

envelopes

When typing a foriegn address, the typist should referr to the return address

onthe envelope of previous correspondence to get the correct order of the

the essential elements in the adress The Letterhead of previous corresponence

can also be checked. (10 marks)

B Envelopes

When typing a foreign address, the typist should refer to the return address on

the envelope of previous correspondence to get the correct order of the essen-

tial elements in the address. The letterhead of previous correspondence can also

be checked.

C (envelopes

When typing a (foriegn) address, the typist should refe(rr) to the return address

on(the envelope of previous correspondence to get the correct order of the

(the) essential elements in the (adress The (Letterh)ead of previous (corresponence)

can also be checked.   (6-2=4)

12

3

A The sentences below each contain one error. Ring the error. In the space provided, write in the correction. (2 marks)

    a) Neither of the films were very amusing. ....

    b) I only arrived yesterday and I feel as though I have been here for weeks.

                                                              ....

B a) Neither of the films (were) very amusing. ....was...............

    b) I (only arrived) yesterday and I feel as though I have been here for weeks.

                                 ....only yesterday............

C a) Neither of the films (were) very amusing. ....

    b) I (only) (arrived) yesterday and I feel as though I have been here for weeks.

                                          ....

                                                                          (0)

4

A Which word on the right is nearest in meaning to the word on the left? Underline only ONE word from each group. (2 marks)

a) commercial	financial commuting mercantile travelling	B a) commercial	financial commuting <u>mercantile</u> travelling	C a) commercial	<u>financial</u> commuting <u>mercantile</u> travelling
b) flexible	electrical adaptable breakable insulated	b) flexible	electrical <u>adaptable</u> breakable insulated	b) flexible	electrical ✓ adaptable breakable insulated (0)

5

A Write in the space the ONE word that is defined.
   a) to obtain
   b) newspaper writer .... (2 marks)

B a) to obtain   acquire
   b) newspaper writer journalist

C a) to obtain   *aquire*
   b) newspaper writer *journalism* (0)

Is your handwriting legible? Work in pairs.
A: Copy out the nonsense words in list A.
B: Copy out the words in list B.

A		B	
1	mmitetoce	*1*	sorsciss
2	rumumr	*2*	ucrco
3	mumsyra	*3*	ecdmomacoat
4	yynsnom	*4*	uflilefdl
5	aetumra	*5*	uaido
6	amerge	*6*	hmyhtr
7	cflususecs	*7*	lasyulu
8	lwloneo	*8*	ryleal
9	sesbarmra	*9*	laltisn
10	drdeass	*10*	usbsnsei

Give your partner the list you have written. Ask him to dictate it back to you. Check each letter from the list above. If your partner cannot read any of the letters, rewrite the nonsense word so that your letters are clear.

The nonsense words you have written make real words if you change the order of the letters. Work in pairs to find out what the real words are.

Pitman Spelling List

The words on this list are responsible for more than 80 per cent of all spelling errors in Pitman Examinations Institute examinations; it should be noted that trap words such as homophones (council/counsel) or look-alikes (quite/quiet) are not included.
* = highest error frequency.

absence
absorption
accessible
accidental
   accidentally
accommodate*
   accommodation*
achieved
acknowledge
acquaintance*
   acquainted*
acquiesce
   acquiescence
acquire*
   acquisition*
aerial
aggravate
agreeable
all right
amateur
analysis
   analyses
ancillary
anxiety
apparent
appropriate
argument
athletic
audio
awful

bachelor
bargain
beginning*
believed*
benefited
breathe
   breathing
budgeted
bureau (x, s)
   bureaucracy
business

category
certainly*
chaos
   chaotic
clothes
colleagues
college
coming*
committee

comparative
compatible
competent
   competence
competition
completely
connoisseur
conscientious
conscious
convenient
   convenience
correspondence*
   correspondent*
corroborate
courteous
   courtesy
criticism

deceive
decision
deficient
definite*
desirable
despair
desperate
deterrent
disappointed*
disastrous
discrepancy
dissatisfied
distributor

efficient
   efficiency
eighth
eliminated
embarrassed
   embarrassment
enthusiasm
equipped
   equipment
erroneous
especially*
essential
exaggerated
excellent
exercise
expenses*
extremely*

familiar
fascinate
favourite
feasible
February
foreign
forty
friend*
fulfilled
   fulfilment

gauge
genius
government
grievance
guarantee
guard
   guardian

harass
   harassment
height
heroes
honorary
humour
   humorous
hypocrite
   hypocrisy

immediately
immigrate
   immigrant
incidentally
incipient
independent*
indispensable
influential
inoculate
   inoculation
install
   instalment
irrelevant
irreparable
irresistible

liaison
livelihood
losing*
lounge
lying

maintain
   maintenance
manoeuvre
medicine
Mediterranean
miniature
minutes
monetary
mortgage
movable

necessary*
   unnecessary*
negotiate
   negotiable
noticeable*

occasion*
   occasionally*
   occasioned*
occurred*
   occurrence
omitted
   omission

parallel -ed
parliament
pastime
penicillin
permissible
physical
planning*
possessive
potential
precede*
   preceding*
predecessor
preference
   preferred
preliminary
privilege*
probably
proceed
   procedure
professional
pronunciation
proprietary
psychology

questionnaire

received
recommend
referred*
   reference*
regrettable
relieved
repetition
responsibility
rhythm

scarcely*
schedule
secretaries*
seize
separate*
   separately*
severely
shining
similar
sincerely*
specimen
statutory
subtle
   subtlety
successful
   successfully
supersede
suppression
surprising*
synonym
   synonymous

tendency
transferred*
   transference*
transient
truly*
twelfth

unconscious
underrate
undoubtedly*
usual*
   usually*

vaccinate
valuable*
view*

Wednesday
weird
withhold
woollen

Index

Abbreviations 36
  in telegrams 21
  terms, in business letters 30, 89–90
Absence report 42
Absence summary 42
Absent card 169
Accident report form 135
Addresses 133
Advertisements 12–13
  job 114
Agendas 59, 140, 154
Airline timetable 75
Alphabet 60
Ambiguity 12
American/British English 101–2
  business letters 102
  spelling 121
any, some, no 56
Apostrophe 55
Application letter 114–17
Appropriateness 158–9
Atlas 87, 89
Attendance record form 41
Audio typist duties 20

Bar graphs 83–5, 87
British/American English 101–2
  business letters 102
  spelling 121
Business letters, see Letters, business
Business reply card 80
Business terms 74, 89–90

Catalogues 1, 9, 11, 31–2, 89, 138, 157
Channels of communication 5–7, 61–3
Charts 75–6, 86–9
  company organisation 61, 93
  flow 48
  map 81
  pie 85
  timetable 75, 78, 89
Cheques 17
Circular letter 167
Collation 80
Commands 149
Commas 92
Commercialese 68
Committee procedures 140
Communication, means of 5–7, 61–3
Comparison 9, 71
Complaints 159
Compound words 21, 23
Comprehension 145–6, 163–4
Conditions 91
Content/function words 21–2, 24

Contents list 132
Correspondence, see Letters
Correspondence, summary of 1, 130
Currencies 88, 91
Curriculum vitae 116, 122–3

Dangling participles 112
Definitions 26, 74
Diagrams 44–9, 61–3, 75–8, 79, 80, 98, 107
  company organisation chart 61, 93
  floor plan 52, 137
  Venn 95–6
Diary 59, 107
Dictionary 89, 90, 132
Direct speech 112
Directions 80–82
Directories:
  airways 89
  internal telephone 89
  street 89
  telephone 89
  telex 89
Documents:
  absence report 42
  absence summary 42
  absent card 169
  accident report 135
  agenda 59, 140, 154
  attendance record 41
  bill 148
  business reply card 80
  cheque 17
  collation 80
  design 94, 157, 171–2
  employee evaluation form 96
  employee progress report 172
  entry form 93
  hotel reservation form 15
  insurance renewal form 15
  invoice 106, 148
  itinerary 76
  notice of meeting 57, 135, 140, 154
  order form 17, 107, 125–30, 157
  personnel requisition form 113
  petty cash voucher 17
  price-list 125, 139
  purchase requisition 125–7, 137
  questionnaire 164–5, 171
  stock cards 126
  telephone bill 148
  telephone message form 32–3
  warning record 43
  and see Forms
due to/owing to 20

Duplicating systems 10–11, 18
  photocopiers 10–11, 18
  stencil 149
Duties:
  audio typist 20
  filing clerk 53
  invoicing clerk 53
  junior 53
  mailing room 61–5
  messenger 53
  receptionist 160
  secretarial 140, 160
  telephonist 53
  typist 53

eg/ie 122
Employee evaluation form 96
Employee progress report 172
Encyclopedia 89
Envelopes 45–7, 133
Examinations:
  definitions 74
  instructions 93, 108–9, 173–4
  letters in 66–8
  pronouns 134
  reports 141
  vocabulary questions 152

Filing 60
  absent cards 169
  alphabetical 44
  geographical 44
  systems 9–10
Filing clerk 53
Floor plan 52, 137
Flow chart 48
Forms:
  composing 94, 157, 171–2
  filling in 93, 157
  and see Documents
Function/content words 21–2, 24

Glossary 26
GMT 88
Graphs 85, 87
  bar 83–5, 87
  line 68–9, 71, 77–8, 85, 87, 142

Hansard 89, 151
Homonyms 12
Homophones 12, 54
Hotel reservation form 15
Hyphens 23–4
  and see Word division

ie/eg 122
Index 131
Indexing 60
Indirect speech 112, 124
Information leaflet 167
Insurance renewal form 15
Interview, job 118
Inverted commas, see Direct speech
Invoice 106, 148
Invoicing clerk 53
ISO paper sizes 46–7, 82
Itinerary 76

Job:
　advertisement 114
　application 114–17
　curriculum vitae 116, 122–3
　description 113
　interview 118
　offers 120
　refusals 120

Keyboard 3, 55

Leaflet, information 167
Letters, business:
　American/British style 102
　circular 167
　complaint 159
　enquiry 27–9, 50–51, 148, 157
　in examination questions 66–8
　from notes 29
　job application 114–17
　job offers 120
　job refusal 120
　ordering 51
　organisation of 27
　paragraphing of 35
　planning 50
　reply 27–9, 50–51, 148
　summary of 1, 130
　tact 130
　thanks 154
　tone 158–9
　vocabulary of 30, 68, 89–90
Line graphs 68–9, 71, 77–8, 85, 87, 142

Mailing room 61–5
Map 81
Meetings 146, 153–7, 165
　agendas 59, 140, 154
　committee procedures 140
　minutes 1, 140, 150–51, 153–4, 156
　motions 150
　narrative minutes 150–51, 153
　notice 57, 135, 140, 154
　resolution minutes 150–51, 153
　resolutions 150
Memo report 136
Memorandums 14–15, 57, 103, 130
Minutes, see Meetings

Narrative minutes 150–51, 153
Negatives 56

no, some, any 56
Notice of meeting 57, 135, 140, 154
Numbering systems for notes and reports 95–8
Numbers: apostrophe with 55

Office manager 53
only 40
Order forms 17, 107, 125–30, 157
Organisation charts 61, 93
owing to/due to 20

Paper sizes 46–7, 82
Paragraphing 35
Participles, dangling 112
Parts of speech 161
　prepositions 110
　pronouns 17, 92, 134, 139, 168
　verbs 54
Personnel requisition form 113
Petty cash voucher 17
Photocopiers 10–11, 18
Phrases, explaining 152
Pie chart 85
Plan of office 52, 137
Post Office Guide 89
Post room, see Mailing room
Postal codes 160
Précis 1
Prediction 160
Prefixes 52, 158
Prepositions 110
Press release 1
Price-list 125, 139
Pronouns 17, 92, 134, 139, 168
Proof-reading 3, 15–16, 36–9, 105, 140, 160
Punctuation:
　apostrophe 55
　commas 92
　direct/indirect speech 112
　hyphens 23–4
　semicolons 18–19, 133
Purchase requisition 125–7, 137
Puzzles 8, 12, 13, 23, 52, 78–9, 82, 161

Questionnaire 164–5, 171
Quotation marks, see Direct speech

Receptionist's duties 160
Reference sources 86–9, 89–91
Registered mail 5
Reports 148
　absence report 42
　accident report 135
　employee progress report 172
　memo report 136
Report writing 136, 141
Reported speech 112, 124
Requisition form 113, 125–7, 137
Resolution minutes 150–51, 153
Resolutions 150
Root words 18, 52, 158

Secretarial duties 140, 160

Semicolons 18–19, 133
some, any, no 56
Spelling:
　British/American 121
　double letters 49
　frequently misspelt words 175
　helping memory 34
　homophones 12, 54
　irregular spelling patterns 65
　one word or two 56
　sequence of letters 8
　silent letters 111
　suffixes 52, 72
　telex code 78–9
　word families 18
Statistics 68–71, 83–5
Statistical year book 89
Stencil duplicating 149
Stock cards 126
Suffixes 52, 72, 158
Suggestions 149
Summary of correspondence 1, 130

Table of contents 132
Tables, see Charts
Tact 130, 149, 158–9
Tautology 56, 73
Telegrams 1, 21–3, 24, 59, 78
Telephone 5, 145–8
　bill 148
　calls 31–4, 170
　directory 89
　messages 14, 31–3, 59, 170
Telephonist 53
Telex 1, 6–7, 21–3, 78–9
　code 78–9
　directory 89
Thanks, letter of 154
Thesaurus 89, 90
Time 88
Timetables 75, 78, 89
Tone 158–9
Transcription 161
Trap words 142–3
Travel guide 89
Two-word verbs 54
Typewriter, instructions at 82
Typewriter keyboard 3, 55
Typewriters, care of 65
Typist's duties 53

US/UK English 101–2
US/UK spelling 121

Venn diagrams 95–6
Verbatim transcript minutes 150–51
Verbosity 73
Verbs 54
Vocabulary:
　questions in exams 152
　and see Word study

Warning record 43
Word division at line-ends 140, 158
Word families 18
Word processors 4

Word study:
  ambiguity 12
  business letters 30, 68
  business terms 74, 89, 90
  comparison 71
  compound words 21, 23
  homonyms 12

homophones 12, 54
prefixes 52, 158
reported speech 124
root words 18, 52, 158
statistics 71, 85
suffixes 52, 72, 158
tautology 73

trap words 142–3
two-word verbs 54
unfamiliar words 24–6
verbosity 7
vocabulary of business letters 30, 68
word families 18

Acknowledgements

Grateful acknowledgement is due to publishers and authors for kind permission to reprint from copyright material by the following:

Alfred Marks Bureau Ltd: *Survey of the Attitudes and Ambitions of Secretarial Students in 1978*; page 70.

Associated Examining Board, The (abbreviated to AEB).

Bank Education Service: cheque on page 17.

Bond, L. C.: *Commerce and the Outside World*, 1978, Pitman Books Ltd; page 2; page 24, Exercise 1.

British Institute of Management: *Improving Management & Productivity in the Smaller Office*, page 52.

British Stationery and Office Products Federation: *Manual of Stationery, Office Machines and Equipment*, ed F. G. Holliday; pages 47 and 92.

British Telecom: page 79 diagram; page 148 bills.

Burd, Stephanie: *The Typist's Desk Book*, 3rd edn, 1974, Pitman Books Ltd; page 26 PS *1–10*.

Delgado, Alan: *The Enormous File*, 1979, John Murray (Publishers) Ltd; page 25, Exercise 3, *4* and *8*; page 122.

Denholm-Young, Sally: *Supersecretary*, 1980, Settle & Bendall (Wigmore House Publishing Ltd – London); page 4, word processing passage; page 24, *6–15*.

Federal Ministry of Establishments, Lagos; Office of the Head of the Civil Service of the Federation, New Secretariat (abbreviated to Nigerian FME).

Fisher, Ken: article in *Memo/2000* August 1980; page 140.

Gosling, K.: *The Clerical Training Office*, 2nd edn, 1975, Pitman Books Ltd; pages 131–2.

Harrison, John: *First Steps in Business Training*, 4th edn, 1975, Pitman Books Ltd; page 17, order form; page 63.

Harrison, John: *Secretarial Duties*, 6th edn, 1979, Pitman Books Ltd; page 80, Exercise 1.

Heinemann Educational Australia Pty Ltd: *Heinemann English Dictionary*, 1979; page 90, *23*.

Her Majesty's Stationery Office: *British Labour Statistics Year Book 1974*; page 76.

Kirklees Metropolitan Council: *About Huddersfield*; page 81.

Leafe, Margaret; article in *Memo/2000* June 1980; page 36, *20*.

London Chamber of Commerce and Industry, The (abbreviated to LCCI).

Longman Group Ltd: Roget's *Thesaurus of English Words and Phrases*; page 90, *25*.

'Lucy', *Girl About Town*, 2 June 1980; page 40.

Mackay, Edith: *The Typewriting Dictionary*, 1977, Pitman Books Ltd; page 3, diagram; page 24, Exercise 2; page 36, *11*; pages 46, 55, 65; page 91, *26*; page 132.

Maclean-Hunter Ltd: *Business Systems and Equipment*; page 145.

Maddox, Harry: *How to Study*, 1967, Pan Books Ltd; pages 68–9.

Merriam, G & C, Co.: *Webster's Secretarial Handbook*, 1976; page 149.

Mills, G. and O. Standingford: *Office Organization and Method*, 6th edn, 1978, Pitman Books Ltd; page 6; page 18 *Photocopying*; page 18, Exercise 3, *1–15*.

Olympia Business Machines Co. Ltd: *Operating Instructions Olympia SM*; page 44.

Owen, J. W. and J. Davies; *Business Punctuation*, 1974, Pitman Books Ltd; page 90, *22*.

Oxford University Press: *Fowler's Modern English Usage*, revised by Sir Ernest Gowers (2nd edn 1965) © Oxford University Press 1965; page 91, *27*.

Paisley, B, and J. Parker: *People at Work*, 1980, Pitman Books Ltd; page 135.

Philip, George, and Son Ltd: *Philips' Modern College Atlas for Africa*, 1980; page 87, climate graphs.

Pitman Books Ltd: *The Pitman Dictionary of English and Shorthand*, 1974; page 90, *24*.

Pitman Examinations Institute (abbreviated to PEI).

Reid, G. A.: *Modern Office Procedures*, 2nd edn, 1978, Copp Clark Pitman; page 18, Exercise 1, *16–18*; pages 20, 45, 48, 64, 92, 132; pages 160–61 A, B, C, D.

Reilly, W.: *Training Administrators for Development*, 1979, Heinemann Educational Books; page 25, *6, 7, 10*.

Reynolds, Maurice: article in *Memo/2000* July 1980; page 164.

Singer, Lynette, and Robin Wood, eds: *Peoples of Africa*, 1978, Marshall Cavendish Books Ltd; page 98.

Spicers Ltd: *The Emgee Catalogue*; pages 11 and 13.

Stananought, Joyce: article in *Memo/2000* January 1980; page 136.

Stonehart Publications Ltd: *Better Buys for Business*; pages 10 and 97.

Sunday Telegraph, article appearing 30 March 1980, courtesy The Daily Telegraph; page 26.

Thurling, F. C.: *Office Practice Today*, 4th edn, 1975, Pitman Books Ltd; page 2; page 9 diagrams; page 25, Exercise 3, *1, 2*.

Trinidad and Tobago Tourist Board: page 92.

Underwood, Graham: article in *The Architect's Journal*, May–November 1980; page 97.

Vigiles Fire Protection, Colchester, UK: page 138.

West, Leonard: *Acquisition of Typewriting Skills*, 1969; Pitman Learning Inc; pages 40, 71.

Zambia Airways: timetable page 75.